W9-CFB-354

A Reader in Peace Studies

Titles of Related Interest

BRECHER & WILKENFELD   Crisis, conflict and instability

BROCKE-UTNE   Educating for peace

GRAHAM   Disarmament and world development

RUSSELL   Exploding nuclear phallacies

THEE   Making peace possible: The promise of economic conversion

Pergamon Reference Works

BRECHER, WILKENFELD & MOSER   Crises in the twentieth century, Volumes I and II

LASZLO & YOO   World encyclopedia of peace

A Reader in Peace Studies

Edited by

Paul Smoker, Ruth Davies

and

Barbara Munske

PERGAMON PRESS

Member of Maxwell Macmillan Pergamon Publishing Corporation

OXFORD · NEW YORK · BEIJING · FRANKFURT
SÃO PAULO · SYDNEY · TOKYO · TORONTO

U.K.	Pergamon Press plc, Headington Hill Hall, Oxford OX3 0BW, England
U.S.A.	Pergamon Press, Inc., Maxwell House, Fairview Park, Elmsford, New York 10523, U.S.A.
PEOPLE'S REPUBLIC OF CHINA	Pergamon Press, Room 4037, Qianmen Hotel, Beijing, People's Republic of China
FEDERAL REPUBLIC OF GERMANY	Pergamon Press GmbH, Hammerweg 6, D-6242 Kronberg, Federal Republic of Germany
BRAZIL	Pergamon Editora Ltda, Rua Eça de Queiros, 346, CEP 04011, Paraiso, São Paulo, Brazil
AUSTRALIA	Pergamon Press Australia Pty Ltd., P.O. Box 544, Potts Point, N.S.W. 2011, Australia
JAPAN	Pergamon Press, 5th Floor, Matsuoka Central Building, 1-7-1 Nishishinjuku, Shinjuku-ku, Tokyo 160, Japan
CANADA	Pergamon Press Canada Ltd, Suite No. 271, 253 College Street, Toronto, Ontario, Canada M5T 1R5

Copyright © 1990 Pergamon Press plc

First edition 1990

CMND 9430-1 is Crown copyright and is reproduced by permission of the Controller of Her Majesty's Stationery Office

Library of Congress Cataloging-in-Publication Data
A reader in peace studies/edited by Paul Smoker, Ruth Davies, and Barbara Munske
p. cm.
Includes index.
1. Peace. I. Smoker, Paul. II. Davies, Ruth.
III. Munske, Barbara.
JX1952.R337 1989 327.1′72—dc19 89–2920

British Library Cataloguing-in-Publication Data
A reader in peace studies.
1. Peace
I. Smoker, Paul, 1938– II. Davies, Ruth III. Munske, Barbara, 1962–
327.1′72

ISBN 0–08–036287–7 Hard cover
ISBN 0–08–036286–9 Flexicover

Printed in Great Britain by B.P.C.C. Wheatons Ltd., Exeter

Contents

Whales*

Whales are memories of the deep
        placid volcanoes
Calm chambers of light
Whales are blue echoes of our past
        Green cathedrals
Scarred myths in motion
And they are intelligent
        compassionate
        and quietly spoken
As their flukes and fins assail the currents of the world
These great sea Buddhas in lines unbroken
Curving down the earth as the dawn is woken
Until that is they are
        Harpooned
    to be converted into
        ambergris
        cat food
        and shaving lotion
    oil lamps
    blubber
    and sexual potions
But then to some of us the idea that a whale has any greater relevance
is a pious ridiculous notion
For whales are simply a product
To be blown out of the ocean
And they should never engage our emotions
Although we will swim with them in our wombs
And fly with them in our dreams
And some of us may remember that once
        long ago
It was they who helped us from the sea.

                      RICHARD BONFIELD

* This poem originally appeared in *Peace News*, 30 October 1987. Reproduced with permission.

Introduction

WHY IS Peace Studies important? We believe it provides important tools for understanding and living in the modern world. In societies that call themselves democracies it is the responsibility of education to provide people with the skills and knowledge they need in order to be active and informed citizens. In addition, it is important that education fosters a global perspective. The accident at Chernobyl, the bombing of Libya and the destruction of the rain forests are all clear evidence that we can no longer pretend to be living in isolated nation-states. Instead we are part of an interdependent global system. Peace Studies aims to foster within a global perspective these skills and this knowledge. It is unusual in bringing together many diverse disciplines which have an interest in these problems.

This book provides an introduction to the field of Peace Studies which we hope will be of interest to the student and to the general reader. Putting this book together has been no easy task as we were confronted with a distinction between our aims and reality. In choosing articles for the book, we invited contributions from authors of all political persuasions, and from many countries. We believed it to be important that this book reflects an international perspective as an understanding of peace and conflict should not be limited to a Western developed viewpoint. Equally important is a balanced gender representation, for too often the experience and insights of women are ignored. The responses to our invitation were varied and left us to select contributions from those offered. Readers will notice that our aims were not fully met. Some groups are under-represented, such as women, conservative writers, people from the Third World and from socialist countries. We realize that to a certain extent, this reflects the nature of our society, and of the academic world especially. We regret, however, that our attempts to avoid this imbalance has not been altogether successful.

This book is a compilation of various articles on peace and conflict. Authors from different political and cultural backgrounds offer their knowledge and opinions as starting points for discussion rather than definitive statements. The reader should take into account these different backgrounds when reading the pieces, and to this end we have tried to give as much information as we can about the authors. These different backgrounds also reflect different styles of writing and use of language. For example, some writers are very careful to avoid sexist language whereas others seem unaware of the importance of this issue. Some authors appear to make their personal involvement in the subject very clear, while others maintain an abstract and distanced approach.

The topics covered here are only a selection from the very broad range that makes up Peace Studies. We believe that some of the most important areas are represented, and that readers will gain some idea of the scope of Peace Studies.

The accusation of bias sometimes made against Peace Studies is justified only to the extent that its central concern is the achievement of a peaceful and just world. This concern has a bearing on the issues which are addressed but not on the academic standards involved. The concern will translate into different approaches; for example, the maintenance of peace is a central concern for both the Ministry of Defence and Dan Smith. Yet, their two articles arrive at opposite conclusions. Equally, Richard Clutterbuck and Noam Chomsky both wish to see an end to terrorism but present very different approaches and solutions.

It is up to the individual reader to decide which, if any, of the approaches represented here are most likely to achieve a more peaceful and just world. We hope this book will encourage students and teachers to explore the field of Peace Studies, and provide a starting point for many constructive discussions. What is more, we hope readers will be motivated to incorporate what they learn into their lives. We do not believe knowledge to be an end in itself, but rather an aid to concerned and active involvement in the world.

PAUL SMOKER
Lancaster, England   RUTH DAVIES
BARBARA MUNSKE

PART 1

Some Theoretical Approaches to Peace and Conflict

Kenneth Boulding begins his article with the assertion that theories are 'attempts by the human mind to reduce the immense variety and complexity of the real world to simpler patterns and components which the mind can grasp'. This is why the first section of this book includes five articles by leading theorists where competing theoretical approaches to peace and conflict are elaborated. These articles provide both a framework for simplifying the complex problems of peace and conflict and a clarification of what can be meant by the terms peace, violence, conflict and cooperation.

Peace Theory

KENNETH E. BOULDING

THEORIES are attempts by the human mind to reduce the immense variety and complexity of the real world to simpler patterns and components which the mind can grasp. A theory has somewhat the relationship to the real world that a map has to the landscape. Thus, chemical theory describes how the world is organized by elements of different valency into compounds of varying complexity. Economic theory studies how the world of human beings and their artifacts is organized by exchange, production, prices, and so on. In the last few decades a new discipline has developed, in English usually called 'peace and conflict studies' (the French call it *polemologie*, from polemics), which studies how the world is organized through conflict, war, violence, nonviolence, and peace. A British meteorologist, Lewis F. Richardson, whose major works were not even published during his lifetime (Richardson, 1960a and 1960b), may well be regarded as the father of this new discipline, although there were precursors and contemporaries (Wright, 1942; Lentz, 1955). There is now an extensive bibliography and a number of journals in this field, and an increasing number of universities are offering programs in it.

The beginning of good theory is the identification of significant classifications of things in the real world. Alchemy never got very far because its elements—earth, air, fire, and water—were hopelessly heterogeneous. Until the chemical elements were discovered—like oxygen, hydrogen, and so on—chemistry did not get very far. Similarly, peace theory begins with the identification of significant classifications of human behavior and organizations. This can begin with the division of human activity into war and 'not-war,' which might be called 'inclusive peace.' Five billion human beings spend about 120 billion hours a day, one-third in sleep, mostly peaceful; two-thirds in waking-time activities: working, conversing, travelling, partying, and so on. Some of these hours can clearly be related to war, which involves producing and using the means of destruction of life and of things that at least some humans value.

A rough measure of the 'war industry' is given by the size of military budgets, which on a world scale run something on the order of five percent of

3

economic activity. Something like half the human race is in the labor force, which occupies something like a third of our time. So about a sixth of human time is devoted to economic activity; five percent of this would mean something less than one percent of human time devoted to war. To this we might add non-war conflict activity: police, the legal profession, quarrelling, and so on, which might bring up the total conflict activity to something like one percent of the 120 billion hours a day which we spend. It is, however, a very visible and dramatic one percent. Conflict gets in the newspapers, is the subject of drama and novels, so it is not surprising that we pay a good deal of attention to it. Nevertheless, as we look at the arts as they reflect human life, at least ninety percent of paintings are of peaceful landscapes and portraits, music is mainly concerned with harmony and the resolution of discord, fortifications are a very small part of architecture, and so on.

The distinction between war and inclusive peace is fairly sharp. Most historians can say whether two countries were at war or not on a given date, though there are a few ambiguous cases. Within this area of conflict we have violent and nonviolent conflict. Within the area of peace we have a great variety of human conditions. One of the pioneers of peace theory, Johan Galtung, identified what he called 'structural violence,' which can be most clearly defined as social structures leading to an expectation of life less than the biological potential, now approaching 75 to 80 years. Where the expectation of life is lower than this as a result of oppression, poverty, nutritional deficiencies, pollution, dangerous work, human ignorance, and so on, structural violence may be said to exist. Inclusive peace includes a great variety of human conditions, some of which may be judged much better than others.

Good theory has to be 'dynamic' in the sense that it must portray not only a flashlight photograph, as it were, of the world at a given moment of time, but also the succession of these photographs, like the frames of a movie, as we move from the past into the future. These patterns in time may include equilibrium systems, like a ball rolling down to the bottom of a bowl, a forest recovering its original state after a forest fire, or a system of peace emerging after it has been interrupted by war. We have to recognize, however, that the world is in constant evolutionary change, that all equilibria are temporary. Nevertheless, there are situations in which a disturbance from some temporary equilibrium results in a movement back towards it: disputes are resolved, a loving couple makes up after a quarrel, and so on. On the other hand, we also have to recognize the long-run evolutionary, irreversible changes. The totality of human knowledge, for instance, has grown almost continuously, even at an accelerating pace, from the first human beings, and this profoundly affects the history of human society and behavior. Both biological and societal evolution seem to have a 'time's arrow' in terms of complexity which seems to be almost irreversible.

An example of peace theory involving a dynamic movement towards a

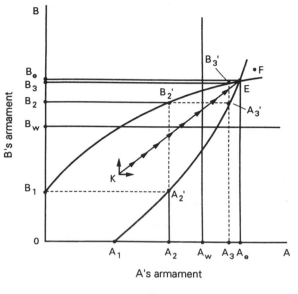

FIG 1.

possible equilibrium is the theory of arms races, first developed by Lewis F. Richardson.* This is expressed in Figure 1.

Here we suppose two countries, **A** and **B**, each of which sees the other as something of a threat to it. We measure **A**'s level of armament horizontally (Axis OA), **B**'s level of armament vertically (Axis OB). Then we suppose two 'reaction curves,' A_1E, which shows the level of armament that **A** wants to achieve for each level of **B**'s armament; B_1E, which shows the level of **B**'s armament that **B** wants to achieve for each level of **A**'s armament. We suppose that even if **B**'s armament level is zero, **A** will have some armament, OA_1; and if **A**'s is zero, **B** will have some armament, OB_1. If we were to start off with both countries' armaments at zero, let us suppose that **B** goes to OB_1, which would make **A** feel insecure. **A** would then go to OA_2, represented by the point A_2' on its reaction curve. This would make **B** feel insecure and he would go to B_2' on his reaction curve, with a level of armament OB_2. **A** would then go to A_3', **B** to B_3', and so on.

In Figure 1, the two reaction curves intersect at E, which would be the point of equilibrium of the 'arms race.' If we had a level of arms in the interval between the curves above E, say at F, we would have a disarmament race, back to E. This is a little reminiscent of the old 'balance of power' theory of international relations. We do not have to assume that the dotted line B_1, A_2', B_2', A_3', and so on, is necessarily the dynamic process. If we were

---

* This type of theory is also explored in Robert Axelrod's chapter entitled 'Building Cooperation' which appears later in this section.

to start from some point such as K within the two reaction curves, both parties would increase their armaments, **A** to A_k, **B** to B_k, ending up as they move towards a reaction line so we might get a dynamic path somewhat like the line KE (marked with arrows).

In Figure 1 we have drawn the reaction lines A_1E and B_1E as curves. The slope of each line at any point shows how much each country reacts to a unit increase in the armaments of the other. This might be called a 'reaction coefficient.' If an increase of 1 unit in **A**'s armament level increases **B**'s by .5 unit, then **B**'s reaction coefficient is .5. An important conclusion is that in order to have an equilibrium such as point E, the reaction coefficients, no matter what level they start at, must fall below 1. If the reaction coefficients are both 1 or greater, the reaction curves will either be parallel or will diverge and will not intersect at all. The arms race will go on until the system breaks down, usually into war. This indeed is why so many arms races have in fact led to war, and why deterrence is fundamentally unstable in the long run. A decline in the reaction coefficient may be a result of economic forces. As armaments increase they become more and more of an economic burden, and one country or the other or both may simply not be able to afford to continue the arms race at a high reaction coefficient. On the other hand, there may also be some level of armaments at which one nation or the other decides that a further increase is intolerable and this frequently breaks down into war. If this level were, say OA_w for **A** and OB_w for **B**, and if the dynamic process were represented by the line KE, then war would begin at the point B_w, since **B** would reach the breakdown point first. This, incidentally, suggests why it is so difficult to define an 'aggressor' in the origins of a war. Which of the two parties starts the war depends on which reaches the breakdown point first. This may be quite arbitrary. When the dynamics of the arms race goes outside the limits of the rectangle OB_wWA_w, war starts.

In this model the 'causes' of war are almost irrelevant. The pattern of economic conflict, for instance, has very little to do with the pattern of war. War emerges because of the existence of government-financed 'unilateral national defense organizations,' which specialize in fighting wars and in preparing for them. These unilateral national defense organizations can only justify their existence and their budgets if they have an enemy or a potential enemy. They tend to create enemies even where there are no severe conflicts. The situation becomes much more complex when we have more than two parties and it can be shown that for an equilibrium of an arms race to exist under these circumstances, the reaction coefficients must be considerably less than 1, and the more parties, the lower the reaction coefficients have to be in order to ensure an equilibrium. This is why unilateral national defense has rarely produced more than an unstable peace, but has always tended to break down into war, quite regardless of the structure of real conflicts.

Another aspect of peace theory which can only be mentioned briefly here is the study of the impact of the different kinds and destructive powers of weaponry on the consequence of using them. An important distinction is between offensive weapons, which are designed to destroy either the opponent's weapons or the opponent and the opponent's properties; and defensive structures, like suits of armor, castle walls, city walls, and so on, which are designed to reduce the destructiveness of the other party's weapons. A change in the capacity of offensive weapons to overcome defensive structures will have a profound effect on social institutions. Thus the development of the effective cannon in the sixteenth century destroyed the feudal system, made the city-state very unstable, and helped to create the national state. As long as the weapons were spears and arrows, the castle wall and the city wall made some sense. With the development of the effective cannon, they made no sense at all. The baron who stayed in his castle got blown up with it. A national state, however, of the size of France or England, Sweden or Russia, could be defended at the borders with cannon. A very important question now is whether the development of the long-range missile and the nuclear weapon has done for the national state precisely what the cannon did for the feudal baron, in that it is no longer defensible by war.

We have seen in the last 150 years a new phenomenon, the development of stable peace between independent national states, in which neither of two countries has any plans to go to war with the other. This begins in Scandinavia in the mid-nineteenth century, spreads to North America by about 1870, and to Western Europe after the Second World War. With the nuclear weapon, this may be the only way in which the national state can achieve security. The conditions of stable peace are fairly simple: both parties must take national boundaries off their agendas, except by mutual agreement; both parties have to have a minimum amount of intervention in each other's affairs. The fact that military conquests and imperialism have not paid off economically on the whole for aggressive powers suggests that a learning process is going on which will expand the area of stable peace.

Peace theory is illuminated and tested by peace history, which is very undeveloped. There are very few historical studies of peace (Melko, 1973), fewer studies of the economic costs of military victory, and still fewer of the benefits of military defeat, which has often in history produced both a cultural expansion and an economic expansion for the defeated. In one sense Germany and Japan, the defeated powers, won the Second World War economically, as they were able to devote a larger proportion of their resources to getting rich rather than being powerful in the military sense. There are also many examples in history, like the defeat of France by Germany in 1870–71, which was followed in France by a great upsurge in art, literature, and music, as well as in economic life. It is peace history that has to provide the data for peace theory, and much of this still remains to be written.

References

Axelrod, Robert. *The Evolution of Cooperation*. New York: Basic Books, 1984.
Boulding, Kenneth. *The Economics of Peace*. New York: Prentice-Hall, 1945 (reissued, New York: Books for Libraries Press, 1972).
Boulding, Kenneth. *Conflict and Defense*. New York: Harper and Brothers, 1962.
Boulding, Kenneth. *Ecodynamics: A New Theory of Societal Evolution*. London: Sage, 1978.
Boulding, Kenneth. *Stable Peace*. Austin: University of Texas Press, 1978.
Boulding, Kenneth. *The World as a Total System*. London: Sage, 1985.
Lentz, Theodore. *Towards a Science of Peace: Turning Point in Human Destiny*. New York: Bookman Associates, 1955.
Melko, Matthew. *52 Peaceful Societies*. Ontario: Canadian Peace Research Institute Press, 1973.
von Neumann, John, and Oskar Morgenstern. *The Theory of Games and Economic Behaviour*, 2nd ed. Princeton, N.J.: Princeton University Press, 1947 (originally published 1944).
Rapoport, Anatol. *Fights, Games, and Debates*. Ann Arbor: University of Michigan Press, 1960.
Rapoport, Anatol, and Albert Chammah. *The Prisoner's Dilemma: A Study in Conflict and Cooperation*. Ann Arbor: University of Michigan Press, 1965.
Richardson, Lewis F. *Arms and Insecurity: A Mathematical Study of the Causes and Origins of War*. Chicago: Quadrangle Books, 1960a.
Richardson, Lewis F. *Statistics of Deadly Quarrels*. Chicago: Quadrangle Books, 1960b.
Singell, Larry D. (ed.). *Collected Papers, Vol. V: International Systems: Peace, Conflict Resolution, and Politics*. Colorado: Colorado Associated University Press, 1975.
Singell, Larry D. (ed.). *Collected Papers, Vol. VI: Toward the 21st Century: Political Economy, Social Systems, and World Peace*. Colorado: Colorado Associated University Press, 1985.

Violence and Peace

JOHAN GALTUNG

Introduction

To discuss the idea of peace we shall start from three simple principles: (1) The term 'peace' shall be used for social goals at least verbally agreed to by many, if not necessarily most; (2) These social goals may be complex and difficult, but not impossible, to attain; and (3) The statement 'peace is absence of violence' shall be retained as valid.

What we intend is only that the terms 'peace' and 'violence' be linked to each other such that 'peace' can be regarded as 'absence of violence'. Everything now hinges on making a definition of 'violence'.

On the definition and dimensions of violence

As a point of departure, let us say that violence is present when human beings are being influenced so that their actual somatic and mental realizations are below their potential realizations. This statement may lead to more problems than it solves. However, it will soon be clear why we are rejecting the narrow concept of violence—according to which violence is somatic incapacitation, or deprivation of health alone (with killing as the extreme form), at the hands of an actor who intends this to be the consequence. If this were all violence is about, and peace were seen as its negation, then too little is rejected when peace is held up as an ideal. Highly unacceptable social orders would still be compatible with peace. Hence, an extended concept of violence is indispensable but that concept should be a logical extension, not merely a list of undesirables.

The definition points to at least six important dimensions of violence. But first some remarks about the use of key words above: 'actual' and 'potential'. Violence is here defined as the cause of the difference between the potential and the actual, between what could have been and what is. Violence is that

Reprinted from 'Violence, Peace and Peace Research' by Johan Galtung from *Journal of Peace Research*, 1969, pp. 167–191, by permission of Norwegian University Press, Oslo.

which increases the distance between the potential and the actual, and that which impedes the decrease of this distance. Thus, if a person died from tuberculosis in the eighteenth century it would be hard to conceive of this as violence since it might have been quite unavoidable, but if he dies from it today, despite all the medical resources in the world, then violence is present according to our definition. Correspondingly, the case of people dying from earthquakes today would not warrant an analysis in terms of violence, but the day after tomorrow, when earthquakes may become avoidable, such deaths may then be seen as the result of violence. In other words, when the potential is higher then the actual is, by definition, avoidable and when it occurs when it is avoidable, then violence is present.

When the actual is unavoidable, then violence is not present even if the actual is at a very low level. A life expectancy of only thirty years during the neolithic period was not an expression of violence, but the same life expectancy today (whether due to wars, or social injustice, or both) would be seen as violence according to our definition.

The meaning of 'potential realization' is highly problematic, especially when we move from somatic aspects of human life, where consensus is more readily obtained, to mental aspects. Our guide here would probably often have to be whether the value to be realized is fairly consensual or not, although this is by no means satisfactory. For example, literacy is held in high regard almost everywhere, whereas the value of being Christian is highly controversial. Hence, we would talk about violence if the level of literacy is lower than what it could have been, not if the level of Christianity is lower than what it could have been. We shall not try to explore this difficult point further in this context, but turn to the dimensions of violence.

The first distinction to be made is between physical and psychological violence. The distinction is trite but important mainly because the narrow concept of violence mentioned above concentrates on physical violence only. Under physical violence human beings are hurt somatically to the point of killing. Psychological violence includes lies, brainwashing, indoctrination of various kinds, threats, etc. that serve to decrease mental potentialities.

The second distinction is between the negative and the positive approach to influence. Thus a person can be influenced not only by punishing him when he does what the influencer considers wrong, but also by rewarding him when he does what the influencer considers right.

The third distinction to be made is on the object side: whether or not there is an object that is hurt. Can we talk about violence when no physical or biological object is hurt? When a person, a group, or a nation is displaying the means of physical violence, whether by throwing stones around or testing nuclear arms, there may not be violence present in the sense that anyone is hit or hurt, but there is nevertheless the threat of physical violence and the indirect effect of mental violence that may even be characterized as some type of psychological violence since it constrains human action. Indeed, this is also the intention: the famous balance of power doctrine is based on efforts to obtain precisely this effect.

The fourth distinction to be made, and the most important one, is on the subject side: whether or not there is a subject (person) who acts. Again it may be asked can we talk about violence when nobody is committing direct violence, i.e., is acting? We shall refer to the type of violence where there is an actor that commits the violence as personal or direct, and to violence where there is no such actor as structural or indirect. In both cases individuals may be killed or mutilated, hit or hurt in both senses of these words, and manipulated by means of 'stick-or-carrot' strategies.

The important point here is that if people are starving when this is objectively avoidable, then violence is committed, regardless of whether there is a clear subject-action-object relation, as during a siege yesterday, or no such clear relation, as in the way world economic relations are organized today. We have baptized the distinction in two different ways, using the word-pairs 'personal-structural' and 'direct-indirect' respectively. Violence with a clear subject-object relation is manifest because it is visible as action. It corresponds to our ideas of what drama is, and it is personal because there are persons committing the violence. It is easily captured and expressed verbally since it has the same structure as elementary sentences in (at least Indo-European) languages: subject-verb-object, with both subject and object being persons. Violence without this relation is structural, i.e., built into structures. Thus, when one husband beats his wife there is a clear case of personal violence, but when one million husbands keep one million wives in ignorance there is structural violence. Correspondingly, in a society where life expectancy is twice as high in the upper as in the lower classes, violence is exercised even if there are no concrete actors one can point to as directly attacking others, as when one person kills another.

The fifth distinction to be made is between violence that is intended or unintended. This distinction is important when guilt is to be decided, since the concept of guilt has been tied more to intention, both in Judaeo-Christian ethics and in Roman jurisprudence, than to consequence (whereas the present definition of violence is entirely located on the consequence side). This connection is important because it brings into focus a bias present in so much thinking about violence, peace and related concepts: ethical systems directed against intended violence will easily fail to capture structural violence in their nets—and may hence be catching the small fry and letting the big fish loose. From this fallacy it does not follow, in our mind, that the opposite fallacy of directing all attention against structural violence is elevated into wisdom. If the concern is with peace, and peace is the absence of violence, then action should be directed against personal as well as structural violence.

Sixth, there is the traditional distinction between two levels of violence, the manifest and the latent. Manifest violence, whether personal or structural, is observable; latent violence is something which is not there, yet might easily come about. For personal violence this would mean a situation where a little challenge would trigger considerable killing and atrocity, as is often the case in connection with racial confrontations. It indicates a situation of unstable equilibrium. Similarly with structural violence; we could imagine a relatively egalitarian structure insufficiently protected against sudden feudalization, against crystallization into a much more stable, even petrified, hierarchical structure.

If peace is now regarded as absence of violence, then thinking about peace (and consequently peace research and peace action) will be structured the same way as thinking about violence. And the violence cake can evidently be cut a number of ways. It has been traditional to think about violence as personal violence only, with one important subdivision in terms of 'violence vs. the threat of violence', another in terms of 'physical vs. psychological war', still another (important in ethical and legal thinking) about 'intended vs. unintended', and so on. The choice here is to make the distinction between personal and structural violence the basic one; justification has been presented firstly in terms of a unifying perspective (the cause of the difference between potential and actual realization) and secondly by indicating that there is no reason to assume that structural violence amounts to less suffering than personal violence.

On the other hand, it is not strange that attention has been focused more on personal than structural violence. Personal violence shows. The object of personal violence perceives the violence, usually, and may complain—the object of structural violence may be persuaded not to perceive this at all. Personal violence represents change and dynamism—not only ripples on waves, but waves on otherwise tranquil waters. Structural violence is silent, it does not show—it is essentially static, it is the tranquil waters. In a static society, personal violence will be registered, whereas structural violence may be seen as about as natural as the air around us. Conversely, in a highly dynamic society, personal violence may be seen as wrong and harmful and still somehow congruent with the order of things, whereas structural violence becomes apparent because it stands out like an enormous rock in a creek, impeding the free flow, creating all kinds of eddies and turbulences. Thus, perhaps it is not so strange that the thinking about personal violence (in the Judaeo-Christian-Roman tradition) took on much of its present form in what we today would regard as essentially static social orders, whereas thinking about structural violence (in the Marxist tradition) was formulated in highly dynamic northwest-European societies.

In other words, we conceive of structural violence as something that shows a certain stability, whereas personal violence (e.g., as measured by the tolls caused by group conflict in general and war in particular) shows tremendous fluctuations over time.

On the definition of 'peace' and 'peace research'

With the distinction between personal and structural violence as basic, violence becomes two-sided, and so does peace conceived of as the absence of violence. An extended concept of violence leads to an extended concept of peace. Just as a coin has two sides, one side alone being only one aspect of the coin, peace also has two sides: absence of personal violence and absence of structural violence. We shall refer to them as 'negative peace' and 'positive peace' respectively.

For the sake of brevity the formulations 'absence of violence' and 'social justice' may perhaps be preferred, using one negative and one positive formulation. The reason for the use of the terms 'negative' and 'positive' is easily seen: the absence of personal violence does not lead to a positively defined condition, whereas the absence of structural violence is what we have referred to as social justice, which is a positively defined condition (i.e., the egalitarian distribution of power and resources). Peace conceived of in this way is not only a matter of control and reduction of the overt use of violence, but of what we have elsewhere referred to as 'vertical development'. And this means that peace theory is intimately connected not only with conflict theory, but equally with development theory. And peace research, defined of as 'research into the conditions—past, present and future—of realizing peace', will be equally intimately connected with conflict research and development research; the former often more relevant for negative peace and the latter more relevant for positive peace, but with highly important overlaps.

To justify this way of looking at peace and peace research, let us see where the many efforts to conceive of peace in terms of only one of these 'sides' or aspects leads us. Such efforts are likely to bring into focus, in theory and indeed in practice, the onesidedness on which they are based.

Thus a research emphasis on the reduction of personal violence at the expense of a tacit or open neglect of research on structural violence leads, very easily, to acceptance of 'law and order' societies. Personal violence is built into the system as work is built into a compressed spring in a mattress: it only shows when the mattress is distintegrating. And on the other hand there may be a research emphasis on righting social wrongs, on obtaining social justice, at the expense of a tacit or open acceptance and use of personal violence. The short-term costs of personal violence appear as small relative to the costs of continued structural violence. But personal violence tends to breed manifest physical violence, not only from the opponent but also inside one's own group—and the aftermath of violent revolutions generally seems to testify to this.

We may summarize by saying that too much research emphasis on one aspect of peace tends to rationalize extremism to the right or extremism to the left, depending on whether onesided emphasis is put on 'absence of personal violence' or on 'social justice'.

Both values, both goals are significant, and it is probably a disservice to try, in any abstract way, to say that one is more important than the other. To realize one of them is no mean achievement either, particularly if we consider the number of social orders and regimes that realize neither.

But the view that one cannot meaningfully work for both absence of personal violence and for social justice can also be seen as essentially pessimistic, as some sort of intellectual and moral capitulation. First of all there are many forms of social action available today that combine both in a highly meaningful way. Secondly, once the double goal has been stated—that peace research is concerned with the conditions for promoting both aspects of peace—there is no reason to believe that the future will not bring us richer concepts and more forms of social action that combine absence of personal violence with the fight against social injustice once sufficient effort is put into research and practice. There are more than enough people willing to sacrifice one aspect of peace for the other—it is by aiming for both that peace research can make a real contribution.

The Reduction of War and the Creation of Peace*

FRANCIS A. BEER

Theories of peace

Peace theory focuses on a particular opportunity and problem—peace. Peace theory draws strength from the fact that we probably enjoy greater peace today than we have at any time in past history. There appears to be a long-run general historical trend toward the diffusion of peace. Wars have become less frequent and the periods of tranquility between them are longer today than in earlier times. Peace theory draws urgency from the contradictory fact that today's wars are more concentrated and severe than before. When wars occur, they are shorter; but casualties have increased both in absolute terms and relative to population (see Beer, 1983, 1974).

Many theorists deal with peace, but peace theory is not a unified whole. It does not begin from abstract axioms, follow through a set of rigorously deduced and exhaustively validated principles, and end with a coherent and consistent set of action recommendations. Rather it is a family of discourse that comes from many diverse traditions, seeing the world in various ways. Space prevents us from considering all of its manifold aspects. We shall focus here on action dimensions of peace theories, on different ways that theorists suggest we may enhance peace.

War reduction

Two major branches of peace theory, defined in this normative way, concentrate in turn on war reduction and peace creation. The first branch, war reduction, accepts the international system as given and tries to alleviate its most extreme dangers by reducing and limiting war.

Some theorists of war reduction concentrate directly on limiting inter-

*The work reported in this article was carried out in the Program on Peace and War, Center for International Relations at the University of Colorado.

national violence. These emphasize the rational management of international crises that might lead to war, and of wars themselves once they occur. Crises management implies special vigilance and control in situations that have a high probability of resulting in war (see Allison, Carnesale, and Nye, 1985). When war does occur, a conscious, organized effort at war management may help prevent smaller incidents of violence from turning into larger ones, keep limited wars limited, and preclude substantial wars from becoming total.

Self restraint and the development of nonviolent techniques may also be important. The future benefits of violence are problematic; the immediate costs—casualties and physical damage—are very real. People are killed and injured; limited 'bushfire' wars sometimes spread out of control, expanding dramatically in space, time, and weapons. It seems more prudent to shy away from using violence as a tool and, instead, to try and prevent it from breaking out or, once it has occurred, to attempt to limit it. Nonviolence is as old as the history of religious leaders and movements. Traditions embodied by Buddha and Christ have inspired successful modern political movements and leaders—the Indian struggle for independence under the leadership of Gandhi and the struggle of the American Blacks for greater equality under the leadership of Martin Luther King, Jr., are but two modern examples (see Sharp, 1973).

Other war reduction theorists aim at military aspects of the international system that are preconditions for violence. Strategic deterrence and arms control are policies with this focus. Strategic deterrence is 'the threat to use force in response as a way of preventing the first use of force by someone else' (Morgan, 1977: p.9). Such deterrence has been quite popular through history (see Naroll, Bullough, and Naroll, 1974), but the advent of nuclear weapons has given it a whole new dimension. Arms control, on the other hand, aims to keep violence in check by putting a cap on forces available to all parties.

Peace creation

War reduction theories appeal to most people because they deal directly with the use of force and weapons. They are, however, limited because they focus on immediately observable symptoms rather than on deeper underlying causes. Theories of peace creation go beyond buffering existing international relations. They focus on balancing and restructuring of the world system.

Balancing

International balancing is an attempt to rearrange the importance of, and relations between, the different levels of the system. The traditional view of international relations has been very state-centered. Historically the international system has consisted of states with sovereignty; and only states could be subjects of international law. Balancing begins from the premise that the national level is over-developed and might usefully be constrained or even diminished. The international, transnational, group, and individual levels might be enhanced through strategies of world order, international functionalism, softening and shrinking the nation-state, and human rights.

World order theories have a strong 'top-down' emphasis. One strand of world order—world federalism—implies that the most desirable approach would be the creation of a single effective world government, perhaps modeled along the lines of modern federal polities, with lawmaking authority. If total unification is not possible, then a partial core union might serve as a growth center for the larger global enterprise (see Clark and Sohn, 1966; and Streit, 1949).

Failing such an ambitious solution, world order approaches the globe as a developing country and aims to forge strong strands of cohesion. World order implies support for continued international legal codification; signature and ratification of, and compliance with, multilateral treaties, agreements, and declarations; international courts and other attempts at adjudication, arbitration, mediation, and conciliation of conflicts and disputes; participation in, contributions to, and compliance with international organizations and the collective decisions reached in them; development of and participation in international transactions, including trade; the establishment of substantial global reserves of commodities in short supply such as money, food, and energy; increased international communication through such means as diplomacy, travel, media, and education (see Falk, 1975; and Mendlovitz, 1975).

International functionalism comes to the world system with less sweeping ambitions. International functionalists tend not to believe in grand solutions to world problems. Instead they take a more piecemeal approach. Following functionalist logic, nations and groups can best build international peace by cooperating on specific projects, one at a time. Such cooperation implies different regimes in different sectors. For example, one set of international cooperative arrangements may exist with regard to the law of the sea, another for trade in oil, and a third for nuclear weapons (see Keohane, 1984; Krasner, 1982; and Haas, 1964).

The most controversial aspect of balancing involves softening and shrinking the nation-state, which has been the basic building block of the modern international system. The nation-state and nationalism have been, and will continue to be, central elements of the global system. They combine subordinate groups, with diverse identities and interests, into political communities with shared territory and aspirations. Yet the sharp edges of nations, like those of international blocs, increase the structural tendencies to violence. National aggrandizement is an important force leading to war.

Expanding states exert lateral pressure on others that, feeling threatened, attempt to defend themselves (see Choucri and North, 1975; and Organski and Kugler, 1980).

Balancing at the lowest level of the world system includes human rights, the protection and development of individual human beings. Peace creation includes a premise that a strong and healthy system grows through the growth of its component parts, rather than at their expense (see Clark, 1977).

Restructuring

We have seen that peace creation involves balancing relations *between* levels of the international system. A second major task of peace creation is to restructure processes and activities *within* different levels of the international system. International restructuring includes demilitarization, as well as the enhancement of equality and stability.

Peace creation implies demilitarization at the international, domestic, and individual levels. This means less emphasis on the law of war, international military peacekeeping, international military alliances, domestic military regimes, military expenditure, and military themes in media and culture.

Restructuring the international system also means moving towards greater equality, a more equal sharing of power, wealth, and knowledge. More groups and actors can participate actively in various dimensions of the world environment. As they articulate and defend their own particular concerns, they will also contribute their resources to the development of a shared human community.

International balancing finally carries a stabilizing logic. Rapid change benefits some, but not all. Changes cannot be implemented all at once through a sudden, apocalyptic global revolution. Rather they must take place gradually over time, through evolution. Revolutionary change is dramatic; but, by historical definition, it often carries with it a good deal of violence. The great revolutions of the modern world—France, the United States, China, the Third World—have been associated with important changes. Nevertheless, many beneficial developments might well have taken place without violent revolution. It is not clear, in any event, that violent revolution necessarily improves international peace.

Constructive actions can and should be undertaken incrementally, in small pieces, as experiments. Policy makers should define their expected impacts in advance and then monitor the results to see if they achieve the anticipated results. If so, additional steps can be taken; if not, little will be lost. Whether the actions succeed or fail, policy makers will have a systematic basis for learning and innovation. They can subsequently try new and better policies aiming at the same end.

Paths to International Peace

Our discussion has suggested a number of possible paths towards the reduction of international war and the creation of greater international peace. Violence limitation includes various strands some of which, like crisis management and war management, are easily applicable to specific situations. Others, restraint and nonviolence, are more difficult in the current context of international politics. Strategic deterrence and arms control are minimalist, narrowly defined, specific, short-term approaches. Balancing the levels of the international system through world order, functionalism, denationalization, human rights—and restructuring it by demilitarization, equalization, stabilization—are obviously maximalist, difficult, and distant goals.

It is often assumed that many of the paths presented here are mutually exclusive. National peace vs. international peace, strategic deterrence vs. arms control, short-term vs. long-term, practical vs. visionary. There certainly are trade-offs between them; yet some of the trade-offs may be more apparent than real. For example, we usually believe that advances in deterrence will set back arms control, or that progress in arms control or demilitarization will hinder deterrence. This is not necessarily true; indeed deterrence and arms control may, to some extent, be preconditions for each other. If deterrence were completely assured, arms control might become easier in areas which were not deemed essential to national peace. If arms control existed to a greater degree, deterrence might be more effective or less important. The Strategic Defense Initiative offers a striking example of this complementarity. Space-based strategic technology will be deployed primarily to provide deterrence (see Jastrow, 1985). Yet much of it will also provide the ability to monitor and enforce arms control. And its vulnerability to attack will, in turn, require arms control measures to ensure its safety.

The short-term and the long-term, the practical and the visionary, are not always at odds. Short-term practical considerations are necessary for us to navigate the shoals and narrows of our present day world; but a longer range vision provides a more stable direction for policy. Even if several of the approaches were mutually exclusive at the present time, they must not necessarily be opposed in the future. Present contradictions may be resolved through subsequent deconstruction, recombination, and synthesis. Survival and reform are not enemies. Both are important components of a comprehensive, coherent, and constructive international peace theory.

References

Allison, G. T., A. Carnesale and J. S. Nye, Jr. *Hawks, Owls, and Doves: An Agenda for Avoiding Nuclear War*. New York: Norton, 1985.

20   Francis A. Beer

Beer, F. A. *Peace Against War: The Ecology of International Violence*. San Francisco: W. H. Freeman, 1981.

Choucri, N., and R. North. *Nations in Conflict: National Growth and International Violence*. San Francisco: W. H. Freeman, 1975.

Clark, J. R. *The Great Living System*. Pacific Grove: Boxwood, 1977.

Clark, G., and L. B. Sohn. *World Peace through World Law: Two Alternative Plans,* 3rd ed. Cambridge: Harvard University Press, 1966.

Falk, R. *A Study of Future Worlds*. New York: Free Press, 1975.

Haas, E. B. *Beyond the Nation-State*. Stanford: Stanford University Press, 1964.

Jastrow, R. *How to Make Nuclear Weapons Obsolete*. Boston: Little, Brown, 1985.

Keohane, R. O. *After Hegemony: Cooperation and Discord in the World Political Economy*. Princeton University Press, 1984.

Krasner, S. D. (ed.). "International Regimes," special issue of *International Organization* 36:2. Cambridge: M.I.T. Press, 1982.

Mendlovitz, S. *On the Creation of a Just World Order: Preferred Worlds for the 1990s*. New York: Free Press, 1975.

Morgan, P. M. *Deterrence: A Conceptual Analysis*. Beverly Hills: Sage, 1977.

Naroll, R., V. L. Bullough and F. Naroll. *Military Deterrence in History: A Pilot Cross-Historical Survey*. Albany: State University of New York Press, 1974.

Organski, A. F. K. and J. Kugler. *The War Ledger*. Chicago: University of Chicago Press, 1980.

Roberts, A. (ed.). *Civilian Resistance as a National Defence: Non-Violent Action Against Aggression*. Baltimore: Penguin, 1969.

Sharp, G. *The Politics of Nonviolent Action*. Boston: Porter Sargent, 1973.

Streit, C. *Union Now: A Proposal for an Atlantic Federal Union of the Free*. New York: Harper, 1949.

Building Cooperation

ROBERT AXELROD

Under what conditions will cooperation emerge in a world of egoists without central authority? This question has intrigued people for a long time. And for good reason. We all know that people are not angels, and that they tend to look after themselves and their own first. Yet we also know that cooperation does occur and that our civilization is based upon it.

A good example of the fundamental problem of cooperation is the case where two industrialized countries have erected trade barriers to each other's exports. Because of the mutual advantages of free trade, both countries would be better off if these barriers were eliminated. But if either country were to eliminate its barriers unilaterally, it would find itself facing terms of trade that hurt its own economy. In fact, whatever one country does, the other country is better off retaining its own trade barriers. Therefore, the problem is that each country has an incentive to retain trade barriers, leading to a worse outcome than would have been possible had both countries cooperated with each other.

This basic problem occurs when the pursuit of self-interest by each leads to a poor outcome for all. To understand the vast array of specific situations like this, a way is needed to represent what is common to them without becoming bogged down in the details unique to each. Fortunately, there is such representation available: the famous Prisoner's Dilemma game, invented about 1950 by two RAND Corporation scientists. In this game there are two players. Each has two choices, namely 'cooperate' or 'defect'. Each must make the choice without knowing what the other will do.

One form of the game pays off as follows:

Player's Choice	Payoff
If both players defect:	Both players get 1 point
If both players cooperate:	Both players get 3 points
If one player defects while the other player cooperates:	The defector gets 5 points and the cooperator gets 0.

This article is included with the permission of the author and the Beyond War National Office, Palo Alto, California.

One can see that no matter what the other player does, defection yields a higher payoff than cooperation. If you think the other player will cooperate, it pays for you to defect (getting 5 points rather than 3 points). On the other hand, if you think that the other player will defect, it still pays for you to defect (getting 1 point rather than 0). Therefore the temptation is to defect. But, the dilemma is that if both defect, both do worse than if both had cooperated. The game is called Prisoner's Dilemma because in its original form two prisoners face the choice of informing on each other (defecting) or remaining silent (cooperation).

To find a good strategy to use in such situations, I invited experts in game theory to submit programs for a computer Prisoner's Dilemma tournament—much like a computer chess tournament. Each of these strategies was paired off with each of the others to see which would do best overall in repeated interactions.

Amazingly enough, the winner was the simplest of all candidates submitted. This was a strategy of simple reciprocity which cooperates on the first move and then does whatever the other player did on the previous move. In the American colloquial phrase, this strategy was named 'Tit-for-Tat'. A second round of the tournament was conducted in which many more entries were submitted by amateurs and professionals alike, all of whom were aware of the results of the first round. The result was another victory for simple reciprocity.

The analysis of the data from these tournaments reveals four properties which tend to make a strategy successful: avoidance of unnecessary conflict by cooperating as long as the other player does; provocability in the face of an uncalled-for defection of the other; forgiveness after responding to a provocation; and clarity of behavior so that the other player can recognize and adapt to your pattern of action.

Live and let live in World War I

One concrete demonstration of this theory in the real world is the fascinating case of the 'live and let live' system that emerged during the trench warfare of the Western Front in World War I. In the midst of this bitter conflict, the frontline soldiers often refrained from shooting to kill—provided their restraint was reciprocated by the soldiers on the other side.

For example, in the summer of 1915, a soldier saw that the enemy would be likely to reciprocate cooperation based on the desire for fresh rations.

> It would be a child's play to shell the road behind the enemy's trenches, crowded as it must be with ration wagons and water carts, into a bloodstained wilderness . . . but on the whole there is silence. After all, if you prevent your enemy from drawing his rations, his remedy is simple: he will prevent you from drawing yours (Hay, 1916, 224–25).

In one section the hour of 8 to 9 am was regarded as consecrated to 'private business', and certain places indicated by a flag were regarded as out of bounds by the snipers on both sides (Morgan, 1916, 270–71).

What made this mutual restraint possible was the static nature of trench warfare, where the same small units faced each other for extended periods of time. The soldiers of these opposing small units actually violated orders from their own high commands in order to achieve tacit cooperation with each other.

This case illustrates the point that cooperation can get started, evolve and prove stable in situations which otherwise appear extraordinarily unpromising. In particular, the 'live and let live' system demonstrates that friendship is hardly necessary for the development of cooperation. Under suitable conditions, cooperation based upon reciprocity can develop even between antagonists.

Conditions for stable cooperation

Much more can be said about the conditions necessary for cooperation to emerge, based on thousands of games in the two tournaments, theoretical proofs and corroboration from many real-world examples. For instance, the individuals involved do not have to be rational: the evolutionary process allows successful strategies to thrive, even if the players do not know why or how. Nor do they have to exchange messages or commitments: they do not need words, because their deeds speak for them. Likewise, there is no need to assume trust between the players: the use of reciprocity can be enough to make defection unproductive. Altruism is not needed: successful strategies can elicit cooperation even from an egoist. Finally, no central authority is needed: cooperation based on reciprocity can be self-policing.

For cooperation to emerge, the interaction must extend over an indefinite (or at least an unknown) number of moves, based on the following logic: two egoists playing the game once will both be tempted to choose defection since the action does better no matter what action the other player takes. If the game is played a known, finite number of items, the players likewise have no incentive to cooperate on the last move, nor on the next to last move since both can anticipate a defection by the other player. Similar reasoning implies that the game will unravel all the way back to mutual defection on the first move. It need not unravel, however, if the players interact an indefinite number of times. And in most settings, the players cannot be sure when the last interaction between them will take place. An indefinite number of interactions, therefore is the condition under which cooperation can emerge.

For cooperation to prove stable, the future must have a sufficiently large shadow. This means that the importance of the next encounter between the same two individuals must be great enough to make defection an unprofitable strategy. It requires that the players have a large enough chance of meeting again and that they do not discount the significance of their next meeting too greatly. For example, what made cooperation possible in the trench warfare of World War I was the fact that the same small units from opposite sides of no-man's-land would be in contact for long periods of time, so if one side broke the tacit understandings, then the other side could retaliate against the same unit.

In order for cooperation to get started in the first place, one more condition is required. The problem is that in a world of unconditional defection, a single individual who offers cooperation cannot prosper unless there are others around who will reciprocate. On the other hand, cooperation can emerge from small clusters of discriminating individuals as long as these individuals have even a small proportion of their interactions with each other. So there must be some clustering of individuals who use strategies with two properties: the strategy cooperates on the first move, and discriminates between those who respond to the cooperation and those who do not.

If a so-called 'nice' strategy, that is one which is never the first to defect, does eventually come to be adopted by virtually everyone, then individuals using this nice strategy can afford to be generous in their opening moves with any others. In fact, a population of nice strategies can protect itself from clusters of individuals using any other strategy just as well as it can protect itself against single individuals.

From national competitiveness to global cooperation

Robert Gilpin (1981, p. 205) points out that from the ancient Greeks to contemporary scholarship all political theory addressed one fundamental question: 'How can the human race, whether for selfish or more cosmopolitan ends, understand and control the seemingly blind forces of history?' In the contemporary world this question has become especially acute because of the development of nuclear weapons. Today, the most important problems facing humanity are in the arena of international relations, where independent, egoistic nations face each other in a state of near anarchy. Many of these problems take the form of an iterated Prisoner's Dilemma. Examples can include arms races, nuclear proliferation, crisis bargaining, and military escalation. Therefore, the advice to players of the Prisoner's Dilemma might serve as good advice to national leaders as well: don't be envious, don't be first to defect, reciprocate both cooperation and defection, and don't be too clever.

There is a lesson in the fact that simple reciprocity succeeds without doing better than anyone with whom it interacts. It succeeds by eliciting cooperation from others, not by defeating them. We are used to thinking about competitions in which there is only one winner, competitions such as football or chess. But the world is rarely like that. In a vast range of situations mutual cooperation can be better for both sides than mutual defection. The key to doing well lies not in overcoming others, but in eliciting their cooperation.

References

Axelrod, Robert. *The Evolution of Cooperation*. New York: Basic Books, 1984.
Gilpin, Robert. *War and Change in World Politics*. Cambridge: Cambridge University Press, 1981.
Hay, Ian. *The First Hundred Thousand*. London: Wm. Blackwood, 1916.
Morgan, J. H. *Leaves from a Field Note Book*. London: Macmillan, 1916.

Mediation

CHRIS MITCHELL

'Intervention between conflicting parties to promote reconciliation, settlement or compromise . . . ' (Webster's Dictionary)

The use of mediators—neutral third parties who help adversaries open
negotiations and (perhaps) end a dispute in a mutually satisfactory
agreement—has a long and varied history in humanity's efforts to manage
the often lethal conflicts that arise from people possessing incompatible
objectives and being willing to pursue them through coercion and violence.
The Greeks used mediators to help end disputes between city-states and we
have records of quite small Greek cities offering to mediate in conflicts
between leading Greek powers, such as Athens and Sparta. The Romans
both used and acted as intermediaries during the time of the Roman
Republic and the Empire. In more recent times there are examples of
mediation initiatives taken between 1973 and 1975 by Dr. Henry Kissinger,
then US Secretary of State, in the conflict between Israel and its neighbours;
in 1982 by the Peruvian President in the brief war between Argentina and
Britain over the Falkland/Malvinas Islands in the South Atlantic; and in
1987 by Senor Perez de Cuellar, the UN Secretary General, in the Iran-Iraq
War. In another realm entirely, anthropologists have discovered individuals
in many tribal societies who have the recognized and accepted role of trying
to end feuds and disputes by acting as a 'go-between' or by getting the
adversaries together to talk on 'neutral ground', while the figure of the
impartial mediator (often, in Britain, from the regional branch of the
Advisory Conciliation and Arbitration Service [ACAS]) is a familiar one in
industrial disputes.

In spite of these last two examples, it is generally believed (incorrectly, as
I will argue later) that mediators acting as peacemakers are mainly active in
trying to help international conflicts (confrontations, crises or wars) to a
peaceful end. The main reason for this view seems to be the commonly
drawn distinction between the usually ordered, secure and peaceful life
existing *within* a country, which means that mediators are seldom necessary,
and the insecure, lawless and unpeaceful nature of 'international society',

with its concentration on arms and military security; its more than 120 wars since 1945; and its absence of agreed laws, courts, police forces to keep the peace, and a government to ensure stability and security for citizens. Put another way, while *domestic* society seems to have been able to establish many ways of managing conflicts without a resort to organized violence (elections, courts, arbitration processes, grievance procedures, collective bargaining and other forms of negotiation, conflicts carried out 'within rules' or boundaries), *international* society appears to have failed to achieve a similar level of sophistication and success. International conflicts are managed much more by traditional methods of diplomatic bargaining, the existence of military force to deter violence by others (a frequently self-defeating strategy!), and the informal help of 'third parties' acting as mediators, moderators or conciliators between countries and their governments in dispute.

It is easy to see that the distinction is somewhat exaggerated. For one thing, it is difficult to argue that all domestic societies are always as peaceful and well-ordered as this model presumes. It can hardly be argued that conflicts are being successfully and peaceably 'managed' presently in Northern Ireland, or the Lebanon, or Peru, or even in the Basque country in Spain. Nor is it true that all parts of 'international society' are characterized by military rivalry, suspicion and an absence of peaceful ways of dealing with disputes regularly and successfully. Relations between Canada and the USA have been adequately managed for well over a hundred years, while the suspicions, conflicts and wars which wracked Western Europe until 1945 have (at least for the foreseeable future) been replaced by disputes dealt with by discussion and negotiation within the framework of the European Community. Finally, it is clearly the case that some ideas for world governments or international institutions to mirror national government in their task of keeping the peace and managing disputes have been taken up and resulted in the establishment of international institutions charged with settling disputes and maintaining 'international peace and security'. The Security Council of the United Nations, for example, was given this task of maintaining international peace and security on a global basis, while the Secretary General can use his good offices to act as fact-finder, conciliator or mediator in international disputes. When it was established in 1963, the Organization of African Unity (OAU) deliberately set up a Mediation Commission to help resolve inter-African disputes. Similarly, the Arab League, the Organization of American States (OAS), the Association of South East Asian Nations (ASEAN) and many other regional organizations all have a specific commitment to maintain regional peace by managing regional conflicts and avoiding violence. In many cases, they attempt to fulfil this role by acting as mediators.

However, it is not the case, even today, that most mediation into international conflicts is undertaken by the representatives of international organizations—although the proportion of such initiatives has gone up over the last 40 years. Traditionally, international mediators tended to be representatives of 'the Great Powers' of the time—Otto von Bismarck, Theodore Roosevelt and Benjamin Disraeli, all acted as important and successful mediators in major conflicts of their time, and Bismarck's phrase about being an 'honest broker' has come to characterize the generally held view of the essential nature of any mediator. In recent years this tradition of 'Great Power' mediation has been carried on by key individuals such as President Jimmy Carter, in achieving a peace settlement between Israel and Egypt at and following the meetings at Camp David in 1978; by Soviet Premier Alexei Kosygin, in bringing about a reconciliation between India and Pakistan at Tashkent in 1966; and by US Secretary of State Alexander Haig when trying, but failing, to prevent a war between Britain and Argentina in 1982. Typically, these key statesmen and diplomats catch media attention as mediators as they shuttle between warring capitals or try to hold quiet conversations about truces, agendas for negotiations and possible solutions with adversaries engaged in war, or the threat of war.

By contrast, little attention is usually paid to many others who can and do quietly take up the role of mediator in particular conflicts, often with success though with little publicity. Such individuals and organizations are often referred to as 'private' mediators, to emphasize both the fact that they hold no official position representing a particular government (so that they can easily be disowned if the initiative 'goes wrong' in some manner) and that their initiative is undertaken with no public resources or high prestige, political influence or aid (both financial and military) to help in persuading the opposing parties to agree to a compromise settlement. Often, such private mediators have no resources other than their goodwill and willingness to help, plus the adversaries' recognition that they are genuinely 'honest brokers', in the sense of being impartial and disinterested in the details of the eventual settlement—which may not be the case with formal official mediators, who often have a direct interest in the kind of settlement eventually negotiated, and who have been characterized as 'biased' mediators by some writers.

A huge variety of individuals and organizations indulge in quiet, private mediation in today's world, their success sometimes being measured in the achievement of a final settlement, but more often in terms of keeping open channels of communication between adversaries, transmitting and validating peace feelers between countries at war, or sounding out opposing governments to see whether the time might be ripe for a formal offer of mediation from a neighbouring country or a regional organization. Historically the Society of Friends (the Quakers) have taken a leading part in such activities as maintaining contacts, transmitting ideas and making suggestions about peacemaking moves to rival governments. Individual Quakers, such as Elmore Jackson, have been active in bridge-building between the Israeli

Government and President Nasser, while members of the Society have tried to act as contact points between the Soviet Union and the USA, Greeks and Turks on Cyprus, and Protestant and Catholic communities in Northern Ireland. Church organizations—usually because of their access to both sides through their humanitarian work—have often undertaken intermediary initiatives to try to end conflicts (rather than just mitigate their effects on those directly involved and harmed) frequently with considerable success. The World Council of Churches, for example, was instrumental in bringing the Sudanese Civil War to an end in 1972, while mediators from the Vatican (following over a hundred year tradition of the Pope acting as peacemaker in Latin American disputes) helped to negotiate a settlement of the Beagle Channel dispute between Argentina and Chile in 1984. On the other hand, a whole range of private individuals have acted as mediators in recent years, including journalists, academics, businessmen (like Tiny Rowlands and Armand Hammer) and clergymen.

While it is true that in contemporary international society there appear to be three basic types of mediators (interested national governments, international organizations and private intermediaries), it is also the case that they all tend to carry out similar tasks in actually being mediators. What do mediators actually do when they are mediating? Writing an article about this several years ago, James Wall listed a total of over fifty activities that mediators could—and did—carry out both in international and industrial mediation. These ranged from suggesting basic negotiation procedures to actually exaggerating the gains made by *both* sides in any compromise settlement.

A rather less complicated answer might be that mediators normally find themselves with four basic tasks. The first is to make contact with those in dispute in order to sound out whether it is worth making an effort to get them into a dialogue. If both sides, when contacted separately, either refuse to see the mediator or appear so hard-line that they are completely unwilling to compromise, then the initiative could end there. One of the first issues for any mediator is whether 'the time is ripe'. Are both sides ready for a compromise or are both determined to fight on to 'victory'? Obviously a mediator's judgement is crucial here, for there is little point in opening contacts and getting the two sides together if there is small chance of any positive progress. A fiasco will help no one.

If the mediator decides there is a good chance for progress, then his next task is to reopen quiet communication between the adversaries. In this, the mediator can find himself operating purely in the role of a 'go-between'— often quite literally, as he shuttles between one side and the other, carrying the latest information about conditions for talks, fundamental bargaining positions and queries about the other side's position on crucial issues. Usually, the mediator finds himself both a message carrier and (more importantly) an interpreter of one side to the other. At this stage it is in this second capacity that a mediator can have a great impact. Is the other side 'really' serious about compromise settlements, or is this just a trick to gain time? How vulnerable to the hawks are the other side's leaders? To what extent is public opinion on the other side ready for a compromise? Any mediator can be asked questions like this and must weigh his replies carefully. This 'go-between' task can be both delicate and protracted as both sides explore whether a face-to-face (or even a 'proximity') meeting is worth undertaking.

If the second task of renewing and monitoring contacts is successful, the next may be for the mediator to arrange, time and conduct face-to-face negotiating sessions between the adversaries. Often this involves providing some safe, private and neutral site for the talks, chairing the meetings to try to ensure that they are productive and do not end in stalemate or one side walking out in disgust. This task is frequently the most difficult, as the mediator has to pace the talks; prevent deadlock; suggest alternatives or new ideas; find ways to help the two sides out of the corners into which they have driven themselves and commitments they feel they must fulfil; reassure each regarding the other's sincerity and trustworthiness; find face-saving formulae for any agreement; yet all the while retain the trust of both parties in his impartiality and credibility. It is hardly surprising that this task usually requires considerable skill and subtlety on the part of the mediator, and frequently ends in failure. It can involve such situations as the mediator adopting one side's new suggestions as 'his own', as they will thus have more chance of being taken seriously by the other side; or of actually keeping the two sides apart from one another for a time (as President Carter did with Israelis and Egyptians at Camp David), in order to prevent a complete breakdown of the talks.

Finally, if the mediator can help the opponents to a successful settlement, the last set of tasks may involve helping both sides to have the settlement accepted 'back home' as being the best that could be negotiated; and also helping them to implement (and sometimes to monitor) the agreement. Experienced mediators know that their role is *not* ended by the press conference announcing the new agreement. Many settlements need some trusted party to check on both sides' observance of some of the terms, or to help in the renegotiation of some, perhaps unworkable, provision or to supply some resources (sometimes something as intangible as trust) which neither possesses. Such tasks are as much part of 'what a mediator does' as making the initial contacts, message carrying, suggesting ingenious compromises at a key moment during deadlocked negotiations, or sensitively exploring the underlying motivations of the two sides (as opposed to their public bargaining positions) in order to open up alternative means of their getting what they want.

Given the complexity of the task of being a mediator, it is hardly surprising that many initiatives break down at one or other stage of the process, either through the unwillingness of the parties to compromise, the intractability of the issues in dispute, or some change in the balance of advantage that convinces one side or the other, yet again, that it can gain more by continued coercion than by making concessions through negotiation. One major difference between institutional mediators (the UN Secretary General, ACAS in Britain, the Federal Conciliation and Mediation Service in the USA) and others, is that the former often have some kind of professional obligation to take up the task of being an intermediary and attempting to reach a compromise. It is somehow expected that the UN should be responsible for reaching a settlement of the Iran-Iraq War, or that the OAU should 'do' something about the dispute over the Western Sahara. Perhaps, this partly explains the growth of what might be called 'institutional' mediation since 1945.

On the other hand, mediation does have a number of great advantages over other means of trying to settle a dispute. Its very informality and flexibility enables new approaches to be explored without commitment and new ideas to be tested out. The adversaries retain the ability to withdraw from discussions if they are going in a direction deemed dangerous or likely to lead to an unacceptable settlement. Mediation initiatives may break down frequently, it is true, but those agreements which are reached are usually reasonably acceptable to both parties (and thus likely to be better kept) compared with settlements that are forced on one side by the other (which are likely to be undermined or overthrown at a later date).

Partly for these reasons, it is interesting to end with the observation that the use of informal mediation processes and the use of unofficial and informal mediators is beginning to occur as much in domestic society as at the international level. Partly, this seems to be happening because in many parts of the world (North America, Scandinavia, Australia and New Zealand, Western Europe), the advantages are being recognized of using a flexible and informal means of getting opponents and parties in conflict together to seek jointly a solution to their disputes. The solution will then not be an imposed one, and the parties can have a major say in how the dispute ends and what their subsequent relationships should be. They 'own' the settlement. The change is also partly the result of discontent with more conventional ways of handling domestic conflicts (e.g., going to court, using political influence to change laws, going through a series of hearings or appeals) both as regards costs or delays and as regards satisfaction with the outcome, even on the part of those who 'win'. This search for more satisfactory ways of managing conflicts had led to the development of a huge range of intermediary techniques, known in North America as 'ADR' (Alternative Dispute Resolution) and to the popularity of such slogans as 'Mediate don't litigate'. ADR has arisen from efforts to discover a means of dealing with a conflict which is basically non-adversarial, non-judgemental and informal. Central to many of the new processes is the figure of some impartial third party, informally helping the adversaries themselves in devising a solution that is acceptable to them. The development of mediation in domestic disputes to date, has led to the growth of such services as neighbourhood and school mediation, family and divorce conciliation, environmental dispute mediation and mediation or facilitation in organizational conflicts. Perhaps this is an interesting example of the transfer of old skills and ways of handling conflict from international to domestic society, for all of the above processes, at base, use similar skills and strategies to those that have been open to international mediators going back to the days of classical Greece.

References

Curle, Adam. *In the Middle: Non-official Mediation in Violent Situations*. Leamington Spa: Berg Publishers, 1986.
Jackson, Elmore. *Middle East Mission*. New York: W. W. Norton, 1985.
Perry, Catherine. *Conflict Resolution, Fellowship Briefing No. 5*. London: Fellowship of Reconciliation, 1984.
Stanford, Barbara (ed.). *Peacemaking: A Guide to Conflict Resolution*. New York: Bantam Books, 1976.
Touval, Saadia. *The Peace Brokers: Mediators in the Arab-Israeli Conflict*. Princeton: Princeton University Press, 1982.

PART 2

Analyses of Different Forms of International Conflict

There are many actors in the international system including states (countries such as the USA, USSR or Brazil); multinational companies (such as IBM, Mitsubishi or Pergamon Press); international governmental organizations (such as UNESCO or the EEC); and national and international non-governmental organizations (such as the International Olympic Committee, International Islamic Organization or the Catholic Church). These actors become involved in a range of political, social, economic and cultural conflicts. This section of the book includes analyses of some of these different forms of international conflict. The chapters have been selected in such a way that a broad range of sometimes contradictory approaches has been included. For example, Noam Chomsky and Richard Clutterbuck have opposing views on terrorism and who should be called a terrorist, while Reinhard Kühnl and Fred Halliday have very different approaches to the East-West conflict.

Capitalism and Global Integration

ANKIE HOOGVELT

Global integration through international trade

At one level global integration has something to do with what you have for breakfast and where it comes from. Your coffee or tea, your oranges and cornflakes have all originated somewhere outside Britain, and much more besides. Shopping for clothes can be taxing if you insist on buying British. You only need to look at the labels to discover there's not much that is made here. And as for that once great pride of British industry, steel and engineering tools, they too now face tough foreign competition in our very own home market. Today, about 30 percent of everything that is produced in the world outside the so called Socialist countries is traded across frontiers. For some countries like Britain the figure is even higher. The combined value of our exports and imports is about 50 percent of the total value of our gross domestic product.

International trade has long been regarded by economists and politicians alike as a 'good' thing, because it encourages nations and people to concentrate on what they are best at, given their skills and natural endowments, and not waste time and resources on that which other nations and people can produce more efficiently. In this way, through international trade, it is thought, all nations can grow and prosper, benefiting from one another's excellence.

The theoretical underpinning for this optimistic view was put forward a long time ago, in 1817, by David Ricardo in his *Theory of Comparative Advantage*. His was such a convincing theory that, at the time, it gave a scientific justification to the expansionist and annexationist policies of the great Colonial Powers: Britain, France, Holland and Belgium. The policy makers of these imperial powers argued that by forcibly commercializing the backward, but hitherto self-sufficient and isolated, communities of Africa and Asia, and by bringing them into a grand worldwide network of international division of labour, not only would jobs be created for the

35

workers at home—'Trade follows the Flag' it was said—but these subjected peoples themselves would ultimately benefit and say 'thank you', their pains of transition forgotten.

These pains included the often violent grabbing by the Europeans of their lands which were turned into plantations or mines producing mineral or agricultural raw materials which would feed the ever expanding industries and workforce of the metropolitan economies; the imposition of colonial taxes which compelled the natives to look for paid work in the white man's plantation and mines or made them grow cash crops for exports; the ruthless dispossession of millions and the violent destruction of traditional forms of social life.

But the forcible introduction of money and markets, of commercialization and of proletarianization, was also accompanied by what the imperial powers were pleased to call 'civilization', namely the inculcation of Western values of education, of Christian notions of individuality and of the sanctity of private property and contract, as well as of Western consumer tastes and lifestyles—of something that the writer Ivan Illich once called: 'Western patent solutions to basic human needs'. The stupendous growth in industrial output fostered by international trade imposed a self reinforcing dynamic: ever widening world market outlets had to be found for the mass produced consumer goods rolling off the assembly lines of the advanced countries' factories. In this way global integration also inevitably implied relentless homogenization of cultures and societies.

Global integration and unequal exchange

The 'old' international division of labour and the emergence of a one-world market system which grew up under the tutelage of Colonialism had one major flaw not foreseen by the neoclassical economists at the time. Instead of equalizing the rates of return to the various participants and thus 'developing' the backward regions of the world as they had hoped, the world market only served to deepen existing inequalities between regions and countries. The already rich nations became richer while the poor nations became poorer still. Why was this so?

There were economic, technical reasons as well as historical and political ones. For one thing, the old division of labour had relegated the colonial territories to become suppliers of agricultural raw materials and foodstuffs, exchanging their commodities for the manufactured products from the advanced countries. The equalizing potential of the free market principle of exchange hinges on a balance of forces of supply and demand. But it so happens that the forces of supply and demand do not operate in the same way for raw materials and foodstuffs as they do for manufactured products. The former suffer debilitating restrictions and bottlenecks which the latter do not. For example, in a growing world economy the demand for raw materials and foodstuffs does not expand at equal pace with that of manufactured goods. There is a limit to the amount of foodstuffs people can consume while the demand for manufactured goods is almost limitless. Again, with industrial progress, raw materials, both mineral and agricultural, are easily replaced by synthetics, while, in addition, technological inventions tend to reduce the volume of raw materials needed to fabricate the same volume and efficiency of function of a manufactured commodity. Just look at your great-grandmother's clock and compare its efficiency with our electronic watch!

There were other, historical and political reasons too, why the global coordination of human activities through the free market system could not benefit rich and poor regions equally. For the rich nations had a head start which made them the more powerful actors in the 'free market' exchange. Labour emancipation through unionization in the aftermath of the Industrial Revolution had yielded a standard of living and wage costs which could not easily be relinquished even in periods of recession. The wage element in manufactured commodities therefore always proved to be higher than that of raw materials. And since it was by and large the companies from the advanced countries which controlled the production and trade of commodities in the colonies, they could buy off labour unrest at home by lowering the prices of the raw materials which they produced in their captive mines abroad. In this way, it has been said, colonial profits helped pay for social advance and social democracy in the metropolitan countries, replacing the imperialism of the ruling class with the 'peoples imperialism'.

Taking all this together it is not surprising that upon independence the newly emerging nations found that they had to work forever harder to stand still, that they had to produce more and more for exports in order to pay for the same amount of imports, and most importantly, that while politically free, they were still in economic bondage.

The realization that the capitalist world market systematically disadvantaged the poorer ex-colonial countries of Africa, Asia and Latin America became, in the 1950s and 1960s, a potent political force which temporarily united these countries into a Third World bloc. This realization gave direction to their domestic development strategies in which economic nationalism and industrialization became paramount. At the international level, in numerous international negotiating forums, organizations and discussions, the Third World countries began to demand fundamental changes in the world market system. They wanted better and more secure prices for their traditional exports; they wanted preferential access to domestic markets in the advanced countries for their infant manufacturing industries; they asked for reforms in the international monetary system and for generous aid flows; and they proposed codes of conduct for multinational companies. In 1974–75, these demands were solemnly enshrined in a United Nations Charter of Economic Rights and Duties of States, and in a Programme of Action for the Establishment of a New International Economic Order (NIEO).

Global integration through international production

But already, long before the ink was dry on the paper of these agreements, profound changes in the world capitalist system had taken place which made these demands obsolete and which eroded the political unity which had given expression to them. For by then the world capitalist system had progressed to a higher level of integration: one which this time was mediated not through trade or free markets, but through enterprise organization. And paradoxically, this higher level of integration was achieved precisely because of the contradictions engendered by the colonially imposed 'old' international division of labour.

What can only be appreciated with hindsight is that the very contradictions of the old division of labour and the resulting nationalistic political and economic aspirations of the newly emerging countries actually neatly dovetailed with the requirements of the already advanced countries. By the late 1950s, the leading branches of industry were in fact no longer manufacturing consumer goods but producer goods such as machine tools and engineering products, plant and equipment. No longer did it make sense to see the ex-colonial areas primarily as market outlets for textiles, matches, cigarettes or bicycles. Instead these areas now needed to be upgraded to become market outlets for spinning and weaving tools, lathe machines and production and assembly lines. In addition, many leading branches of industry such as aerospace, telecommunications and arms producers depended for their growth and profits on contracts from governments. The springing up of many small independent national units—the number of 'independent' nation-states trebled between 1945–75—all of them adopting a 'development and industrialization' ideology and feverishly wishing to 'catch up with the West', and seeking Western patent solutions to basic human needs, corresponded nicely with the level of industrial sophistication achieved by then in the metropolitan countries. The technological backwardness of the 'developing' countries as they were now called, provided fresh opportunities for Western capitalists to make money: the industrialization drive of these countries meant that they had to invite foreign companies to set up subsidiary companies in their countries, and help them produce locally what previously had been imported. But the Third World countries were not alone in this: there were parallels in other parts of the world. For example, the postwar reconstruction of Europe became a driving force behind the massive expansion of American companies there.

By 1971 the total value of international production (that is the total value of production by multinational companies in countries other than their 'home' countries) was greater than the total value of international trade. Today some 200 multinationals contribute about one-fifth of the non-socialist world's gross product. Each of the 50 largest corporations with an annual turnover of over $10 billion exceeds in economic size and strength most of the world's Third World economies and some of the largest companies can match dollar for dollar all but the largest of the world's advanced economies (see Table 1). International trade in the conventional sense of economic exchanges between independent producers and consumers in different countries has been overtaken by the 'in-house' or infra-firm transactions of globe-girdling corporations. This means that the invisible hand of the market which we habitually credit with the fine quality of efficient resource allocation, is in its turn being led by the global profit seeking calculus of a handful of incumbents in the upper echelons of international corporate organizations.

In other words, global integration, or the coordination of human activities on a worldwide basis, now takes place *not* within a world market but within the planned, administrative embrace of world companies.

Initially, the new global integration through international production emerged as a defensive reaction on the part of companies who saw their former markets threatened by trade restricting domestic ambitions and policies. If it was no longer possible to sell Coca Cola or Widgets across frontiers, then of course subsidiary plants would have to be set up in each foreign location to produce Coca Cola or Widgets. But a new and still more sophisticated pattern of integration developed when multinational companies began to take full advantage of the diversity of financial, fiscal, economic and industrial legislation enacted in a world of some 150 sovereign but competing nation-states. They began to fragment the production process itself, farming out different component activities to different national locations depending on country specific legislation and local circumstances, e.g., labour intensive activities to low wage countries, research intensive activities to places with generous government subsidies and a highly skilled work force, final assembly to locations near large markets, profit remittances to 'tax havens' where tax rates are near zero. And so on. Such global production in which each affiliate carries out some part of the production process but not the whole has technologically and economically integrated human activities across national frontiers on a scale far exceeding any interdependencies that had already been created by the existence of a 'world market'. It is an integration that is arguably less systematically unequal between rich and poor nations than the integration achieved under the old division of labour. For, the new globally integrated 'organic' mode of production implies a macro-rationality that goes beyond the plans of each part and even beyond the plans of the leading part (i.e., the home base of the multinational enterprise concerned). The centralized management strategy of the multinational company requires not only control over resource

TABLE 1.   *The World's Top One Hundred: Nations and Global Companies Ranked by Total Value of GDP or Sales (in millions of US Dollars, 1984).*

Rank	Nation/Company	GDP/Sales	Rank	Nation/Company	GDP/Sales
1	United States	3,634,600	51	Libya	30,570
2	Japan	1,255,006	52	Egypt	30,060
3	Federal Republic of	613,160	53	Greece	29,550
	Germany		54	Dupont	29,483
4	France	489,380	55	Malaysia	29,280
5	United Kingdom	425,370	56	United Arab Republic	28,840
6	Italy	348,380	57	General Electric	28,285
7	Canada	334,110	58	Pakistan	27,730
8	China	281,250	59	Standard Oil	27,215
9	Brazil	187,130	60	IRI	26,758
10	Australia	182,170	61	Toyota	26,040
11	Mexico	171,300	62	EMI	24,460
12	India	162,280	63	New Zealand	23,340
13	Spain	160,930	64	Atlantic Richfield	22,357
14	Netherlands	132,600	65	Israel	22,350
15	Iraq	109,440	66	Kuwait	21,710
16	Saudi Arabia	109,380	67	Unilever	21,627
17	General Motors	96,372	68	Chrysler	21,255
18	Sweden	91,880	69	Matushita	20,749
19	Switzerland	91,110	70	Hitachi	20,525
20	Exxon	86,673	71	Pemex	20,380
21	Republic of Korea	83,220	72	Shell Oil	20,309
22	Royal Dutch Shell	81,743	73	Hungary	20,150
23	Indonesia	80,590	74	Elf	20,105
24	Belgium	77,630	75	Chile	19,670
25	Argentina	76,210	76	Française Petroleum	19,267
26	Poland	75,410	77	Portugal	19,060
27	Nigeria	73,450	78	Peru	18,790
28	South Africa	73,390	79	US Steel	18,429
29	Iran	66,000	80	Ireland	18,270
30	Austria	64,460	81	Nissan	18,226
31	Mobil	55,960	82	Singapore	18,220
32	Norway	54,720	83	Phillips	18,079
33	Denmark	54,640	84	Siemens	17,833
34	British Petroleum	53,101	85	Volkswagen	17,832
35	Ford Motor	52,774	86	Daimler-Benz	17,800
36	Finland	51,230	87	Nestle	17,159
37	Algeria	50,690	88	Petrobas	16,046
38	IBM	50,056	89	Angola	16,038
39	Venezuela	47,500	90	Syria	15,930
40	Turkey	47,460	91	United Technologies	15,749
41	Texaco	46,297	92	Phillips Petroleum	15,676
42	Thailand	41,960	93	Bayer	15,598
43	Chevron	41,741	94	Tenneco	15,400
44	Yugoslavia	38,990	95	BASF	15,072
45	AT & T	34,909	96	Occidental	14,510
46	Colombia	34,400	97	Fiat	14,193
47	Philippines	32,840	98	Samsung	14,193
48	Cuba	32,238	99	Mitsubishi	14,112
49	Korea	32,238	100	Hyundai	14,025
50	Hong Kong	30,620			

Source: Company data from *Fortune*, May and August 1986. Nation data from World Bank, *Development Report*, 1986.

allocation in the foreign affiliates coupled with substantive 'administered' trade beween the geographically dispersed parts, but it also implies the ability and the need to choose the location of profit making centres in accordance with the long-term viability and growth of the firm. These need no longer be in the home countries from where the multinational companies originate. The fact that, today, one-half of the largest 100 British multinationals have finance subsidiaries in countries other than Britain is indicative of this trend.

With this macro-rationality of management, the umbilical cord that used to tie the multinationals to their home nations (making them a vehicle for imperialism between nations) is severed. In this sense it is more appropriate to call these companies transnational rather than multinational. The flip side of this is that global production has integrated the world economy in a manner that escapes democratic social control in any country. Even in the advanced countries which boast strong traditions of democratic government, people are beginning to wonder if their is any point in casting their votes when the government of their choice cannot fulfil its electoral pledge of lower interest rates, or job creation, or the holding down of prices, because international capital can shift massive funds in and out of a country, relocate industrial activity to other nations, or mark up prices at will.

Last but not least, the thickening network of contemporary global integration has its counterpart in 'peripheralization' and 'marginalization' of those areas of the globe no longer of interest to global capital. The declining participation of subSaharan Africa in world trade (see Table 2) is one example of this phenomenon; the continuing long-term unemployment levels in the depressed areas of the north of Britain is another.

TABLE 2.   *Share of World Exports and Imports (in percent and by Region and Economic Grouping).*

	Exports			Imports		
	1950	1970	1985	1950	1970	1985
WORLD	100.0	100.0	100.0	100.0	100.0	100.0
Developed Market Economy Countries	60.8	70.9	65.6	64.9	71.6	68.3
Socialist Countries Eastern Europe	6.8	9.8	9.0	6.3	9.7	8.6
Developing Countries and Territories	31.1	18.4	23.9	27.2	17.9	20.9
By region						
South and Central America	12.4	5.5	5.4	10.1	5.5	4.0
Africa North	2.1	1.6	1.5	2.5	1.2	1.6
Africa subSahara	3.1	2.4	1.7	2.8	2.2	1.5
Asia West	2.3	3.3	5.4	2.2	2.0	4.6
Asia South and South East	10.9	4.8	9.2	8.9	5.8	5.5

Based on UNCTAD, *Handbook of International Trade and Development Statistics*, 1986. Supplement tables 1.9 and 1.10, pp. 26 and 27.

References

Bush, Ray, Gordon Johnston and David Coates (eds.). *The World Order: Socialist Perspectives*. London: Polity Press, 1987.

Harris, Nigel. *The End of the Third World: Newly Industrialising Countries and the Decline of an Ideology*. London: I. B. Tauris & Co. Ltd., 1986.

Griffin, Keith. *World Hunger and the World Economy*. London: Macmillan Press, 1987.

Hoogvelt, Ankie M. M. *The Third World in Global Development*. London: Macmillan, 1982.

Kruijer, Gerald J. *Development through Liberation: Third World Problems and Solutions*. Basingstoke: Macmillan Education Ltd., 1987.

The Race Factor in International Politics

HUGH TINKER

Western writers on international relations have tacitly ignored race as a factor in world conflicts. While acknowledging the existence of a gulf between 'North' and 'South' they feel more comfortable describing this as an economic gap, almost as a technical difficulty, which can be characterized by labelling the deprived countries of the Third World as less developed countries (LDCs). The peoples of the Third World are in no doubt about the causes of the basic division between white affluence and black and brown poverty and the continuing determination of the whites to preserve this division by reference to their innate superiority. As one Asian commentator declares: 'The West is still hamstrung by the anachronistic idea that White can always do things (including, of course, rule) better than Black, Brown or Yellow, whatever its Ideological commitment to human freedom and equality.'[1]

Whenever Western writers are brought to consider race as a problem in international politics they like to make the point that racial tensions are as serious among the Third World peoples as they are between white and black. They point to the hostility of the indigenous peoples to the overseas Chinese in Southeast Asia or to Indians and Pakistanis in East Africa. We may agree that these tensions are very real, but they do not create the global divisions which can be ascribed to white racial dominance. To the Third World, white racism is a continuing legacy of white imperialism and an aspect of the still pervasive force of neocolonialism. (Incidentally, the black-brown tensions mentioned above may also be attributed to a kind of sub-imperialism in which until very recently Indians and Chinese were agents of white imperialism.)

This article is adapted from the original which appeared in the *International Journal*, Vol. XXXIV, No. 3, Summer 1979. Used with the permission of the author and of the Canadian Institute of International Affairs.

43

How far are we all prisoners of the past: both the recent past, in which the world was, effectively, the stage for Western expansion, and that remote past, in which the light-skinned Aryans foisted upon the dark-skinned Negritoid, Veddoid, and other subjugated races the syndrome of values which equated 'light' and 'fair' with good, and 'dark' and 'black' with evil? For this is where the racial factor begins; with a primordial sense of the superiority of white over black. Formerly, students of race relations employed as a key concept the idea of prejudice. It was assumed that because of unfamiliarity, or social distance, or merely lack of adequate education, individuals and groups were 'prejudiced', while rational, informed people were absolutely or relatively unprejudiced. Through more complete knowledge, the incidence of prejudice could be reduced and better race relations would follow.

When this approach was seen to be wholly inadequate, students of race relations embraced the 'problem' explanation. Hostility to those of another race arose out of environmental shortcomings: poor housing in short supply, educational inequalities, competition for jobs, institutional inflexibility (such as police suspicion of the wanderer, the displaced). Even when this explanation was in the context of liberalism—involving a declared intention to make good these shortcomings—there was a clear understanding that the problem arose from the insertion of what one eminent English judge called 'an alien wedge' into the 'host' society.[2]

The problem was caused by the arrival of black and brown groups within white society: almost nobody (except a few radicals) saw the problem as that of white racism. Any acknowledgement that there is an innate hostility to 'lesser breeds without law' among almost all the whites of the world is slow to arrive. A kind of rearguard action is still being fought. During the twilight of the British Empire, progressives might agree that right-wing imperial administrators were guilty of colour prejudice; but not themselves. Today, British intellectuals (or some of them) might agree that the British working class, the alleged supporters of Enoch Powell and the National Front, are racialists; but not of course themselves. The idea that deep in the white subconscious there is the conviction that White is Wonderful and Black is Beastly is resisted and rejected by all right-thinking (white) people. Hence, the proposition that black and brown people are on one side and white are on the other would be dismissed as obscurantist—indeed, racist—by right-thinking (white) people.

The proposition, in terms of international configurations, was advanced long ago by non-white thinkers. The black American sociologist W.E.B. Du Bois insisted that 'the problem of the 20th century would be the problem of the colour line—the relation of the darker to the lighter men in Asia and Africa, in America, and the islands of the sea.'[3] The Indian poet, Rabindranath Tagore, told an international conference: 'I regard the race and colour prejudice which barricades human beings against one another as the greatest evil of modern times.' The World Conference for International Peace through Religion, held in Geneva in 1928, identified causes of race friction in different areas of the world arising from migration, economic imperialism ('the crushing wealth of the West'), religious imperialism, the rising tide of nationalism in the East, and 'international discourtesy' displayed by the Western nations.[4] The conference was asked to recommend that the League of Nations establish a court of racial justice.

The conference achieved nothing, of course, and was followed shortly after by yet another long series of wars in which whites destroyed blacks, including the Italian invasion of Ethiopia. Although this invasion aroused worldwide censure, it was condemned by white critics as an ideological deviation, a manifestation of fascism. It was left to folk who were then almost invisible and inaudible on the world stage—the blacks of the United States and the Caribbean and young African intellectuals such as Kwame Nkrumah—to protest against the racist implications of the invasion: the extinction of the last independent black nation, the last symbol of black dignity.

When an international issue was belatedly recognized as having racial elements it was the Nazi persecution of the German Jews (the oppression of whites by fellow whites) which aroused the conscience of the Western world. The Nazi extermination policy led to the coining of the term genocide, and the adoption by the United Nations General Assembly of the Convention on the Prevention and Punishment of the Crime of Genocide (1948). The equally devastating extermination of black and brown peoples, such as the wiping out of the North American Indian tribes or the Herero tribe of South-West Africa, had aroused no such international concern.

The Nazi treatment of the Jews remains the reference point for any consideration of race as a factor in international conflict. It was this terrible crime against humanity which caused the infant United Nations to press on with the Universal Declaration of Human Rights (1948). These acknowledged rights represent the freedoms slowly acquired in Western liberal societies: equality before the law, freedom of thought, conscience, and religion, freedom of opinion and expression, freedom of assembly, and so on.

Because the application of this code was qualified by the members accepting it, in that the United Nations should not intervene in matters of domestic jurisdiction, the Declaration has remained little more than a statement of ideals. The same applies to the conventions which flowed from that declaration, including the International Convention on the Elimination of All Forms of Racial Discrimination (1965). This convention states that racial discrimination is 'any distinction, exclusion, restriction or preference based on race, colour, descent or national or ethnic origin'. This apparently sweeping definition of forms of racial discrimination is modified by the provision that the convention does not apply to 'distinctions, exclusions,

restrictions or preferences made . . . between citizens and non-citizens';
another evocation of the 'domestic jurisdiction' principle. The Convention
calls for the encouragement of 'integrationist multi-racial organizations and
movements' and sets up a committee of experts to whom complaints about
non-observance of the Convention may be referred to. Thus far the
committee and the Convention have made only a limited impact upon
international peace questions and the channels of the United Nations have
been largely used as pressure points in the overall confrontation between the
superpowers and their allies and clients.

Meanwhile, the Third World states have increasingly to be reckoned with
in the United Nations. A mere dozen at the time of the organization's
foundation, the march forward into independence increased their number to
75 by December 1964 and to over 100 by 1979.[5] These new states represent
every kind of interest, and these interests are frequently in competition or
conflict. There is no coherent Afro-Asian bloc and their priorities are often
mutually divergent. But they unite when issues seen as originating in white
dominance are before them. One issue, now recognized by all the world, is
the prolongation of white dominance in southern Africa, a continent
otherwise liberated from white imperial domination. The second issue,
increasingly identified as racial by Afro-Asian nations, is thought by the
West to lack such a connotation: this is Israel's occupation of the lands of the
Palestinians.

South Africa is now so isolated as a global pariah that it is easy to forget
how, until recently, the West was prepared to condone the system of white
dominance as a part of the natural order. During the early years of the
United Nations, whenever any questions concerning South Africa—
including South-West Africa (now Namibia)—was brought into the international arena, the West either opposed intervention or abstained from
taking sides. Britain, Australia, New Zealand, the United States, the
Netherlands, and even the Scandinavian states, were quite clear that South
Africa should not be put on trial for its internal policies towards non-whites.
It was only after the entry of black African states into the United Nations in
1960 and immediately thereafter that the West began to reconsider its
approach. South Africa remained secure in its economic strength and in its
ties with the multinationals and seemed still able to ride out the storm.

The United Nations passed resolution after resolution, by the combined
voting strength of the Third World and the communist bloc, without any
practical effect. The climax was the adaptation by the General Assembly of a
resolution establishing an International Convention on the Suppression and
Punishment of the Crime of Apartheid (1973). This was ratified by 38
countries, none belonging to the West. The convention refers specifically to
racial oppression and envisages the setting up of an international tribunal to
try those guilty of the crimes enumerated.[6] This massive condemnation by
world opinion seemed to leave the South African government unmoved;

especially as the British government of the day announced that it could not accept the legality of the Convention.

However, when Portugal withdrew from Angola and the Popular Movement for the Liberation of Angola (MPLA) with Cuban military support, took over that country, South Africa began to revise its policies. South-West Africa was the most vulnerable terrain, and, having stonewalled for 30 years over its future, the government of B. J. Vorster unexpectedly indicated that it was prepared to negotiate with the United Nations. Within a few months, the whole apparatus of apartheid was demolished in South-West Africa/Namibia. The prohibition upon interracial marriages, the confinement of Africans to separate residential locations from whites, the classification of jobs on racial lines, the separate educational systems: all this was (in law) brought to an end. How, philosophically, South African whites could reconcile the contradiction between accepting multiracial practices in one of their territories alongside apartheid elsewhere must be a mystery! Negotiations then began for an agreement on the transfer of power to a new multiracial Namibian administration. At this point, the Western powers (the United States, Britain, France, West Germany, Canada) came forward as mediators between South Africa and the United Nations. All of them had investments in Namibia, some of massive proportions, and doubtless the move was to provide for a smooth transfer which would safeguard these investments. The plan does not seem to have worked out. At the time of writing it is still not clear whether Third World opposition to racialism or white solidarity will finally determine how Namibia emerges; whether through acceptance of African claims or by armed struggle. What has become clear is that the last ideological bastion of white exclusiveness has been breached, and South Africa's white friends have been compelled to recognize that the view of the Third World must prevail.

It may be argued that South Africa is a special case, a kind of historical accident, a fossil of white colonialism preserved when all the rest had dissolved away. Doubtless, the West would like to treat the South African case as an unpleasant inconvenience; but one that will not recur to be categorized as a special kind of 'problem', and that, given special treatment by the West, may, perhaps, eventually go away.

The emergence of Israel as another global outsider provides uneasy evidence that the introduction of race into international relations is not just a will-o'-the-wisp, as Western experts would like to say; it is a strategy promising a vigorous response. To mobilize Third World support, the Palestine Liberation Organization (PLO) and other Arab spokesmen have portrayed Israel as a paradigm of South Africa, and Zionism as a manifestation of racism. In 1975 came the United Nations resolution describing Zionism 'as a form of racism and racial discrimination'. The 72 states which voted for this resolution included most of the Afro-Asian world, as well as the Soviet bloc. (It was one issue which united the Soviet Union and China.)

Only 35 states, led by the United States, voted against the resolution with another 32 abstaining.

Perhaps less dramatic but equally significant in its way, was the 1978 resolution directed against Israeli policies and practices which proclaimed 'the inalienable right of the peoples of Namibia, South Africa and Zimbabwe, of the Palestinian people and of all peoples under colonial or alien domination . . . to self-determination, national independence, territorial integrity . . . without external interference'. It has been a regular feature of conferences of non-aligned states to make these connections between southern Africa and Israel as areas of foreign (that is, white) occupation of essentially brown and black lands.

In consequence of these developments the former Israeli strategy of building friendships in Asia and Africa by providing advice and expertise on practical development now lies in ruins. Israel has been compelled to rely almost exclusively upon Western support, especially that of the United States. Prime Minister Begin worked hard at convincing his friends that his opponents are terrorists, comparing the PLO to the Nazis. Paradoxically, the Arabs and their communist allies hurl the same charge at Begin and accuse Israel of Nazi methods towards prisoners and the subject Arab population. It appears as though the agreed measurement for racism remains the treatment by whites (Germans) of fellow whites (Jews).

It seems inevitable that the problems created by white hegemony in South Africa and by Arab resistance to Israeli expansion will continue to haunt the international community right into the twenty-first century. Increasingly, the West will be forced to make a choice: to support its 'natural' partners (those on top) or to acquiesce in the Third World's assessment of these situations as unacceptable. Even those as skilled in international finesse as the French may find that the price of enjoying international influence is to make a definite choice. The choice may still be taken in terms of the realities of power; the Third World remains powerless. The consequences will be the increasing polarization of forces between those who dominate and those who are dominated: a division line which the white 'North' will seek to minimize while the black 'South' maximizes what is one of its moral advantages. For the international morality of the late twentieth century is agreed that racism is deplorable.

If race does become a dominant feature of international politics it will emerge as in the subtle undertones of the Israeli-Arab confrontation and not in the dramatic form of a race war. Two probable areas where racial undertones may become more pronounced are the Caribbean and the Pacific. The Caribbean is recognized as potentially dangerous for the West's protagonist, the United States, and the Pacific could also be a danger area under vastly different circumstances for both the United States and Australia. They still have memories of fighting for survival in this area. In both these vast areas the factor of race stems from historical experience: from the forcible transportation of black, brown, and yellow peoples to labour in the interests of whites. The plural societies thus created still perpetuate white dominance.[7] This dominance is closely tied in with the economic dominance of multinationals owned by and controlled from the West. Attempts to create a New International Economic Order will involve the emergence of a new racial order. In some aspects the confrontation between the races will be internal, as in Australia, New Zealand and Hawaii, and on much reduced scale in Puerto Rico, Bermuda, and the Bahamas. These internal confrontations will also, in certain cases, be between non-white rivals, as in Sri Lanka, Guyana and Fiji.[8] But, just as 'racial' differences escalated in Palestine/Israel from internal group conflict into international confrontation, so there is the prospect of local, internal conflicts being escalated until they become involved in international politics.

In the Caribbean, there is already a focus for this process: this is Cuba, which has now established cordial relations with most of its neighbours and has been declared by Castro to be an Afro-Latin culture. At present there is no such catalyst in the Pacific. Japan, which created this role in the past, is too firmly an honorary member of the white world, and perhaps its coming leader. As yet, the possible contenders are still under Western influence; but somewhere there may be a 'Pacific Castro', already studying at university or working for a trade union.

Along with the prospects of confrontation between whites and non-whites there are many potential conflicts between different brown and black peoples who see each other in terms of racial differences.[9] As the image of classical Western imperialism begins to fade, so we may expect its emotional power to be transferred to the image of racism: a power so much older than the oldest empire and (alas) likely to retain its potency until the end of time.

Notes

1. *Asia Week,* 25 November 1977, in a review of the present writer's book, *Race, Conflict and the International Order.* The reviewer concluded: 'What this portends is the increasing polarisation of the world along racial lines.' By contrast, a review of the same book in the British Labour weekly, *Tribune,* on 14 October 1977, dismissed its 'unconvincing final prophecies of global polarisation along race rather than class division'.
2. Lord Radcliffe, 'Immigration and Settlement: Some General Considerations', *Race,* July 1969.
3. It was Du Bois who first declared that there is 'Beauty in Black'.
4. C. F. Andrews, 'Racial Influences', in Arthur Porritt (ed.). *The Causes of War: Economic, Industrial, Racial, Religious, Scientific and Political.* London: 1932, pp. 63–113.
5. What or who constitute the Third World? Somewhat arbitrarily, the present body count does not include the countries of Latin America but does include those of the Caribbean.
6. The crime of apartheid includes, inter alia: 'Denial to a member or members of a racial group or groups of the right of life and liberty of persons' by murder, bodily or mental harm, infringement of freedom or dignity, torture, arbitrary arrest and illegal imprisonment, or deliberate imposition of living conditions calculated to cause the physical destruction of a racial group or groups, and 'any legislative and other measures calculated to prevent a racial group or groups from participating in the political, social, economic and cultural life of the country'.
7. Except perhaps in Fiji, where British colonial policy established the Fijian aristocracy as the

powerholders, with Indians, Fijian commoners, and other groups as the governed. In 1987, we have seen this chiefly dominance challenged—but to the further detriment of the Indian majority still seen as intruder by the 'sons of the soil'.

8. The tension between Sinhalese and Tamils in Sri Lanka escalated into virtual civil war. Because there are 30 million Tamils in India, the Indian government intervened, introducing a military 'peace keeping force' into northern Sri Lanka in 1987. An example of how an internal racial conflict may be internationalized.

9. Tom Mboya was taken by the Australians to visit Papua New Guinea when it was still a trust territory. He is supposed to have observed, after meeting the Papuans: 'If I had realised that they were black I would never have agreed to Indonesia taking over West Irian.'

Cold War

FRED HALLIDAY

Ideas of Cold War

The idea of 'Cold War' is very much a product of the post-1945 epoch. Although the term had been used before, to denote drawn-out and inconclusive conflicts, its modern usage refers to the postwar confrontation between the USA and the USSR and their broader alliance systems in West and East. It was popularized by the American columnist Walter Lippman in a book of that name published in 1947, and its central meaning is that, while the two blocs have not gone to war directly, i.e., have not engaged in 'hot' war, they are involved in a protracted contest for global power and for military advantage.

Historians have tended to use the term to refer to a particular period of postwar history, that dating from around 1947 until after the death of Stalin in 1953. This was a period of almost no East-West diplomatic contact, of confrontation in Europe short of outright war focused on Berlin, and of major wars in the Far East. Some writers have argued that the period after 1979 can also be seen as a Second Cold War because, in its broad essentials, it equalled the first Cold War in intensity and confrontation.

At the same time, the term 'Cold War' has been used more broadly, to refer not to specific phases of East-West conflict but to the conflict as a whole. In this sense Cold War refers to the overall rivalry between the communist and capitalist systems, and to the course of that rivalry ever since the first communist state was established after the Bolshevik Revolution in Russia in 1917. Used in this way, Cold War is not only something that has been in progress for decades, but is also likely to continue for many decades to come, until either all communist, or all capitalist, states disappear. Yet while Cold War in this sense has been in existence since 1917, it has acquired a new character since 1945, for two major reasons: first, because the conflict between East and West has become *the* dominant one in world politics, in a way that was not true of the interwar and World War II years; and, secondly, because this conflict has been expressed above all through the nuclear arms race and competition for greater strength in the military field. The conflict between East and West has not been the only divisive issue of the postwar epoch and it has not been confined to the nuclear arms race: but it is above all these two characteristics of world affairs since 1945 that have made the Cold War so central to international relations.

The development of Cold Wars

The depth of rivalry between East and West was not generally recognized during World War II, because of the need to ally against the Axis powers, and because it was widely believed that the experience of World War II would lead states to become more cooperative and united in their goals than had hitherto been the case. The hopes for a more collaborative postwar world were concentrated in the United Nations and in the organization of the Security Council, where the five permanent members, including Russia and the USA, had a predominant power. Within two years of the end of the war, however, relations had deteriorated greatly. The focus was in Europe, along the dividing-line between the Soviet-occupied and the Western halves, and above all in Berlin, an enclave within Soviet-occupied eastern Germany where Russia, the USA, Britain and France had separate sectors, and where for a number of months in 1948 and early 1949, the USSR imposed a land blockade in an attempt to force the western sector to submit.

But the Cold War had a much wider scope than Berlin or Germany alone. In France and Italy there developed sharp conflicts between radical, communist-led, labour movements and the postwar governments backed by the USA. In Greece, there was a civil war between conservative and monarchist forces, backed by Britain and the USA, and a communist-led guerrilla movement that had gained considerable strength during the struggle against German occupation. In Eastern Europe, the Soviet Union, which had initially permitted a range of political freedoms, had by 1948 used its occupation forces to impose communist regimes, most spectacularly in Czechoslovakia where the Communist party took power in February 1948. Unexpectedly, however, the Eastern European country which had seen the strongest communist-led guerrilla movement, Yugoslavia, was not willing to follow Soviet orders and in 1948 broke with Stalin's leadership.

The Cold War also affected the Middle and Far East. The first major clash between East and West came in early 1946 over the question of Soviet troop withdrawals from Iran—these forces had been sent there during the war, in alliance with British troops, and the Russians were now reluctant to withdraw them. Soviet relations with Turkey also deteriorated at this time. The bloodiest confrontation was, however, in the Far East: in China, where the Japanese occupation was followed by civil war that ended only with the communist victory in 1949; in Indochina, where France was fighting communist insurgents in Vietnam, Laos and Cambodia; and, with greatest international repercussions, in Korea, where in June 1950 the communist government of the North launched a sudden invasion of the pro-Western South, drawing both US and Chinese troops into a war that ended, with stalemate, only in 1953.

Over all these specific areas of conflict, there towered the rivalry of the blocs themselves. This was partly expressed in the nuclear arms race: the USA had exploded nuclear weapons in 1945, and the USSR did so, much to the West's surprise, in 1949. It was also expressed in the ideological conflict, with both camps proclaiming themselves to be the defenders of freedom and democracy and denouncing the others for tyrannical behaviour. It seemed by the late 1940s as if the world had been divided into two hostile camps, with little contact between them and, at some point in the future, an almost inevitable war.

A comprehensive war did not occur, although both sides continued to arm themselves to an ever-greater extent, in periods of diplomatic relaxation as much as in periods of confrontation. In the period after Stalin's death in 1953 tensions eased somewhat, with compromise peaces in Korea and Indochina, and the beginnings of Soviet-US summit talks. In the two decades or more that followed, there was continual rivalry especially in the Third World, and on one occasion, during the Cuban Missile Crisis of 1962, the USSR and the USA appeared to be nearing a nuclear confrontation. But the situation in Europe was less tense, and the USSR successfully contained resistance to its control that emerged in East Germany (1953), Poland (1956) and Hungary (1956). At the same time, the USA and the USSR began the arms control process, with the Nuclear Test Ban Treaty of 1963 and the Strategic Arms Limitation Treaty of 1972. While continuing, the ideological confrontation appeared somewhat less ferocious, and the inevitability of war less certain. By the early 1970s East and West were engaged in a process of relaxation of tensions, or détente, which seemed to promise a continued progress away from Cold War confrontation.

This was not to be. In the late 1970s East–West tension increased again, and from 1979 onwards there began a period referred to by many writers as the 'New' or 'Second' Cold War. Again, there was a virtual breakdown in East–West diplomacy and no progress on arms control. The USA, feeling that it had lost ground to the USSR in the arms race, embarked on a major new military procurement policy, in the field of long-range or strategic missiles and, later, in the field of space. The USA also felt that the USSR had taken advantage of détente to promote its allies in the Third World—in Nicaragua, Angola, Ethiopia, Afghanistan and Cambodia—and from 1980 onwards the USA came to assert itself much more forcefully in the Third World, both directly and by providing assistance to states and guerrilla movements sympathetic to it. In Europe, there was no repeat of the Berlin Blockade or the Greek Civil War, but tension was heightened by the deployment of a new generation of intermediate-range nuclear missiles— the SS-20s by the USSR and Cruise and Pershing by the USA. While less acute than the first Cold War in terms of ideological confrontation and the reduction of diplomatic contact, the Second Cold War was potentially more dangerous because of the very much higher levels of nuclear weapons possessed by both sides, and the very short periods of time needed to ready and deliver them.

Four analytic questions

A number of analytic questions concerning both specific Cold Wars and the more general rivalry of East and West underlie much of the discussion of the historical record. The first is that of *causation* of which bloc can be said to have been primarily responsible for the outbreak of these confrontations. Predictably, writers in the West blame the 'expansionist' and 'totalitarian' character of communism, and of the USSR in particular, while Soviet writers blame the 'imperialist' West for its hostility to socialism and to the Soviet camp. More particularly, Western writers blame Stalin's imposition of communist control in Eastern Europe for the outbreak of the first Cold War, and the Soviet pursuit of nuclear strength and Third World influence for the second, Soviet writers see the West as using its superior military and economic position after World War II to try and force the USSR into a defensive position, and, later, of distorting the East-West military balance, and the Soviet role in the Third World crises of the 1970s, to justify launching the Second Cold War.

More measured analysis might suggest that the Cold Wars were caused by both East and West. There is little doubt that in the nuclear arms field, it has been the West which has held the initiative for almost all of the postwar period and which was the main instigator of further twists in the arms spiral. There has also been a recurrent reluctance in the West to accepting either that the USSR has legitimate security anxieties, or that it can play any legitimate role in the crises of the Third World. A considerable amount of what is written in the West about Soviet military and foreign policy is distorted. On the other hand, the USSR has used its military power to impose on Eastern Europe, and to maintain there, communist regimes that are rejected by much of the population. It is also committed to rivalling the West in the Third World for strategic influence: throughout the postwar period, the USSR has supported political and guerrilla movements that are in conflict with the West. Ultimately, the two blocs are based on distinct, and necessarily competitive, ideologies and political systems which must, with whatever relaxations and interruptions, lead to continued conflict between them, but which need not necessarily end in outright war.

A second analytic issue concerns the place of the arms race, and of *nuclear weapons* in particular, in the overall rivalry of the Cold War. In some accounts, the rivalry of the USA and the USSR is almost reduced to being one about nuclear weapons, with the implication being that if these can be controlled or abolished then the root cause of the tension will have been removed. At the same time, it has been nuclear weapons that have to a large extent inhibited the leading powers from going to war, because the cost to both sides of so doing would be too great. In the words of the French writer Raymond Aron, nuclear weapons have 'slowed down' history, by preventing the USA and the USSR from using military power more directly, Nuclear weapons have stimulated the conflict, but have also kept the war 'cold' rather than 'hot'. The nuclear arms race has clearly been a major component of the overall Cold War confrontation, both because these weapons represent in the starkest form the threat which each side poses to the other, and because they have become the most readily available symbol of the power of each bloc. At the same time, arms control negotiations, and agreements, have come to symbolize a willingness of East and West not only to reach compromises on nuclear weapons, but also to lessen tensions more generally. Yet for all their prominence in the East–West confrontation, nuclear weapons are not the only element within it: ideology, and competition in the Third World, are equally important and would continue to fuel the conflict even were nuclear weapons to be greatly reduced, or abolished.

The place of the *Third World* in East–West rivalry and in the two Cold Wars is another important analytic issue. It is of great importance for at least three reasons. First, it is in the Third World that the main fighting of the postwar period has taken place. Of the more than 20 million people who have been killed in wars since 1945 nearly all have died in Asia, Africa and Latin America. While many of these wars have had causes far removed from East–West rivalry, most have acquired an East–West dimension and have both stimulated, and been stimulated by, that competition: the Arab-Israeli and Indo-Pakistan conflicts are good examples. In the Third World the Cold War has often taken a 'hot' and very lethal form. Secondly, it is in the Third World that the frontiers of East and West are uncertain. Whereas in Europe the dividing line laid down in 1945 is clear, no such definition applies in the Third World, and many in the Third World reject the idea of their belonging to East or West at all. This fluidity makes for much greater uncertainty, but also allows for conflicts and wars to occur without this forcing either the USA or the USSR to resort to a full, and almost inevitably nuclear, response as would be the case in Europe. Finally, however, and despite this greater margin of conflict in the Third World, it is there that the greatest danger of an overall nuclear confrontation would appear to exist: the Cuban Missile Crisis of 1962, and a number of other cases when the use of nuclear weapons was considered, indicate the risks which Third World crises present to the world as a whole, in addition to the horrors which they inflict on the peoples of the countries concerned.

The fourth major analytic issue raised by study of Cold War is that of *ideology,* and how far the belief systems of the two camps contribute independently to the overall rivalry of East and West. It is commonly argued that the communist bloc has an ideology whereas the West does not, and equally commonly argued that neither side really believes any more in its proclaimed value systems. The communist world may be more explicit about the values it espouses, but the West too has a set of shared, and competitive, ideas about how society and politics should be organized and which forces to support, and which to oppose, in the contemporary world. Moreover, while there is an element of scepticism and manipulation in the use of such ideologies on both sides, it would be mistaken to assume that they are without impact, both on the governments and on the populations of the countries concerned. This belief in political ideologies, about capitalism or communism, is the stronger because in both the USA and the USSR it is conjoined with another ideology, namely that of patriotism, and an identification with the country and its political system.

The Cold War has by no means been the only constituent of conflict in the postwar world. The North–South divide, conflicts within the Eastern and Western blocs, and international economic rivalries have also been of major importance. But to a considerable extent the overarching conflict has been that between the Soviet-led and US-led blocs. It has known periods of greater and lesser intensity, but, in its broader meaning, it is likely to endure for many years to come.

References

Calvocoressi, Peter. *World Politics Since 1945*, 4th ed. London: Longman, 1982.
Crockatt, Richard and Steve Smith. *The Cold War, Past and Present*. London: Allen & Unwin, 1987.
Halliday, Fred. *The Making of the Second Cold War*, 2nd ed. London: Verso, 1986.
Lacqueur, Walter. *Europe Since 1945*. Harmondsworth: Penguin.
Steele, Jonathan. *The Limits of Soviet Power*. Harmondsworth: Penguin, 1985.
Thompson, Edward, *et al. Exterminism and Cold War*. London: Verso, 1982.

Images of Peace and the Reality of War

REINHARD KÜHNL

One could argue that arms and war have always been financed by the productivity of the working classes. It was the same in ancient Greece and Rome as it is today. The ordinary working people provided the foot soldiers for the campaigns, they had to kill and let themselves be killed, and in the main it was they who bore the consequences of the acts of devastation. It has been said that as a consequence there has always been a certain awareness amongst the working classes, often only in the form of a dark suspicion, that things do not have to be the way they are, that they could and should be different. They have dreamed of a Utopia in which people can work and live together in peace and friendship, that class domination and war are neither natural phenomena nor the irreversible will of the gods.

The motif of peace plays a central role for the most part in these conceptions of utopia. Something approaching an 'archetype of the peace-able International' is developed in several passages of the Old Testament of the Bible: The nations shall

> beat their swords into ploughshares, and their spears into pruning hooks: nation shall not lift up sword against nation, neither shall they learn war any more. But they shall sit every man under his vine and under his fig tree; and none shall make them afraid.

This thought reappears in the utopia of the Stoics, which was founded 'on the principle of world citizenship', the 'unity of the human race'; it appears again in the early Christian social utopia in its 'communism of love and in the International of whatever bears a human face however poor', in Augustine's City of God and finally in the utopias of declining feudalism from Joachim de Fiore to Thomas Munzer. Such thoughts are also to be found in Asian religions and philosophies. For thousands of years it is said that these

Kühnl, R./Schönwälder, K.: Sie reden vom Frieden und rüsten zum Krieg. Friedensdemagogie und Kriegsvorbereitung in Geschichte und Gegenwart. 1. A. Kleine Bibliothek 408. Köln: Pahl-Rugenstein Verlag, 1986.

thoughts have been rooted there in the consciousness of the masses, they have had their political effects in the liberation movements of these countries, e.g., the case of Gandhi, and they have also been adopted in the politics of a number of states which feel committed to non-alignment.

In all these utopias both social oppression and exploitation are abolished as well as war, and so is the state power apparatus which organizes both. This is reflected in the Hebrew word *shalom* which does not only mean peace but also harmony, wholeness and fullness of joy. These utopias bear witness very vividly to how terrible were people's sufferings, which war inflicted upon them, and to show how infinitely large therefore was their yearning for a world without war. For thousands of years this was scarcely more than a vague hope which had no basis in reality. If it is true that ideology is shaped by the ruling elite, this would explain the location of such utopias outside the present reality, in a past Golden Age or as a paradise in the hereafter.

This yearning gained a new quality however with the bourgeois Enlightenment. From then on, supported by the power of reason, the old models of authorization of the ruling ideology, which were tradition and divine revelation, were turned on their heads and rational criteria were developed. Any politics had therefore to justify itself according to these new criteria. The verdict was passed on war that it was an act of barbarism from a past, dark age.

Immanuel Kant perceived then a truth which has only been fully developed and reached public awareness in our time. He said that the 'greatest evils are inflicted on us by *war*, but not so much the war that has already taken place but rather the preparation for the future war, which never diminishes and indeed increases incessantly'. In his work *On Eternal Peace*, which was written, not by chance, in the years of the French Revolution (1795), he attempted to formulate the conditions which are necessary for the conquest of evil. For example he demanded:

> No doubts should be incurred by the state in respect of foreign trade by the state [and] no state should forcibly interfere with the constitution and government of another state.

The connection between internal social rule and external warfare came under scrutiny at this time as well. Johann Gottlieb Fichte saw in political and social equality the guarantee for peace within and without. He wrote that:

> It is impossible for a whole nation to decide to turn a neighbouring country into a battlefield for the sake of booty. . . . A war of conquest is only possible and understandable in a country where the advantage favours the few oppressors, while the disadvantage, the effort, the costs, fall on the army of countless slaves.

The works of German Classicism were also imbued with this new spirit.

Peace was now understood to be the fundamental condition for the perfection of the individual and of the human race. Voltaire even developed the thought that peace could only then be guaranteed when the person who started a war was punished as a common criminal. More than one and a half centuries and two World Wars had to pass before this thought became binding under international law. However, the social subject that could bring about the conditions formulated by the Enlightenment and Classicism was not yet in sight as far as these utopias of peace were concerned.

With the development of the labour movement, Marxism claimed to recognize a social force capable of securing such a transformation of society into one which is classless and peaceful. In connection with this transformation, Marxism looked for the causes and driving forces which lead to war, and found them in the interest structure of society. As early as 1845 Friedrich Engels wrote:

> The present society which sets the individual person at odds with all others produces in this way a social war of all against all. . . . We abolish the conflict between individual people and all others—we counter the social war with social peace.

The motto, 'All men are brothers', which played a decisive role from the Old Testament to early socialism, now gained a firm, social dimension and at the same time its political direction 'Workers of the world unite'. According to this idea, once class society was overcome, then the causes of war would also be overcome; socialism means that 'in contrast to old society, with its economical miseries and its political delerium, a new society is springing up, whose international rule will be *Peace,* because its national ruler will be the same everywhere—Labour'. The struggle against war was no longer founded purely on honourable motives and subjective concern. These had shown themselves to be very susceptible in the history of class society to the ideological manipulation of those in power, but it now gained a scientific basis. The hatred felt by the rulers for Marxism is understandable in this respect.

With the Labour movement there now developed a social power in whose material interests it was to struggle against war. Its position within the productive process enabled it to lead the struggle with a real prospect of success. Marxism argues that the fight for liberation from exploitation and war could now be tackled in an organized way, i.e., it could go beyond the level of individual actions. Organization guarantees that the experiences of struggle are not lost with the death of the individual fighters, but can be passed on to the following generation, so that the struggle gains a continuity which was historically not possible before. The smashing of the labour movement by fascist terror in Italy 1922, Germany in 1933, Spain in 1939 and Chile in 1973 had the function, amongst other things, of destroying this continuity. By means of its position in the productive process, this organized force is also 'able to command peace where their would-be masters shout war'. At present many scientists and academics are also realizing that the struggle for peace must be organized if it is to have a chance of success—a very difficult insight considering such people's socialization.

The new historical quality which was reached in the struggle for peace by means of the labour movement and Marxism was made real by the socialist revolutions in an increasing number of countries. From 1917 onwards, and above all since the end of the Second World War, social orders were established where, one might argue, property relations no longer provided an impetus for armament and wars of conquest. Such countries therefore demand disarmament constantly, especially in the face of the growing dangers of war and destruction, and are increasingly supported in this by the countries of the Third World. The socialist states do indeed see the economic, political and ideological antagonism between socialism and capitalism, including the struggles for national and social liberation in the Third World, as inevitable. However, they stress—following the principle of peaceful coexistence—that military conflict between socialism and capitalism is not only avoidable, but is seen as a catastrophe which must be avoided at all costs. In addition, for these states arms are

. . . a heavy financial strain, which inhibits their overall economic and social development. Even if parts of the social apparatus, because of their special function, may over-emphasize the necessity of—fundamentally defensive—arms to balance the potential for offensive weaponry that exists on the other side, they do not however find (as in the capitalist states where leading areas of monopoly capitalism act independently) strong forces, on which they could rely, which see in excessive armament above all its usefulness in terms of business management, its profit, but not the damage to the national economy it always causes.*

In our epoch then, peace is no longer simply a utopia which one could only yearn for or hope for as an act of mercy from higher powers or ruling forces. Rather it is a goal, for which real, strong forces are working worldwide, in order to put a definite end to a history of suffering for mankind which has lasted for over five thousand years.

---

* W. Abendroth, 'Nach zwei Weltkriegen die Gefahr des dritten?' *Blätter für deutsche und internationale Politik* 5/84, p. 564.

Does Terrorism Work?*

RICHARD CLUTTERBUCK

Terrorism was best defined by Sun Tzu over two thousand years ago: 'Kill one, frighten ten thousand.' Guerrillas and freedom fighters may or may not use terrorism as a technique. A resistance fighter who kills a soldier who invades his country, moral reasons aside, is not a terrorist, because he does not frighten ten thousand other soldiers—indeed he galvanizes them. If, however, he takes innocent hostages from his own village and shoots them to deter others from collaborating with the enemy, then he is a terrorist—just as much as the occupying soldier who shoots hostages to deter support for the resistance. By these criteria, the Palestinians, the *Shia,* the Irish Republican Army, Irish National Liberation Army, Ulster Volunteer Force and the Ulster Freedom Fighters are terrorists, regardless of their cause.

In fact, the efficacy of terrorism is largely a myth. It achieves dramatic short-term dividends but seldom advances the long-term aim. The terrorism of Begin's underground organization *Irgun* did not advance the independence of Israel, which was achieved by Ben Gurion's officially recognized Jewish Agency and the militia organization *Haganah.* Begin embarassed them as much as the IRA embarasses the Dublin government in seeking reunification. Begin's terrorism ensured violent Arab hostility, just as 35 years later his terror bombing of refugee camps and his actions in Lebanon ensured that it will continue. Similarly, PLO terrorism has not recovered one acre of Palestine for the Arabs and has ensured that the Israelis will fight to the death rather than accept terrorist bases in the hills of Judea. The short-term dividends, however—publicity, release of prisoners, ransoms—are so spectacular that more and more political and religious groups, frustrated by their inability to get their way, turn to terrorism, above all for publicity. It is because totalitarian state-controlled media can deny such publicity that the Soviet Union suffered only 62 of the 6700 terrorist incidents recorded between 1968 and 1980.

Can the liberal democracies deny the terrorists this 'oxygen of publicity'

---

* Reproduced with permission from *The Tablet,* 3 August 1985.

(to use Mrs Thatcher's phrase) without so restricting freedom of the press as to do more harm than good?

In June 1985 a TWA airliner carrying many American passengers was hijacked by the *Shia* demanding the release of Arab prisoners by Israel. There is no doubt that the highly emotive publicity on America's competing television networks enormously strengthened the hand of the TWA hijackers. To abandon the gallant Captain Trestrake or to fail to save the husband of the weeping wife linked to him live on television was unthinkable and the terrorists knew it. True, a platoon of soldiers, cut off in battle, could expect no similar political sacrifices to save it; nor could a kidnapped ambassador—but soldiers, diplomats and policemen accept that their lives are on the line.

In the long run, America's concern for individual lives is one of the things which makes her so much stronger and more resilient than the Soviet Union. Nevertheless, the media should recognize that they did help the terrorists. The answer must lie, not in censorship or government control, but in a voluntary code—which may be a vain hope because the scoops will go to those who break it.

A glimmer of hope lies in the success of the British police in negotiating a media blackout in four kidnap cases since 1975, saving all the hostages and capturing all the kidnappers. The art lay in briefing all the media together, convincing them that life was at risk, that publicity would increase that risk— and woe betide any journalist who broke faith.

It is more difficult if the story itself has already got out—as it inevitably will in the case of a hijack through the foreign press. However, Chancellor Schmidt achieved media silence in the later weeks of the Schleyer case in 1977 when the head of the West German employers' organization was kidnapped and then killed by the Red Army Faction. Again in 1980, after an appalling start, the whole world's press respected the parents' plea for a blackout of the closing stages of the Schild family kidnap in Sardinia.

In the case of the TWA hijack, had President Reagan at the outset briefed all the editors and journalists, he might have got them to agree on a common degree of restraint.

In other respects, the President's handling of the crisis was good. Regardless of the media, fanatical terrorists with lives in their hands hold almost all the cards in dealing with a humane society. A rescue attempt in Algiers would have destroyed a useful working relationship. A rescue attempt in Beirut—with the airport held by *Shia* militia—could only have recovered dead bodies. Bombing *Shia* bases in populated areas would have been a form of terrorism itself, as counterproductive as Begin's own terrorism in Lebanon. So President Reagan courageously swallowed his pride and sought help from the only people who would bring any pressure to bear on the terrorists—Assad and Berri (the President and Justice Minister of Lebanon)—counting on the fact that neither wished to see Lebanon relapse into even greater chaos. They did not want to alienate the Americans too far. The President's ability to apply pressure by economic boycott and destabilization will have counted more with them than military action, and in the long-term these are by far the West's strongest cards.

Nevertheless, joint action by liberal societies—like that by journalists—is too often nullified by greed and self-interest. Are we in a Third World War? In one sense, yes. The Soviet Union set out to extend its power by fair means or foul in 1945—unsuccessfully in Western Europe and East Asia, successfully in Eastern Europe, Cuba, parts of Africa and the Arab world and Afghanistan. One of the most effective methods used by the Soviets has been to exploit internal conflicts and to support any terrorist groups which destabilize Western democracy, almost regardless of the political beliefs of the terrorists. They exploit and support rather than sponsor. They did not (and did not need to) create the IRA, the Red Brigades, the PLO or the Islamic fundamentalists. There is little or no evidence of causes of tactical direction by the Kremlin, though there is of help with weapons (usually through an intermediary state), money, training, propaganda and intelligence, through the ubiquitous KGB under cover of embassies, trade delegations and so forth.

How should we fight it? Not so much by international conventions as by bilateral cooperation at working level between police, intelligence services, soldiers and rescue squads. Such bilateral cooperation is already excellent between such services in, for example, Australia, Britain, Canada, the Netherlands, the United States and West Germany. We must extend this to others, including friendly Third World countries. The West has a lot to offer and can make their cooperation worthwhile.

Where the actions of police, military and the judiciary are concerned, we must always act within our own laws, no matter how great the temptation to do otherwise. Preemptive terror and clandestine assassinations, as well as undermining our whole moral case, will rebound, as the widely documented use of terrorism and torture by the French against the Algerian independence movement rebounded against them.

If the terrorists make our liberal judicial procedure unworkable, by intimidating witnesses and juries, for example, then we must pass emergency laws to make procedures that are workable. The West Germans did it, the Italians did it and we did it in Northern Ireland—all with success. The killings in Northern Ireland in 1972 were 467. In 1973 we passed the Northern Ireland (Emergency Provisions) Bill introducing trial without jury for terrorist offences. In that year, killings fell to 250, where they remained on average for the next four years. From 1977 to 1984 they averaged 90, and only 64 in 1984. The saving of life in Italy after the package of laws was introduced in 1979 was even more dramatic.

The IRA, the UVF, the Palestinians and the *Shia* terrorists all believe fervently in their cause. So do some of their own people, but this does not give them the right to murder those who do not. The right of a minority to kill must never override the right of the majority to live in peace.

The words of the Pope, spoken in the heart of Ireland, cannot be quoted too often: 'We must not call murder by any other word than murder.'

International Terrorism: Diplomacy by Other Means

NOAM CHOMSKY

'The evil scourge of terrorism', as Ronald Reagan termed it, became the focus of general concern in the early 1980s, in part through the efforts of the Reagan administration to heighten awareness of this plague and the need to eradicate it. The source was identified as the Soviet Union, accused by Secretary of State Alexander Haig of 'training, funding and equipping' international terrorism. According to his successor, George Shultz, the goal of these 'depraved opponents of civilization itself', inspired by their Soviet master, is to 'shake the West's self-confidence, unity, and will to resist intimidation'. The charge was taken up by many commentators as well as specialists in the new discipline of terrorology, who allege that terrorism occurs 'almost exclusively in democratic or relatively democratic countries' (Walter Laqueur), sure evidence of its Soviet origin. A poll of editors selected terrorism in the Mideast/Mediterranean region as the top story of 1985, and the problem continues to rank high on the agenda of concerns, as it should, considering the human cost of atrocities that 'represent a return to barbarism in the modern age' (George Shultz).

To confront the threat of terrorism we must determine the locus and agency of these crimes, concentrating on the most serious cases and their origin; that is the reasoning of those who trace terrorist acts to the Soviet Union as the manipulator behind the scenes. But the problem arises in pursuing this rational course. Like many other terms of political discourse— 'democracy', 'freedom', etc.—the term 'terrorism' has two meanings: its ordinary sense, and a technical Orwellian sense designed for service to power. These must be clearly distinguished.

For the ordinary sense, we may follow the official US code, which defines 'acts of terrorism' as an activity that 'involves a violent act or an act dangerous to human life' intended 'to intimidate or coerce a civilian population' or 'to influence the policy of a government by intimidation or targeting large populations, from the *retail terrorism* of the weak. If we are serious about the matter, our prime concern will be wholesale terrorism, generally conducted by states or their agents, *international terrorism* if conducted beyond state borders.

The Orwellian sense of the term is quite different. The usage is designed to protect one's own state from scrutiny, so we restrict attention to acts conducted by *them,* not *us,* keeping to retail terrorism, preferably chargeable to the account of some official enemy, identified as its source. The extensive literature on terrorism follows these guidelines closely. Hence it provides the useful conclusion that, whatever the facts, the primary source of terrorism is the Soviet Union, those designated as its clients, or other official enemies, because nothing else counts as terrorism. Let us, however, keep to the proper sense of the term, which is not restricted by political preference.

International terrorism must be distinguished from the far more serious crime of aggression: the Soviet invasion of Afghanistan, for example, or the US attack against South Vietnam (later all of Indochina) from the early 1960s, each naturally described by the aggressor and its minions as 'defense' of the population under attack. It is sometimes less clear to which of these categories acts of violence should be assigned. Thus the Israeli bombing of Tunis in October 1985 was condemned by the UN Security Council as an 'act of armed aggression', but the United States, which abstained, rejected this characterization after having initially welcomed the attack. Similarly, the International Court of Justice in June 1986 condemned the US attack against Nicaragua as 'an unlawful use of force', while former CIA director Stansfield Turner, testifying before Congress on the US 'proxy army' (the term used by its US lobbyists in documents circulated internally at the White House), described its acts as 'terrorism, as State-supported terrorism'. In such cases, let us give the benefit of the doubt to the US and its clients, categorizing such acts as these as international terrorism rather than aggression.

Adopting this principle, the most serious single act of terrorism in the Mideast/Mediterranean region in 1985 was the Israeli bombing of Tunis, to be surpassed the next year by the US bombing of Tripoli, with some 100 killed. But these acts of international terrorism during the peak years of concern over this 'return to barbarism' pale by comparison with Central America, where the proxy army attacking Nicaragua has killed thousands of civilians with the avowed intent 'to influence the policy of a government by intimidation or coercion', fitting the State Department definition with precision. And these atrocities do not compare with the state terrorism in El Salvador conducted by a mercenary army organized by the United States 'to intimidate or coerce a civilian population'. Its purpose was to destroy 'the people's organizations fighting to defend their most fundamental human rights', in the words of Archbishop Oscar Romero, soon to be assassinated by elements of the US-backed security forces, while pleading vainly with President Carter not to send arms to the ruling junta which would use them for these ends, as it did, with mounting US support as the terror intensified. Note that this is international terrorism, given the US role in directing, training and supplying the forces that carried out large-scale slaughter, torture, rape and mutilation, with more than 50,000 killed. State terrorism in Guatemala in the same years, also supported by the Reagan administration, claimed a still higher toll.

International terrorism is not limited to these regions, and is not a new phenomenon of the 1980s. Thus in Africa, the UNITA forces supported by South Africa and the United States boast of having shot down civilian airliners with hundreds killed; holding hundreds of foreign teachers, doctors and missionaries—'taken hostage', according to UNITA commander Jonas Savimbi, and not to 'be released until Prime Minister Thatcher offered his organization some kind of recognition' (*New York Times*); and so on. In the terminology of the Reagan administration, these terrorist acts qualify Savimbi as a 'freedom fighter', and 'one of the few authentic heroes of our times' (UN Ambassador Jeane Kirkpatrick). In earlier years, the main target of international terrorism was Cuba. From shortly after the failed Bay of Pigs invasion, Cuba was subjected to regular attack by CIA-trained paramilitary forces operating from US bases that bombarded hotels, sank fishing boats, attacked industrial installations and Russian ships in Cuban harbors, poisoned crops and livestock, attempted to assassinate Fidel Castro, etc., in missions that were running almost weekly at their peak.

These and many similar actions on the part of the US and its clients, however, are not the subject of conferences and learned tomes, or anguished commentary in the media, and do not affect the conclusion that acts of terror occur 'almost exclusively' in Western countries. The conclusion is accurate, as long as we adhere to the approved Orwellian usage.

The terrorist acts that accord with the Orwellian usage, and thus enter the canon of Western discourse, are largely traceable to Lebanon, beginning in 1982, when Israel invaded Lebanon to demolish the civilian society of the Palestinians, leaving chaos and destruction in its wake. The terrorist attack of the Ankara synagogue, the Karachi hijacking, and the shootings at the Rome and Vienna airports in December 1985 are among those reported to have involved young men who survived the Sabra-Shatila massacre. The 1985 TWA hijacking was an effort to obtain hostages to compel the release of hundreds of Lebanese held prisoner in Israeli-run torture chambers in southern Lebanon or in Israel proper; these, in turn, were hostages held to ensure compliance with Israel's dictates in southern Lebanon.

The goals of the 1982 invasion had been plausibly explained in its early phases by Israel's leading academic specialist on the Palestinians, Yehoshua Porath. The fact that the PLO had scrupulously observed a cease-fire despite Israeli terror operations was seen by Israel as a 'veritable catastrophe', he suggested, threatening the policy of evading a political settlement. 'The government's hope,' he continued, 'is that the stricken PLO . . . will return to its earlier terrorism; it will carry out bombings throughout the world, hijack airplanes, and murder many Israelis', thus losing 'the political legitimacy it has gained'. If he is correct, the invasion achieved the aim of inspiring a wave of terror.

Lebanon had been subjected to Israeli attacks from the early 1970s, with hundreds killed and hundreds of thousands driven from their homes, for reasons explained by Israeli diplomat Abba Eban: 'there was a rational prospect, ultimately fulfilled, that affected populations would exert pressure for the cessation of hostilities.' Translating this into plain language: the population of southern Lebanon was held hostage and terrorized to induce them to accept Israel's arrangements for the region, including control over the territories conquered in 1967. Similar reasoning explains Israel's murderous 'Iron Fist' operations in southern Lebanon in 1985. For years, Israel has been conducting piracy and kidnapping on the high seas, sometimes sinking ships in international waters, all acts of terrorism in the ordinary sense of the term but exempt under Orwellian usage, all supported by the US, which again qualifies as the source of international terrorism by the logic of terrorology as applied to the Soviet enemy.

These are only a few examples. We should be concerned over the 'evil scourge of terrorism', and we might act to reduce it drastically, since the source, very often, is under our influence and control.

References

Chomsky, Noam, and Edward S. Herman. *The Political Economy of Human Rights*, 2 vols. Boston: South End, 1979.
Herman, Edward S. *The Real Terror Network: Terrorism in Fact and Propaganda*. Boston: South End, 1982.
McClintock, Michael. *The American Connection: State Terror and Popular Resistance, El Salvador, Guatemala*, 2 vols. London: Zed, 1984.
Chomsky, Noam. *Pirates and Emperors: International Terrorism in the Real World*, New York: Claremont, 1986.
Walker, Thomas (ed.). *Reagan versus the Sandinistas: The Undeclared War on Nicaragua*. Boulder, Colorado: Westview, 1987.

Reporting 'Terrorism': The Experience of Northern Ireland

BRIAN HAMILTON-TWEEDALE

The experience of reporting a violent political conflict on its own doorstep has profoundly challenged the liberal values of the British media, and in doing so has undermined the legitimacy of its claim to perform a vital role in the democratic process. In theory, where governments and communities are in conflict, but not in a state of war, newspapers and television should perform their duties independently from the executive, the legislature and the judiciary, defending each against the excesses of the other and upholding, in the process, the public interest. In practice, where Northern Ireland is concerned, the British media have become committed to a perspective of the conflict which, since the early 1970s, has increasingly equated the interests of the public with those of the state. In the process a strategy for reporting events in the North has evolved which, though falling short of direct censorship, effectively denies the public the information and analysis it requires to arrive at a meaningful understanding of the conflict, and makes it difficult for it to engage in an informed debate as to how it can be best resolved.

The conflict in Northern Ireland is, above all else, a political conflict and one with deep historical and social roots. Yet in so far as it has featured as an issue in the British media, the story has been predominantly one of violence. In his analysis of news during two periods in 1974 and 1975 (each of which contained a major election campaign in an effort to maximize the level of political reporting) Philip Elliott found that violence and law enforcement stories accounted for 72 percent of the coverage accorded to the North by national television, 58 percent of the coverage in the quality press, and 65 percent in the popular press. In all only a third of the stories dealt with politics and other matters. Elliott contrasted this approach with that of the Irish media which not only carried more stories (a ratio of about 5 to 1) but were also much more concerned with the political dimension.[1]

British media coverage of events in the North has not only focused on violence at the expense of politics, it has also tended to present violence in a de-contextualized form with little if any attempt being made to go beyond the immediate details and human tragedy of reported incidents, or to place them within a broader and more analytical framework. However, while this style of reporting may make for graphic and at times moving detail, it excludes much of what could give some sense or meaning to the violence and thereby renders it less, rather than more, explicable: the result is a continual procession of violent episodes differentiated only by the scale and location of the violence and the personal characteristics of those involved.

According to statistics published by the *Irish Times*, 2304 people had been killed in Northern Ireland up to June 1983 as a direct consequence of the conflict. The figures showed that republican paramilitaries had been responsible for 1264 of these deaths, loyalist paramilitaries for 613, the army and police for 264, while a further 163 were 'non-classified'. Further statistics showed that of the civilian victims 775 were Catholic, 495 were Protestant, and a further 29 were not natives of the North.[2]

The complex pattern of state, anti-state, and intercommunal violence suggested by these statistics has been largely obscured by newspapers and television which have tended to be preoccupied with the violence of those who oppose rather than those who represent authority. Critics have noted a strong tendency within the British media to cast the army and police in a positive light; to minimize and at times ignore their involvement in violence even when it clearly breaches democratic and legal standards and, when army and police violence is reported, to treat it in an uncritical and sympathetic manner.[3] An editorial carried by *The Star* following the controversial shooting by the SAS of three unarmed IRA members in Gibraltar is illustrative of the general attitude of many papers towards violence emanating from 'official' sources. Under the headline 'Their just deserts', the paper informed its readers that:

> There will be howls of protest from Irish Republicans over the killing of three terrorists in Gibraltar.
>
> They will say the victims were unarmed. That their suspect car did not contain explosives.
>
> SHED NO TEARS.
>
> This was not the cold blooded killing of three innocents. It was the destruction of a bomb gang who planned to massacre hundreds of people.
>
> That they FAILED is down to the vigilance of our security forces and the efficiency of the SAS.
>
> Three evil monsters have got what they deserve.
>
> (8.3.88)

However, while journalists have been quick to condemn 'unofficial' violence, they have generally refrained from exploring on the public's behalf the complex factors which give rise to it. Instead the tendency within British journalism has been to present the violence of Northern Ireland as being the product of 'psychopaths', 'terrorists', and other such terms of convenience. A point clearly illustrated by the coverage accorded to the Enniskillen bombing in November 1987 which was widely interpreted as being the work of 'evil men' (*Daily Mirror*), 'Maniacs' (*The Star*), 'terrorist Godfathers' (*Today*), 'cowardly bigots' (*Sun*) and 'men whose infatuation with blood transcends their dopey belief in a federal, socialist, united Ireland' (*Daily Express*). Needless to say, the repetitive use of such labels serves only to obscure and mystify, rather than clarify and explain, the social and political factors which may underpin the violence. In doing so they feed off, and in the process reinforce, a view of the violence as being largely inexplicable.

British journalists have not only been preoccupied with 'terrorism' as opposed to other forms and sources of violence, but even within this narrowly defined category they have been selective and sometimes tendentious. As has been noted above, loyalist groups have been responsible for as many as 600 of the 2304 deaths recorded up to June 1983, and almost all of their victims have been civilians. Yet despite this the British media has tended to present 'terrorist' violence as if it were the sole preserve of the IRA and other republican groups. So much so that the casual observer of British media coverage could be forgiven for arriving at the conclusion that the IRA are almost exclusively to blame for the violence in Northern Ireland. Philip Elliott, for example, notes that while IRA violence has dominated the headlines the involvement of loyalists in acts of violence has been played down to such an extent that 'protestant extremists have themselves complained about the lack of attention paid to their efforts'.[4] During the period examined by Elliott the death toll in the North was sixteen Catholics, six Protestants, one member of the security forces, and one other. Yet despite the fact that Catholics were the main victims, the media blamed most of the violence on the IRA or some other republican group.

The publicity so often accorded to 'terrorist' violence contrasts sharply with the attention paid to the views of the various paramilitary groups, which over the years have been studiously ignored. Television interviews with representatives of republican groups in particular have been extremely rare, and as the recent outcry over the *Real Lives* programme 'At the Edge of the Union' clearly demonstrated, have provoked instant outrage from politicians and the press. Liz Curtis, for example, can trace only four occasions when the BBC has transmitted interviews with people speaking on behalf of the IRA or INLA, and four such occasions featuring only the IRA on ITV.[5] The record of the British press, which has consistently criticized such interviews as providing a propaganda platform for the enemies of the state, has scarcely been any better.

All sides to the Irish conflict have recognized the importance of propaganda, and all sides have been equal in their efforts to get their point of view across to the public. Their chances of succeeding, however, have been far from equal: the speed and efficiency of the information services operated by the army and the police; the pressure on journalists to seed out official accounts; the fact that official sources carry with them the authority of the state, and the generally held view that the word of the 'terrorists' cannot be trusted, have all tipped the scales heavily in favour of the authorities. As the journalist Simon Hoggart has commented:·'When the British press prints an account of an incident as if it were established fact, and it is clear that the reporter himself was not on the spot, it is a 99 percent certainty that it is the army's version which is being given.'[6] Thus while the 'terrorists' have scored the occasional propaganda victory, the advantage remains firmly with the army and the police.

The problem in Northern Ireland, however, is that on occasions official sources have proved to be as unreliable as the 'terrorists' are so often assumed to be. Since the early 1970s evidence has continued to accumulate that the army, and more recently the police, have deliberately exploited their strategic position as a news source to manipulate and mislead journalists; usually to implicate the IRA in violence committed by loyalists, often to cover up their own involvement in illegal or questionable activities, and frequently to discredit their political opponents.[7] Despite this evidence however, British journalists, increasingly starved of resources, are more reliant upon and less critical of these sources today than at any other time in the past.

Since the early 1970s as the violence has tailed off, British media interest in Northern Ireland has diminished, and is now only temporarily revived when something spectacular like the Enniskillen bombing occurs. Reading a British paper in 1988, and a popular newspaper in particular, it is often difficult to remember that there is still a conflict taking place in the North. The problem with this pattern of reporting is that it contributes to an image of 'normalcy' which is belied by the reality of the political situation in the North.

Notes

1. Elliott, Philip. 'Reporting Northern Ireland: a study of news in Britain, Ulster and the Irish Republic'. In *Ethnicity and the Media*. Paris; UNESCO, 1977.
2. *The Irish Times*, 4 November 1983.
3. Curtis, Liz. *Ireland: the propaganda war*. London: Pluto Press, 1984.
4. Elliott, Philip. Op. cit., 1977.
5. Curtis, Liz. Op. cit., 1984. Chapter 7.
6. Hoggart, Simon. 'The army PR men of Northern Ireland'. *New Society*, 11 October 1973.
7. See Curtis, op. cit., 1984.

In addition to the above see also:

Kirkaldy, John. 'Northern Ireland and Fleet Street'. In Yonha Alexander (ed.), *Terrorism in Ireland*. London: Croom Helm, 1983.

Schlesinger, Philip. *Putting Reality Together*. London: Constable, 1978.

Schlesinger, Philip, Graham Murdock and Philip Elliott. *Televising Terrorism*. London: Comedia, 1983.

PART 3

Various Aspects of Nuclear Technology and Related Decision-making

The nuclear issue is in many ways central to contemporary discussions of peace and war. On the one hand there are those who argue for nuclear deterrence and the vital role it has played in keeping the peace since the Second World War, on the other are those who advocate non-nuclear defence policies which emphasize non-provocative defence and common security. Both points of view are represented in this section together with a chapter analyzing decision-making on nuclear weapons in Britain. Those who advocate 'peace through strength' sometimes argue for the economic advantages or spin-offs gained through military research and development. The opening chapter considers these arguments for a major defence system, the Strategic Defence Initiative (Star Wars). Those who argue for 'peace through disarmament' are sometimes criticized for failing to take into account the possibilities for cheating on any disarmament agreement. The final chapter considers the problem of verification and the technical aspects of nuclear disarmament.

Decision-making on Nuclear Weapons in Britain

OXFORD RESEARCH GROUP

Before a nuclear weapon decision reaches the final point of Cabinet approval, hundreds of people have been at work on it. Their influence falls within six areas which are illustrated in Figure 1;

The Ministry of Defence
The 'Special Relationship' with the USA
Membership of NATO
The Cabinet and Cabinet Office
The Treasury
The Foreign and Commonwealth Office

The size of each drawing indicates the relative amounts of influence which we estimate these bodies to have on nuclear weapons decision-making in Britain. It is an approximate picture, because little information is available to the public. We have drawn together as balanced as possible an account of the process using only published sources and unclassified information; but because of the extent of secrecy on these issues, there will obviously be gaps and omissions. Britain has a system of accountability for major decisions of national importance, but when it comes to nuclear weapons decisions in key respects it does not apply.

The Ministry of Defence

The Ministry of Defence (MoD) coordinates and controls the most important internal influences on weapons policy in Britain: intelligence, research and development (R&D), science advice, nuclear policy, military strategy, weapons procurement, and budget. The MoD comprises one-third of the civil service with a payroll of half a million people under the control of a hierarchy of the senior grades, and responsible to five ministers of the government—the Secretary of State for Defence and four junior ministers.

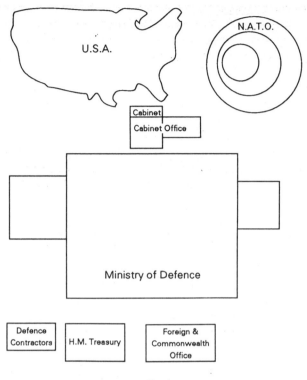

FIG 1.

The intelligence community plays a key role in nuclear weapons decisions, especially at the very early stages. The combined sources of defence intelligence put forward a 'threat assessment' to senior military and planning staff, indicating their estimate of current and future dangers, new foreign weapons development, tests, allocation of budget to new concepts and so on. Data is gathered primarily by the Defence Intelligence Service within MoD (whose Director General reports directly to the Chief of Defence Staff), but with input from the Secret Intelligence Service (MI6), the Security Service (MI5), and the Government Communications Head-quarters (GCHQ) at Cheltenham. Internally within MoD, intelligence estimates are channelled in three directions, to the policy-makers, to the operational requirements people and to the procurement people. Outside MoD, the data is interpreted and evaluated by four committees, the most important of which are the Joint Intelligence Committee, housed in the Cabinet Office, and the Permanent Secretaries Committee on Intelligence Services. This 'threat assessment' forms the basis for future weapons requirements. Intelligence information is apparently also made available to

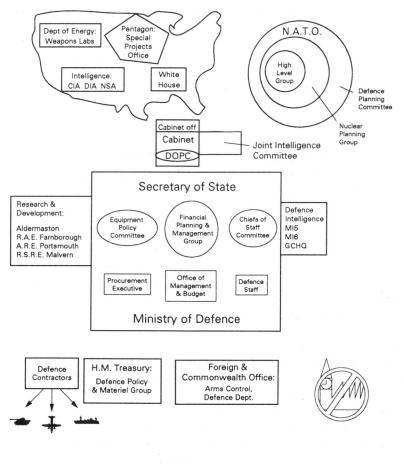

FIG 2.

the defence industry. Intelligence gathering has become almost a military operation in its own right.

Research and Development. Most modern nuclear weapons comprise an explosive warhead and a 'delivery system'—the missile or other device which guides it to its destination, and the submarine, aircraft or helicopter from which it is launched. For its major systems, Britain buys missiles from the USA. The British research and development community is largely concerned with warheads for the missiles, airdrop and depth bombs, and all the component parts of the various delivery systems. The main R&D establishments which concern us are:

The Atomic Weapons Research Establishment at Aldermaston
The Royal Aircraft Establishment at Farnborough

The Admiralty Research Establishment at Portsmouth
The Royal Signals and Radar Establishment at Malvern

Scientists and designers at these establishments formulate the technical possibilities for new weapons or refinements of existing ones and lobby for them in Whitehall. Lord Zuckerman, himself Chief Scientific Adviser to MoD and then to the government from 1960–71, says that 'it is the man in the laboratory, . . . not the commander in the field who starts the process of formulating the so-called military need'. New weapons proposals are in due course considered by the Equipment Policy Committee. This is chaired by the Chief Scientific Adviser at MoD who channels advice from the three services to the Secretary of State. One of his four assistants is responsible for specifically advising ministers on the implications of nuclear defence policy.

Nuclear Policy is formulated in the Strategy and Policy Group of the unified Defence Staff department of MoD, which handles all longer-term military policy work including UK nuclear participation in NATO, UK nuclear strategy, nuclear security, weapons, targeting and deployment.

Procurement of weapons is the responsibility of the Procurement Executive, whose Chief reports directly to the top MoD civil servant, the Permanent Under Secretary. He has under him Systems Controllers who deal with ordering and purchase of equipment for each of the three services. Only programmes with estimated R&D costs of more than £25 million or production costs of more than £50 million must be approved by the Equipment Policy Committee.

Expenditure has always been a key element in deciding what kind of weapons Britain should have. A new department, the Office of Management and Budget, has been set up within the MoD to deal with long-term financial planning. There is a clear relationship between this new office and the key MoD committee—the Financial Planning and Management Group. The brief of this committee is to match the defence programme to the available resources. The committee brings together the eight most powerful staff in MoD and is chaired by its top civil servant, the Permanent Under Secretary.

The 'Special Relationship' with the USA

Ironically, it was the US refusal to continue atomic cooperation with Britain after the end of World War II which prompted the Attlee government to take the decision to build Britain's own first bomb in 1947.

Today, things are very different. Britain has what is known as the 'Special Relationship' with the USA—a remarkable web of political and strategic links in which nuclear affairs have been and are a key strand. Never before in history have two nations maintained such close ties in such sensitive areas. A British nuclear capability was one way of ensuring that British interests received adequate consideration in Washington and NATO discussions. The US has profoundly influenced British nuclear policy through the transfer of data and components of nuclear weapons systems.

Weapons supply and collaboration

The Bilateral Agreement for Cooperation on the Uses of Atomic Energy for Mutual Defence Purposes was signed in 1958. Since that time all British warheads have been tested in the US; the agreement, and a further one the following year, enabled Britain to buy from the USA component parts of nuclear weapons systems, to receive information on the design and production of nuclear warheads and to exchange British plutonium for US enriched uranium.

In 1960, National Atomic Coordinating offices were set up in Washington and London. The 1963 Polaris Sales Agreement set British nuclear policy for decades—whereby its most important and expensive nuclear weapons have depended upon American designed and made missiles.

The next important nuclear weapons development was the British-designed improvement to the Polaris system—the Chevaline project. Chevaline was a new 'front end' for Polaris missiles, designed to defeat anti-ballistic missiles which the Soviets were thought to be building. The move seems to have been designed to inject a degree of reciprocity into the Anglo-US relationship, and remove fears that the eight-year (1966–74) suspension of British nuclear testing would lead to a decline in the relationship. The entire project was kept secret from the British people and the British Parliament. The Chevaline project overran both in time and cost. This strongly influenced the next major British decision; to purchase Trident missiles from the US. President Carter's willingness to sell Trident to Britain may have been a quid pro quo for Britain's willingness, agreed by Prime Minister Callaghan with Carter at the Guadeloupe Summit in 1979, to take Cruise missiles as part of the Euro-missile decision. The decision in favour of buying Trident from the US was eventually taken by the Conservative Government in May 1979, which later agreed to buy the more advanced Trident II. Britain agreed to man US Rapier air defence systems round US Air Force bases in Britain throughout the life of the Trident programme and to maintain its naval deployments in the Indian Ocean, in exchange for contributing only £116 million to the R&D cost of Trident II (estimated at £9 billion).

Terms of agreement

Once an American President has made a decision to cooperate with a foreign country on the military application of nuclear energy, he directs the departments concerned to prepare to enter into negotiations, carried out by

US representatives. 'When the bilateral executive agreement on nuclear co-operation is signed, the President must, under Section 123(d) of the Atomic Energy Act, submit the agreement to the Congress for formal approval. The projected agreement does not go into effect until it has been explicitly approved by the Congress.'[1] The agreement is unclassified.

> The Executive Branch then enters into two kinds of technical implementing agreements: a formal Program of Co-operation covering one or more specific nuclear weapons delivery systems, and a (military) service-to-service stockpile agreement. Programs of Co-operation and stockpile agreements have been concluded with each NATO country where the United States has nuclear weapons deployed. The stockpile agreement states that the location of nuclear weapons storage sites is to be determined by SACEUR (the Supreme Allied Commander Europe) in agreement with US military authorities and the government of the country concerned, that the costs are to be borne by the user nation unless NATO agrees to fund the site costs under its infrastructure program, that US personnel will have custody of the weapons and that external security will be the responsibility of the user government.

US bases

There are over 130 US military bases and facilities in Britain, ranging from tiny offices to gigantic airbases. Nearly 400 US Air Force aircraft including approximately 150 F-111 fighter-bombers are normally based in Britain. In war or crisis, the number of bases and aircraft in Britain would treble. Nearly half the military aircraft in Europe would use British bases.

The use by US forces of bases and facilities in Britain is governed by the agreement reached in 1951. All that the British public know of it is contained in a joint communique of January 1952:

> Under arrangements made for the common defence, the US has the use of certain bases in the United Kingdom. We re-affirm the understanding that the use of these bases in an emergency would be a matter of joint decision by His Majesty's Government and the United States Government in the light of the circumstances prevailing at the time.

Control

This raises the issue of control over the release of nuclear weapons stationed in Britain. The same communique quoted above goes on:

> The release of nuclear weapons can only be authorized by the President of the United States (or, for British weapons, the British Prime Minister).

Before releasing or ordering the use of nuclear weapons in Europe the President is bound to consult *if time and circumstances permit*. [our italics]

Joint targeting

The US Single Integrated Operational Plan is prepared by the Joint Strategic Planning Target Staff at Omaha in Nebraska—headquarters of American Strategic Air Command. A small British team works there, as part of a NATO team, and British nuclear forces receive their data on the British share of strike targets. There is no input into this war-planning from politically-elected or politically-accountable people in Britain.

Intelligence links

The intelligence relationship between the US and Britain has been close since 1974 when a secret treaty, known as UKUSA, linked GCHQ with the embryonic National Security Agency. The two agencies have an extraordinary joint capacity to intercept and decode signals worldwide.

GCHQ is formerly part of the Foreign Office, but in effect is responsible to the Joint Intelligence Committee in the Cabinet Office, which began supplying the US with intelligence estimates as early as 1943.

Membership of NATO

NATO is an alliance of sixteen sovereign nations, based on the principle of collective security.

NATO is an inter-governmental, not supra-national, organization. The defence policies of NATO nations are national responsibilities: the function of NATO is to provide an organizational framework for coordination of policies.

NATO nuclear policy formulation

Until the mid-1960s nuclear decisions in NATO were an exclusively American affair. This led to a European mood of alienation and periodic mistrust. The Americans too were unhappy about the situation, wanting to familiarize European politicians with the challenges of modern strategic planning. Therefore, out of the NATO Defence Planning Committee grew the Nuclear Defence Affairs Committee in 1966 and its prestigious sub-group, the Nuclear Planning Group. Today it is this group which meets at the level of Defence Ministers twice a year, to discuss central issues of NATO nuclear affairs. In 1977 the Nuclear Planning Group took the unusual step of setting up a new subcommittee of senior officials from national defence ministries to prescribe nuclear policy requirements for the future. This group has met regularly since that time and is called the High Level Group: it is chaired by the US Assistant Secretary of Defense for International Security Affairs, its activities are unpublicized and no communiques of its meetings have ever appeared. The UK representative is the Deputy Under Secretary at MoD in charge of Plans and Policy in the Defence Staff.

The High-Level Group is not supposed to be a decision-making body, but an analysis of the progress of the 1979 Euro-Missile decision shows a sequence of events which demonstrate an extremely strong policy directing influence. By February 1978, the High-Level Group had concluded that new American missiles were required for Europe. In January 1979 President Carter convened the Guadeloupe Summit meeting with Prime Minister Callaghan, Bundeskanzler Schmidt and Premier Giscard D'Estaing. From then on American diplomacy intensified behind the evolving decision to 'engineer' total political unity in NATO-Europe prior to the announcement of the decision itself. In the summer of 1979 the High-Level Group worked out final details of the deployment programme for the new weapons. At the end of November the permanent representatives at NATO headquarters in Brussels approved the High-Level Group's decision, and three weeks later it was endorsed by NATO's defence and foreign ministers. *The decision was not debated in the British Parliament until 1982.*

The integrated military structure

In 1985 Britain devoted 95 percent of its total defence budget to NATO commitments. In the nuclear weapons realm the British Navy, Army and Air Force all deploy nuclear forces committed to the NATO alliance. Britain's fleet of four Polaris submarines is currently under the core of Britain's 'independent nuclear deterrent'. They are deemed to be a 'contribution' to NATO's nuclear forces; they are targeted for use in wartime 'in accordance with Alliance policy and strategic concepts under plans made by Supreme Allied Commander Europe (SACEUR), save where Britain's supreme national interests otherwise require'. This last phrase—the kernel of British 'independence'—means that British, not NATO, political authorities can have ultimate say over the use of Polaris and other British nuclear forces.

The influence of the Cabinet and Cabinet Office

Decisions on defence and foreign policy are usually assumed to be made by the Prime Minister and Cabinet. By the time weapons decisions have reached this point, however, the options are limited. Options such as non-nuclear alternatives, for example, would not normally be under consideration.

The Cabinet Office plays a crucial role in the formulation and consistency of defence and foreign policy: it houses the Joint Intelligence Organization, as well as the Secretariats for each of the Cabinet Standing Committees. By the time the papers on a defence decision reach the Overseas and Defence Secretariat, the proposals have worked their way through the various processes and committees described, to a point where the Secretary of State for Defence is in agreement with his own civil servants about the decision to be taken and is prepared to defend it in Cabinet. Considerable amounts of money will have been spent on a particular weapons system by this stage, and the briefs prepared by the Overseas and Defence Secretariat will strongly recommend one particular course of action.

The Cabinet by no means always decides on particular questions as a whole Cabinet. Decisions are often taken in subcommittees, which bind the full Cabinet through the concept of 'collective responsibility', although other ministers may be ignorant that such a committee even exists. These committees are vital, but very little is known about them. In 1984 there were thought to be some 25 known Standing Committees, and about 110 of the even more secret special project Ad Hoc Committees, which are identified by the prefix 'MISC' (for miscellaneous) followed by a number. No one outside a central core of top ministers and officials actually know how many there are. The Defence and Overseas Policy Committee, a Standing Committee, ultimately officially takes decisions on nuclear systems. However, the secret Ad Hoc Committee known as MISC7 dealt with the replacement of the Polaris force with Trident, and MISC91 with the choice of the ALARM anti-radar missile. These three committees are chaired by the Prime Minister, who also selects the membership. The Prime Minister can thus effectively determine the outcome of decisions made in these key committees. The Cabinet Secretary is also chief secretary to every Cabinet committee chaired by the Prime Minister. He plays a crucial role in government business.

Parliament knows nothing of these decisions until the government decides to tell them. Even the House of Commons Select Committee on Defence, or the Public Accounts Committee, has no power to require government to announce or debate such a decision.

The influence on the Treasury

The purpose of the Treasury is to assist the government to control public expenditure and to promote satisfactory funding of the UK economy. Staff in the central Treasury number just over 1400 of whom only 175 are in the senior grade.

The Defence Policy and Material Group, known as 'DM', is the main section in the Treasury which deals with defence projects and expenditure. It has about 24 staff in total and has a huge responsibility of monitoring the defence budget (£18,060,000,000 for 1985–86). At ministerial level, DM normally deals with the Chief Secretary of the Treasury, who is also a member of the Cabinet. The Chancellor is concerned on major issues, such as nuclear projects, which are discussed by ministers collectively in Cabinet or Cabinet subcommittee.

The DM is badly understaffed for the job it has to do. Its staff simply do not have the weapons expertise to argue merits of a complex new technology with MoD.

Each year, MoD negotiates with the Treasury a total amount of expenditure for existing programmes; within this total it is up to MoD to decide what it will spend on what. There is a separate procedure for major new projects: every project which will cost more than £12.5 million in development or £25 million in production must have Treasury approval. MoD does however have the (crucial) right to deflect money between programmes during the year.

The influence of the Foreign and Commonwealth Office (FCO)

Arms control policy is the responsibility of the Foreign Office. The Foreign Secretary or his junior minister are answerable to Parliament. At the official level, a Superintending Under Secretary is responsible for two main departments—the Arms Control and Disarmament Department, and the Defence Department. The latter is described as being responsible for liaison with MoD on international aspects of defence although in practice both departments do so. The Defence Department is concerned with the bilateral talks between the USA and USSR. The longer-standing international forums for arms control negotiations, the UN Conference on Disarmament and other UN talks are the responsibility of the Control and Disarmament Department. Arms control policy in Britain is directly linked, through a process of 'clearance', with defence policy. But the link is one way. While arms control policy must be 'cleared' with MoD, defence policy need not be cleared for its arms control implications.

The role of Parliament

Under British Parliamentary tradition, Cabinet Ministers are accountable to the House of Commons in certain ways: answering parliamentary questions, replying to letters from MPs, taking part in debates. Many questions on nuclear issues, however, are simply not answered. There are long periods when there are no debates on nuclear weapons at all, for example between 1967 and 1980, a period during which plans were laid for massively increasing Britain's nuclear capability.

In theory the possibility is always open to the opposition to call for a debate on government policy. If the government majority is small, and if the opposition can win over government backbenchers, it can pass a vote of 'No

Confidence'. If that happened the government would normally be forced to resign. In practice this has not happened on nuclear issues, for two reasons. Firstly, because insufficient information has been made available to enable a fully-fledged debate on crucial decisions, and secondly because the Labour Party in opposition has until recently been deeply split on the issue. The Conservative Party has had a substantial majority, and in opposition would have been uninterested in calling a debate on nuclear weapons. The Defence Estimates are made public in a White Paper, usually in January each year, and voted upon. The figures in the defence budget are set out under different headings, but nowhere do Members of Parliament see what US legislators see, namely the 'line items' which describe the cost of each weapon separately, in its research development, testing and manufacturing stages. Only in that way would they be able to recognize and to control the development of new nuclear weapons.

Commons Select Committee

One way in which the House of Commons tries to exercise control over government actions and to obtain information is through the Select Committees. The Defence Committee is one of 14 departments. While it may call for evidence from and question ministers and civil servants, and recommend changes and expenditure, the Committee does not have the power of appropriation of funds to give effect to these recommendations (as does the US Senate Armed Services Committee, for example)—this would require substantial constitutional change. Ministers retain the right to withold information 'in the national interest', and the committee does not have access to papers containing the advice which civil servants give to ministers.

This committee represents the furthest limit to which inquiry can be made on defence issues by representatives of the people of Britain. As with any interrogation or dialogue, the success of Select Committees depends on the ability of MPs to ask the right questions and the willingness of civil servants to answer them: neither of which can be absolutely relied upon.

The Defence Committee regularly publishes reports of its inquiries, but it should be noted that a substantial proportion of its hearings are held in camera and the reports are dotted with deletions of what is considered to be sensitive evidence.

The Public Accounts Committee

This is not the most powerful committee in the House of Commons consisting of 15 backbench MPs, and chaired by a former cabinet minister from the opposition. It has been a public watchdog since 1862, keeping a check on the billions of pounds for which heads of departments have to account. It is the only Select Committee to have a larger specialized staff working directly for it: the Comptroller and Auditor General and his staff of 600 are independent auditors who examine the accounts of each government department to ensure that expenditure is in accordance with the law and Parliament's intentions. The Comptroller, however, failed to inform the PAC of the escalating costs of the Chevaline project, although he had access to the relevant papers at the time. The Committee was reduced to publishing an indignant report after the event.

What emerges from this brief discussion is that the mechanisms for accountability in Britain which have evolved gradually over the centuries were not designed for anything remotely like nuclear weapons. Accountability cannot begin until there is adequate information to question, challenge, debate and control the specific proposals which determine British nuclear policy.

Notes

1. This and the following material is from *U.S. Security Issues in Europe*, Sub-committee on US Security Agreements and Commitments Abroad of the US Senate Committee on Foreign Relations, December 1973.

Suggestions for Further Reading

Statement of the Defence Estimates Vol. I, Cmnd. 101–1. London: HMSO, 1987.
House of Commons Ninth Report of the Committee of Public Accounts: *Chevaline Improvement to the Polaris Missile System*. London: HMSO, March 1982, HC269.
Campbell, D. *The Unsinkable Aircraft Carrier* and *American Military Power in Britain*. London: Michael Joseph, 1984.
Gowing, M. *Independence & Deterrence*, Vol. I. London: Macmillan, 1974.
McLean, S. (ed.). *How Nuclear Weapons Decisions Are Made*. London: Macmillan, 1986.
Miall, H. *Nuclear Weapons: Who's In Charge?* London: Macmillan, 1987.

Nuclear Weapons and NATO Strategy

MINISTRY OF DEFENCE

The basic principle at the heart of NATO strategy, supported for nearly 40 years by all members of the North Atlantic Alliance, has been nuclear deterrence. At once simple and yet paradoxical, it is based on the idea that the surest way to preserve peace between East and West, without jeopardizing the freedom of our peoples, is to face a potential aggressor with a clear risk that the costs of aggression would amply outweigh any conceivable gain; and that the use of force is hence no longer a rational option. Thus the purpose of NATO's possession of nuclear forces is to ensure that circumstances never arise when we might have to consider using them.

NATO could not achieve such deterrence by conventional weapons alone. An adversary who no longer faced the risk of nuclear retaliation might once again regard force as a usable option, since the costs of aggression might no longer appear prohibitively high. Moreover, a defence based solely on conventional weapons would have no prospect of success against a nuclear-armed adversary. For it would always be open to an adversary who retained his nuclear weapons to use them, or threaten their use, to overcome any conventional resistance. Indeed, the more successful the conventional defence, the greater the incentive might be for a nuclear-armed power to resort to nuclear weapons. NATO's one-sided abandonment of such weapons might therefore increase the risk not merely of conventional war but also of nuclear use against NATO.

In 1987 it is easy to forget that in the first half of the century the world was twice plunged into immensely destructive global conventional war, precipitated on both occasions by a state numerically weaker than the combination of states that faced it. In the last century Europe was torn asunder by several major wars. By contrast, in the 40 years since the end of the Second World War—40 years of nuclear deterrence—there has been no war in Western

Europe, either conventional or nuclear, in spite of deep ideological hostility between East and West. This is a striking achievement, which those opposed to nuclear weapons, whether on moral or other grounds, would do well to ponder. They must explain how it is morally preferable to make Europe once again 'safe' for conventional war—a war in which modern weapons could bring destruction on a scale never seen before, and which could in the end provoke the very use of nuclear weapons that they seek to avoid.

Nuclear weapons on their own are not, however, sufficient for a credible deterrence strategy. Indeed the nature and scope of the nuclear component of the Alliance's deterrence forces have varied over time. In the early 1950s, faced with massive conventional forces in Eastern Europe, the NATO countries relied principally on the ability of the United States to inflict a massive nuclear strike on the Soviet Union. But the growth of the Soviet nuclear arsenal in the late 1950s and 1960s—and in particular the Soviet acquisition of long-range nuclear weapons capable of striking the United States—meant that NATO needed to widen its options for responding to either a conventional or a nuclear attack. So NATO evolved in the 1960s a new strategy of 'flexible response'; and this remains its strategy today.

For the strategy to work it requires existence of the US nuclear guarantee, backed by a strong US conventional presence in Europe. But it is a fundamental principle of the Alliance that the risks and benefits of a collective security policy be fully shared. In the nuclear field, concrete expression is given to this by the direct participation of European nations in the provision of the Alliance's deterrent forces. Belgium, the Federal Republic of Germany, Greece, Italy, the Netherlands, Turkey and the United Kingdom, all provide delivery systems and units trained in nuclear operations for the delivery of weapons that remain under US custodial control. Among these are dual-capable aircraft and artillery, and nuclear-dedicated systems such as Lance and Pershing missiles. The United Kingdom also assigns all its own nuclear forces to the Alliance, including both our strategic deterrent and theatre air-delivered weapons for aircraft and ship-borne anti-submarine helicopters. In addition, Alliance nations provide base facilities for US nuclear-delivery units, which are part of US forces in Europe. These include bases for US Poseidon submarines and the US Air Force and Army units in the Central and Southern Regions of Allied Command Europe.

For a country to reject NATO nuclear strategy, while continuing (as NATO membership implies) to accept US nuclear protection through the Alliance, offers no moral merit. Nor would it offer the United Kingdom greater safety, for whether nuclear weapons are based here or not, our country's size and location make it militarily crucial to NATO and so an attractive target in war. A 'nuclear free' Britain would mean a weaker NATO, weaker deterrence, and a greater risk of war; and if war broke out we would if anything be more likely, not less, to come under nuclear attack.

To implement a strategy of nuclear deterrence, NATO has to maintain an effective stockpile of nuclear weapons. But deterrence does not require ever-increasing numbers of such weapons. On the contrary, NATO is firmly committed to deploying only enough nuclear weapons to ensure deterrence, while at the same time seeking to negotiate deep reductions in the stockpile of both sides.

This was demonstrated by the decision of NATO Ministers in October 1983 at Montebello to withdraw 1400 warheads from the land-based nuclear stockpile in Western Europe in the period up to the end of 1988. The decision, taken together with the withdrawal of 1000 warheads that had already taken place before October 1983, brought the total number of warheads to be removed from Europe since 1979 to 2400. Furthermore, one existing warhead is being removed for each Pershing II or Cruise missile deployed by Western Europe, so that such deployment results in no further net increase. Critics of this decision have argued that it is of little import, since the warheads withdrawn were in any case obsolete. This is not only untrue—many of the weapons being withdrawn are still very effective—but misses the point: for NATO might have decided to retain a larger stockpile and subsequently to replace these weapons with equal numbers of modernized versions.

This reduction by NATO was unreciprocated by the Warsaw Pact. Deterrence could be assured at lower levels of armaments provided the Soviet Union were prepared to reduce too, so that there was balance between the two sides and both were assured of their own security. For many years the search for balanced, equitable and verifiable measures of arms control has been a slow one; but over the past 12 months real progress has been made.

As we record here, however, nuclear weapons cannot be treated in isolation. It is also necessary to consider the wider balance of forces between East and West and the Warsaw Pact's massive superiority in chemical and conventional weapons. The ever-increasing strength of these Soviet armaments casts a shadow over Western Europe. Reductions in nuclear weapons increase the importance of eliminating these other disparities and ensuring a stable overall balance. But as long as the basic tensions between East and West are undiminished, NATO will need to continue to rely on a strategy of nuclear deterrence based on an effective mix of systems. Nuclear weapons will remain as vital for keeping the peace—for preventing conventional as well as nuclear war in Europe—as they have been for the past 40 years.

Non-nuclear Defence

DAN SMITH

However strong the case against nuclear weapons, it is perfectly fair to ask how Britain would defend itself without them. Obviously, much of the answer depends on the circumstances in which Britain gave up nuclear weapons. If it were part of a universal move to nuclear disarmament, that would be a very different context in which to assess conventional defence than if the rest of the world—and especially the USA and USSR—retained nuclear weapons. Equally, the roles and structure of British conventional forces might be very different depending on whether Britain remained a member of NATO or withdrew from it.

There are so many possible political and strategic scenarios, that it would not be very useful to list them and design an appropriate conventional British defence policy for each one. Instead, it seems better to look at the main principles which have emerged out of several years of research and discussion in Western Europe, the USA and, most recently, the USSR.

One thing which has emerged in the 1980s debate on nuclear weapons and security is that there is a series of competing assumptions about the subject which produce entirely different conclusions. It may be helpful to list them:

	Orthodox View	*Alternative View*
1] The threat is:	the USSR's desire for global aggrandizement	the East-West confrontation
2] War is most likely to start with:	Soviet aggression (like Hitler in 1939)	a crisis getting out of control (like World War I in 1914)
3] Therefore we must concentrate on:	deterring Soviet aggression	avoiding crises and reducing confrontation
4] This means:	strengthening our armed forces so they can retaliate	keeping defensive forces strong and minimizing offensive ones

In the alternative view in the right hand column, the orthodox view leads to actions which make the dangers worse because they intensify confrontation.

Indeed, by raising the stakes to the point where NATO is prepared to respond to conventional attack with the first use of nuclear weapons—that is, by starting a nuclear war—the orthodox view mounts deterrent threats which are not only massive but possibly incredible. Yet if they are credible, in a crisis that may tempt the other side to strike first.

The way out of this vicious circle for advocates of non-nuclear defence is not, initially at least, simply to question whether the USSR is such a threat (though we will get onto that), but to pose a completely different way of thinking about security. It has three elements:

1. *Security is more than a military affair.* Threats to the well-being and prosperity of ordinary people do not come only from the USSR or the East-West confrontation, but from a host of other sources—economic, environmental, depletion of energy sources, etc. Military responses to such threats are self-defeating. Even those threats which do arise from East-West politics (however they are interpreted) require diplomatic and political as well as military responses.
2. *Security is indivisible.* In the nuclear age, it is a wild goose chase to think you can improve your own security at the expense of somebody else's. All that does is accelerate the arms race and make the confrontation worse.
   It increases the atmosphere of insecurity, mutual suspicion and hostility which could be a recipe for disaster in a major crisis.
3. *Defence must be defensive.* Whatever is done in the name of defence must be, as far as possible, obviously defensive. That is how it must look to the other side. It has to aim for security without confrontation, defensive strength without offensive capability.

From these three points can be pulled the two key notions of non-nuclear defence policy.

The first is *Common Security*. This contrasts with the idea of collective security on which both NATO and the Warsaw Pact are founded. The idea of common security works from the perception that security is indivisible.

The second is *Non-provocative Defence*. This is also known as *defensive defence*. It looks for armed forces which can provide defence, but cannot attack. This means doing away with those capabilities which are needed for major offensives—heavy armoured forces on the ground, long-range attack aircraft, capabilities for sea-borne invasions.

One thing has to be stressed at this point. The idea of non-provocative defence is not based on the idea that some weapons are defensive and others offensive. With very few exceptions throughout history, weaponry is offensive or defensive according to how it is used. The most obvious example to take is a shield, with which a medieval knight, Roman legionary or Scottish clansman *defended* himself. Using the shield to defend himself, he was able to use his sword, lance, mace or whatever, to *attack* and kill.

In the modern age, the offensive–defensive distinction still cannot be applied to distinguish between individual weapon systems. For example, tanks are the basis of land offensives, but they can also be used as part of a defence.

Where the distinction does apply is when you look at a state's overall force structure—the way its armed forces are constructed. The fact that the USSR, for example, has laid great emphasis on armoured forces, especially tanks, gives rise to justifiable fears that it is contemplating aggressive action. Equally, the USA's deployment of aircraft carriers with medium-range bombers and its large force of Marines gives rise to justifiable fears about aggression on the other side.

So in a policy of non-provocative defence, those forces which could be interpreted as laying the military foundations for aggression would be minimized. There might be some tanks—but not enough for a major offensive. Long-range strike aircraft would be eliminated, and air defence would be carried out by fighters and surface-to-air missiles, not by trying to destroy the other side's airfields. Naval forces would provide for coastal defence, not for the ability to threaten the other side's coastline.

All of this is technically possible and has the great advantage of being a good deal cheaper than the way that forces are structured according to the orthodox view of things. The weapon systems which would be eliminated are the ones which are the most expensive.

Many of the arguments for non-provocative defence are based on the effort to understand how the other side feels. This is an essential part of realising that security is indivisible. If we mount a military capability for reasons of defence, but the other side sees in it a way in which it could be used for an offensive, it will take counter-measures which we shall probably interpret as threatening—and so on, in an endless arms race and worsening confrontation until a crisis provides the spark to detonate this huge barrel of gunpowder.

Almost all of the common objections to non-nuclear, non-provocative defence can be traced to the orthodox view that the threat we face is the USSR's desire for global aggrandizement. The alternative view provides two answers to that.

First, even if it is true that the USSR seeks global expansion, the West's response is unnecessarily dangerous. It provides no basis for security because it is based on a gamble with awesome stakes. The threat to use nuclear weapons is, ultimately, either pointless or self-destructive or both—*in any scenario*. Used first, it starts a nuclear war—self-destructive, because of retaliation and nuclear winter. Used second, it simply adds to destruction after the deterrent has failed—pointless. Of course, if the USSR does want to invade Western Europe, the threat of a nuclear war would undoubtedly give it reason to hold off. But if its expansionist tendencies cause a crisis somewhere else, and war looms, it will probably strike first, specifically to destroy those nuclear weapons which otherwise would be used against it. So even if the USSR is as bad as Western hawks paint it, it still makes sense to develop defence policies which do not hold these risks, which do not tempt the USSR into a preemptive strike.

Second, however, the USSR is not the threat it is made out to be. There is no evidence that, since it took over the Eastern European states after World War II, it has had—or that its leaders have thought it had—a basic interest in either conquering or incinerating Western Europe. Like the USA, it seeks influence and power on the world stage, and this is dangerous. Its military strategy in Europe does place great emphasis on the offensive, but this is not because it wants to conquer Western Europe; it has enough problems in the rest of its sphere of influence without wanting to add to them. Rather, its emphasis on the offensive comes from its view that the best place to have a war is anywhere but on its own territory. The USA, with its policy of forward defence in Europe and Northeast Asia, has shown it has a similar point of view. The USSR's forces will be launched in a westwards offensive only if the USSR believes war is inevitable because of a major crisis in which both it and the USA have major interests at stake. And it could decide that war was inevitable, not just because of the nature of the crisis, but also because of the nature of the West's armed forces. The USA might decide the same thing, because of the nature of the USSR's forces.

Somewhere and somehow, a start has to be made to break out of the traps which the orthodox view lays for us. It sees threats which don't exist, and fosters threats it refuses to see. In the name of security, it mounts forces which make everybody insecure.

Non-provocative defence provides a way to skirt these traps—to make crises less likely, and less explosive if they occur. It does not hold all the answers to the problems of security—because not all the answers can be provided by any military set-up. But it provides some, and it has the advantage that if and when politicians start to talk peace and reconciliation, the actions of the armed forces they command will not be talking a different, more threatening language. And it has the further advantage that, while the more states that introduce it the better, it can be begun by individual states. Indeed, in Europe, Sweden, Switzerland and Yugoslavia all have military policies which provide security without suggesting to anybody that they have offensive intentions.

They are non-aligned nations, and many advocates of non-provocative defence argue that the policy could not be adopted by states which remain in NATO or the Warsaw Pact. Yet there is actually nothing in the North Atlantic Treaty which would prevent Britain or any other member shifting to non-provocative defence.

Suggestions for Further Reading

Alternative Defence Commission. *Defence Without the Bomb.* London: Taylor & Francis, 1983. This is the first report of the ADC and is a major treatment of all the military and strategic issues involved in thinking about non-nuclear defence. It looks at military and non-military possibilities for defence and assesses whether a non-nuclear Britain would do better inside or outside NATO.

Alternative Defence Commission. *Without the Bomb*. London: Paladin, 1985. This is a short version of the ADC's report. It makes essentially the same arguments, but misses some of the detail.

Alternative Defence Commission. *The Politics of Alternative Defence*. London: Paladin, 1987. The ADC's second report, looking at the political issues which are involved in thinking about non-nuclear defence.

Palme Commission. *Common Security*. London: Pan, 1982. Produced by an independent group chaired by the late Swedish Prime Minister, this is the book which gave the name to one of the basic concepts of alternative thinking on defence. It takes a global view and is more concerned with the political issues than with the details of non-nuclear defence.

Verification: Nuclear Disarmament and the Practicalities of Checking on Compliance/Cheating

PATRICIA LEWIS

Introduction

There is little point to arms control or arms reduction treaties unless the parties to them comply with them. Consequently each party to a treaty wants to know that the other party or parties are keeping their side of the bargain. The means of finding out if any country is keeping or breaking its word is called 'verification'.

Verification is defined as the action of demonstrating or proving to be true by means of evidence or testimony. In arms control this is translated as the action of demonstrating compliance. In reality, it means satisfying yourself that the other countries are sticking to the agreement.

Verification as a check on compliance assumes at least some desire to comply with an agreement. Because of the nature of the relationship between those engaged in an arms race, a desire to comply cannot be so easily assumed. Verification is then better described as checking on cheating.

The difference between checking on cheating and checking on compliance is a difference in attitude. The procedures for both attitudes are somewhat different in their approach. Generally speaking, checking on compliance is far less intrusive and is a lesser threat to national sovereignty than checking on cheating.

The relationship between the superpowers is, historically, lacking in trust and, as a result, verification regimes attached to a treaty have incorporated the checking on cheating attitude. This desire to see into every nook and cranny of each other's sensitive territory has, however, had to be tempered with respect for national commercial and military secrecy. The strictness of

97

verification has also had to take into account technical limitations, with the result that no system for checking on cheating is ever totally foolproof. Nor is total, 100 percent foolproof verification ever necessary. For each treaty is an 'adequate' or 'effective' verification regime.

Verification does not have to be foolproof to be effective. The police use this principle when enforcing traffic regulations: a sign saying 'police speed trap in operation' will make you think twice about breaking the speed limit even though you may suspect a bluff. In arms control verification the deterrence is even greater because there really are traps along the route. The amount of verification deemed necessary for each arms control agreement varies from treaty to treaty. The more crucial a treaty, in terms of its military significance, the more sure we have to be that the parties are complying. For example, a treaty to dismantle about 1000 ground-launched nuclear weapons in Europe, such as the INF treaty, does not need as strict a verification system as a treaty to remove *all* nuclear weapons in Europe.

Verification consists of a number of activities:

Monitoring—the gathering of data either on a systematic basis or on a 'one-off' dedicated mission.

Information Processing—the data is then assembled in a readable form.

Analysis—the stage at which the data is interpreted (e.g., does the satellite photograph show a missile base or not?).

Identification of the interpreted data—it is at this point that a decision is taken as to whether there is a violation. It is very difficult to state categorically that there has been a violation of a treaty unless there is corroborative evidence from various sources of information and so at this juncture, intelligence from a range of avenues is collected and compared.

Response—so everyone in the intelligence department agrees that a violation has occurred, how do they respond? The reaction depends on the significance of the violation, the state of relations between the accused and accuser, the internal politics of the accusing country and the global political climate.

Practicalities of verification

Missile reduction

The first stage in the verification of a missile reduction treaty is to agree on how many weapons in the limited category each side possesses. This is always tricky. The determination of how many weapons are actually deployed is usually agreed by consensus but it is very difficult to know how many are stockpiled. Fortunately those that exist in the stockpile, so long as it can be checked that they are never deployed, do not pose a major obstacle.

The next step in the negotiations is to agree on the number of weapons to be removed or dismantled. It is always easier for verification purposes if all of a certain type of weapon is prohibited. Verification becomes very difficult if some are allowed to remain because it could always be possible that more are deployed than allowed. When all of a particular type of weapon are disallowed then any sighting of that type of weapon signals a violation of the treaty. In fact verification problems was one of the main reasons for negotiating the 'Zero-Zero' treaty for the Intermediate-range Nuclear Forces (INF) reductions.

So how is a treaty prohibiting a class of weapons verified? The first steps are relatively easy.

Removal and dismantling

The parties agree on the timing for the decommissioning of the weapons and the stages of the procedure. They will also need to satisfy themselves that they have destroyed the missiles and warheads in the manner agreed but each will wish to protect its military secrets. The dismantling procedures will have to take both of these desires into account.

First they must agree to the dismantling sites. Some way to dismantle the weapons with the monitors watching but without them being able to see the exact design of the warheads or delivery vehicles has to be devised. In the case of warheads one approach is to have the owners seal the warheads under the eyes of the inspectors, take them to the dismantling sites and unseal them, again in the presence of inspectors. The removal of the fissile material, the guidance components and other sensitive equipment in the warheads can then be done in another secluded area so that it can only be viewed remotely by video camera.

The remainders of the warheads in the dismantling zone can then be seen and checked by the inspectors. The premises can also be checked before and after the operation to the satisfaction of the inspectors. The nose cones and associated components can be crushed in a similar manner to the way that an old car is crushed at a car-wrecking plant.

The missile itself is somewhat harder to deal with because of the highly explosive rocket fuel required to transport the missile and warhead to the target. There are ways, however, to render the missile inoperable and the problem lies primarily in solid fuel propelled missiles.

One method is to rupture the fuel containers so that any attempt to launch them would fail—this is a delicate and dangerous operation. Another is to fire the missiles with dummy warheads and destroy them in flight or they could be burnt on a huge bonfire.

What to do with the nuclear material in the warhead is a bone of contention. Those who wish to achieve global nuclear disarmament at some point in the future want the fissile material removed and kept by the International Atomic Energy Agency (who could either dilute it and store it in a similar manner to nuclear waste or could bank it for possible future use). Those who wish to retain nuclear weapons point to the so-called 'shortage' of plutonium and say that its re-absorption into the stockpile is necessary. Certainly if the current trend in nuclear weapon development continues, more and more plutonium is going to be used in the developmental testing and manufacture of new designs.

Once the weapons have been destroyed according to the terms of the treaty (which will take a few years in all), there has to be a way of checking that no more are manufactured or deployed. Checks also have to be made on storage facilities to ensure against surprise deployment of stashed-away weapons.

Verification of absence

National Technical Means

National Technical Means (NTM) of verification has come to mean the detection and identification of events and objects by satellite. It is a standard term in arms control which means the legitimate collection of verification data using the monitoring countries' own resources.

Large missiles which are deployed in fixed position silos and a host of associated facilities are readily seen by military satellites. Mobile missiles, such as ground-launched Cruise Missiles, are also stationed at fixed position sites and these sites can be observed by satellite. There is always the possibility, however, that the missiles could be taken away on their mobile launchers and hidden from view. The likelihood for this covert action going undetected is small. The missiles have been developed to be highly accurate and for such accuracy they have to be launched from pre-positioned sites. In addition, the personnel required to operate them would need training and would have to take the missiles out for exercises. The risk of being detected by satellites when out on an exercise would be too high.

On-site inspection (OSI)

Another way to verify the absence of a type of missile is to have provision in the treaty for on-site inspections and challenge inspections.

As the name implies OSI allows inspectors from a treaty signatory to visit sites in the countries of the other parties to the treaty. Some sites are more difficult to inspect than others. For example, it is much easier to have access to a missile base than to a submarine. On-site inspection can take several forms. One is the routine inspection at declared, pre-agreed sites. Routine

OSI is favoured because it allows the nations to prepare for the visit and does not pose a large threat to national security. Routine checks do not imply any accusation of cheating because they are already stipulated by the treaty. Provision for non-routine inspections on demand can also be written into a treaty. There can be a quota of these or an unlimited number and they can be either to all areas or to declared, agreed sites. In practice these inspections can only be negotiated if they are limited to agreed sites and are limited in number. Any form of 'demand' or 'challenge' inspection implies at least a suspicion of cheating. It is this form of OSI which has been a stumbling block for treaty verification.

The on-site inspection procedures for verifying the absence of a class of missiles depend on the type of missiles and on the treaty. In the case of the INF Treaty, for example, there are long-term provisions for visiting the missile bases. The original US proposals for verifying that all but 100 of the weapons had been removed were much more complicated. They included continuous on-site monitoring of the production, storage and repair facilities as well as a right to short-notice challenge inspections. Once the USSR agreed to remove all of the long-range INF, the US dropped the stringent verification demands.

Tied up with this issue is the legal question of whose sites to inspect. In the USSR the production, storage and repair facilities are under governmental control. In the USA, however, the manufacture of the weapons is carried out by commercial defence contractors. It seemed highly unlikely that they would grant free access to Soviet inspectors to look around their factories. After the initial US proposals for stringent verification there were many voices of concern in the US defence industry on this issue.

Another major factor in the verification strictness debate is that the number of weapons dismantled by the INF agreement is a small fraction of the total number of nuclear weapons in the world (less than 5 percent). It is not so crucial in terms of military significance if some 'slip through the net'. In the case of more significant disarmament, such as the proposed 'drastic reductions' of 90 percent of the strategic arsenal, then the need to be sure becomes more acute. On achieving total nuclear disarmament the verification procedures will have to be such that the whole world is confident that no nuclear weapons exist.

Dual capability

A proportion of nuclear weapons can carry conventional or chemical warheads instead. In the event of large reductions of nuclear weapons it would be very important to be sure that conventional warheads were just that.

In order to determine whether or not a warhead was nuclear the verification inspectors could employ nuclear detection techniques. These require the presence of inspectors close to the warheads using complicated nuclear detection equipment. The verification procedures are then highly intrusive or highly cooperative.

Verification of a comprehensive test ban

From the time of the first nuclear test in 1945 there has been a consistent call for controls on the development of nuclear weapons. While a total test ban would not necessarily mean the end to the arms race it would halt major developments in weaponry. Scientists and the military would not certify a weapon for stockpiling unless it had been tested to their satisfaction. Certainly if we are ever to achieve total or near total nuclear disarmament a ban on testing would be a key factor in that achievement.

In 1958 a group of experts set up to investigate a nuclear test ban concluded that a ban could be verifiable down to about 20 kilotons and, as a result, the USSR and the USA initiated the Conference for Discontinuance of Nuclear Weapons tests. On 22 August 1958 the US announced a one year-unilateral moratorium on nuclear testing to take effect from the first day of the conference (October 31). The USSR responded by agreeing to refrain from testing if the Western powers did likewise. The talks made little headway but the moratorium was extended and observed. Then on 13 February the French tested their first nuclear bomb and the talks broke down some months later. In September 1961 the Soviet Union broke out of the moratorium, blaming the French testing programme. Since then, and until the Soviet unilateral moratorium (August 1985 to February 1987), the USSR and the USA have continued to test nuclear warheads (although since 1964 all have occurred below ground).

It must be said, however, that between then and now, there has been some headway. In 1963 the Limited Test Ban Treaty (banning above-ground nuclear explosion) was signed by the USA, USSR and the UK. In 1968 the Non-Proliferation Treaty, halting the spread of nuclear weapons to non-nuclear states, was signed by many countries and in 1974 the bilateral Threshold Test Ban Treaty (limiting underground tests to a maximum of 150 kilotons explosion) was successfully negotiated. The Peaceful Nuclear Explosions Treaty, which needs intrusive verification procedures, was successfully concluded in 1976.

The negotiations for a Comprehensive Test Ban, between the UK, USSR and USA, began in Autumn 1977. Initiated by President Carter, progress was excruciatingly slow. Talks were suspended after the Soviet invasion of Afghanistan in 1979.

The current situation is that, while negotiations have been suspended, the technical issue of verification is still being discussed in Geneva.

There are two objections voiced to a Comprehensive Test Ban Treaty. The first is that it is impossible to verify, the second is that there is a need to test the weapon stockpile for reliability and safety. However, according to many weapons designers, stockpile tests are not necessary. To check out a warhead it is sufficient to inspect the components and replace those which have corroded or which function inadequately. A test has to be carried out only if a modification to the design is desired.

The central issue in negotiations for a CTBT has always been verification. The way to verify a test ban is through seismic detection coupled with information obtained from satellites. All sorts of vibrations travel through the Earth and they can be detected by instruments which respond to small movements on or in the ground. These instruments are called seismometers or seismographs (as they produce graphs of the vibration patterns). Large disturbances in the Earth's crust, such as earthquakes or underground explosions, show up very easily in the output from the seismographs and the magnitude of the vibrations tell us about the size of the disturbance.

The waves which travel through the Earth fall into two categories, those that travel along the surface of the Earth and those that travel through the volume (called body waves) and both types of wave carry useful information about the nature of a disturbance. They can be detected thousands of kilometres away from the source of disturbance. It is generally easy to distinguish between an earthquake and an underground nuclear explosion because the waves from each have different characteristics. In particular the very high frequency waves that are produced are very different for different types of disturbances and research into the use of monitoring these frequences is encouraging.

Discrimination gets tricky when a small nuclear explosion is suspected. Even those who do not wish to see a CTBT concede that nuclear explosions down to tens of kilotons yield are easily distinguished and verifiable. The arguments start when we ask: 'How low can we get?'

A crucial point in the debate is the concept of verification itself. It is important to realize that if the *risk* of getting caught is high enough to inhibit any desire to cheat, then we have an *effective* verification regime. So, at low yields, what are the risks of getting found out? Short answer—considerable. Long answer—it depends on how much money and effort is put into seismic array networks around the test sites and around the world.

It is generally agreed that if the USSR were to agree to some 25 to 30 tamper-proof, high frequency monitoring stations on its territory and on-site 'challenge' inspections, then we would be able to verify down to one kiloton yield, with a high degree of confidence. Many scientists are convinced that it would be possible to detect and identify explosions of much lower yield.

Some argue that it would still be possible to cheat if a large cavity were mined in, say, salt deposits and a small nuclear device exploded in such a manner that most of the vibrations were prevented from travelling through the ground—this is called cavity decoupling. The likelihood of such an exercise going unnoticed is tiny. Photoreconnaissance satellites would quickly pick up any large-scale mining activities (and large they would have to be—a cavity about the size of an Egyptian pyramid is one estimation). In addition it is never possible to fully muffle the seismic signals from an explosion and recent research shows that monitoring the high frequencies considerably reduces the effects of muffling and hence foils attempts to cheat. In fact tests carried out in the US have shown it to be, so far, technically impossible to evade detection in this manner.

Because there seems to be consensus that a test ban could be verified down to one kiloton yields, there are proposals for a One Kiloton Threshold Test Ban Treaty. This would allow any number of tests below the threshold and either none or some quota above (then we would have a Quota Threshold Test Ban Treaty). There are problems associated with such schemes. A One Kiloton Threshold Test Ban would remove verification obstacles but would set the scene for a series of accusations of violation, it would also still allow limited research into the development of warheads. It would have, however, more support and hence is more likely to be negotiated successfully.

A Quota Threshold Test Ban would be more acceptable to the military, primarily because it could be structured to make very little difference to their programmes. It would probably take the form of allowing, each year, a few tests between 20 and 150 kilotons, several tests between 1 and 20 kilotons and an unlimited number below one kiloton. So it would make very little difference *unless* it were a *Graduated* Quota Threshold Test Ban—in other words year by year the numbers of tests would decrease until a Comprehensive or a One Kiloton Threshold Test Ban Treaty would come into effect.

Verification technology and you

There are other technologies and practical means of verifying arms control and disarmament treaties which have not been included in this section. There are also other technologies which could be researched and developed to make them useful for verification problems. Almost all of the verification technology research is carried out by government scientists in the weapons laboratories. These scientists are in a difficult position. They are researching ways of weapon reduction while their colleagues are designing new types of weapons. In addition, all of the information that reaches governments about the compliance activities of other states comes from military sources and governmental intelligence sources. Most of the detailed information is classified. This means that you, as a citizen, have to accept the word of your government on the compliance or non-compliance behaviour of other states. If the verification data and analyses were in the public domain, ordinary civilians would have access to this vital information.

Many scientists around the world are now debating this problem. Several groups have been formed to promote treaty verification research by civilian scientists. For example, there is a team of US civilian seismologists gathering seismic data in the USSR both during and in between nuclear tests. The data they are collecting have hitherto been unobtainable and are resolving many of the finer points of the verification of nuclear test bans. There are other scientists who are now looking at commercially available satellite data in order to gain expertise in image analysis for arms control verification. Such efforts will eventuate in public awareness of treaty compliance and will allow countries who cannot afford their own verification research access to information previously denied to them.

PART 4

Political and Economic Aspects of Development in the Third World

Like the East-West conflict, North-South relationships are also central to our understanding of peace and development. This section deals with political and economic aspects of development in the Third World and considers some of the very difficult problems that we now face. The Third World perspectives on peace and development presented here analyze the consequences of colonization, decolonization and neo-colonialism on the development process in the Third World and the major food, development and debt crises that have as a consequence been generated. These crises are exceptionally severe in Africa and the chapters by Aguibou Yansane and Girma Kebbede focus on this region. The Third World debt crisis has major consequences for peace and development throughout the southern hemisphere and Susan George considers how the debt was incurred, how the debt is being managed and what can be done to bring an end to the crisis. The final chapter by Renato Dagnino details the additional difficulties created in the Third World as a consequence of global trends in military expenditure.

Decolonization and the Development Crisis in Africa

AGUIBOU Y. YANSANE

Introduction

Colonization interfered with the internal, cultural, economic and political evolution of most African states. Western European colonization transformed territories in Africa, Asia and the Americas into colonies. The first purpose of the colonies was to form sources of cheaply produced raw materials and minerals. Another objective of the colonies was to be safe, stable markets for European merchandise and commercial services. Colonization established railroads, ports, shipping lines, navigation companies and transformation industries. Many colonists and colonial enterprises acquired substantial financial guarantees and ended up making huge profits through their ventures. A further purpose of colonization was to 'civilize' the traditional 'indigenous' societies by bringing to them technological advances in health and education as well as commercial, industrial and moral benefits.

In view of these first two objectives, colonization carried the seeds of its own end. How about then, decolonization? Decolonization may be defined as the formal transfer of political and international sovereignty from a colonial state to formerly colonized people. The colony's populace then hold autonomous power to decide on political, economic, cultural and social policies of the new nation-states.[1] Unfortunately, decolonization has bred a series of self-defeating problems. This is illustrated by the experience of state formation and nation-building in Africa over the past thirty years. History shows that decolonization, a necessary step in the development of formerly colonized people, must be implemented with lucidity in analysis of

109

politics, economics and business management. Otherwise it creates more problems than it can solve.

Colonization interfered with Africa's nation-building

Between the fifteenth and nineteenth centuries, Africans were building their nations at the same time that European countries were forming. They had empires, kingdoms and city-states. They had at least several identifiable types of government: the village council and the somewhat centralized monarchies, such as Ghana and Mali. There were strongly centralized structures in Songhay, Kanem-Bornu and the seemingly decentralized monarchies of the Coastal Guinea (Ashanti, Yoruba states, etc.) in which the king's power was limited by customs, the constitution and by religion. No one of these political systems attempted to exclude the others.[2] The people had generally peaceful relations among themselves. At times when they had conflicts, they resolved them by warfare or negotiations.

The colonial system interfered with Africa's nation-building process. There was much African resistance to colonial conquest in the nineteenth century by such peoples as Algeria's Abdel Kader, West Africa's Hadj Omar Tall, Uthman Dan Fodio, Samori, Behanzin, and South Africa's Shaka.[3] Those are just a few resisters. They and their followers struggled against the consequences of colonial conquest, but they could not prevent the destruction of many of Africa's highly organized systems. This led to Africa's loss of independence, loss of sovereignty, mixed economic balance, and certainly international humiliation. There grew up the assumption of the inferiority of Africans and people of African descent to rationalize the African slave trade, prejudice and racism. The many disastrous effects on the psyche of modern Africans and people of African descent are evident. It is fortunate that most Africans seem to have recently transcended and overcome the negative aspects of the colonial syndromes. They have built meaningful relations with the former colonial rulers.

Colonization had a mixed balance sheet

Colonization created, in Africa, colonial boundaries where none had existed. Any local governments may have been subdued or taken over to coexist with the colonial administration. In either case, the role of the local government was minimal.

Colonization created a colonial political and administrative order. At the top echelon of this order were the colonists and settlers—citizens transplanted from the European metropole or mother country. The machinery of colonial rule was used to protect these colonists and settlers. They enjoyed most of the benefits of colonization, earning huge salaries for their administrative or business positions. In British colonies, these metropolitan citizens were the real holders 'in trust' of colonial territories under direct or indirect rule.[4] The holders in trust were supposed to prepare the 'indigenous' people for independence once the 'trust territories' were socially, economically and politically mature or capable of self-rule.[5] In the transition to self-rule, a leader of the government was named; but the British governor was still the head of government. He alone apportioned or allocated to British citizens in the colonies the portfolios of defence, external affairs and finance during self-rule.

The French, inspired by the ideals of the French Revolution of 1789, promised the colonized people assimilation into a single republic, with liberty, equality, and fraternity for all.[6] Unfortunately, this assimilation could not be pursued to its logical end as the metropolitan French themselves were deprived of many things such as education and health.

The Belgians hoped to 'civilize' the Congolese people (today's Zairians) through the Calvinist gospel of work. They aimed at making the local citizens good burghers.[7] The good burghers would have benefited more from paternalism à la Plato's Republic in a society indoctrinated with the Roman Catholic conception of the hierarchy whereby the ruling Belgians should have provided the conditions of good life for the ruled Congolese.

By the fourth quarter of the nineteenth century, the Portuguese colonies were much smaller than the British, French and Belgian. Their colonialism was more oppressive and exploitative, and the end products would have discriminated against Africans permanently.[8] They made Africans a source of reserve labour in their colonies.

In many countries Africans suffered great alienation as a result of the loss of cultural heritage.[9] This may explain the number of long protracted liberation wars. The protracted wars took place especially in settler colonies, such as Kenya, Algeria and Zimbabwe (previously Southern Rhodesia). There settlers had driven the 'natives' to the arid and less suitable lands so that they might settle in more fertile sections. This deprivation of land and deep alienation can be given as explanations for the violent nature of the nationalist movements and decolonization in Kenya, Algeria, Zimbabwe, the Portuguese colonies, and in South West Africa.

In all cases, the colonial states were centralized, authoritarian and oppressive. They were staffed primarily to protect the colonial order and economy. The new way of life was based on Western social attitudes, cultural values and work ethics. It was supposed to be supported by an evolutionary theory according to which nation-states and industrialized capitalism represented the most advanced forms of human organization. It was argued that it was the duty and right of higher civilization to conquer lower civilizations, thereby bringing progress. The metropolitan colonial language was the main vehicle of communication; the legal and institutional framework was Anglo-Saxon, French, or Iberian in inspiration.

The colonial economy extended the imperial system. After the abolition of the slave trade, the colonial governments established control over the indigenous mode of production in the transition from West Africa's slave economies to enclave economies based on cash crops and mineral extraction. This control over the mode of production is characteristic of imperialism. Elements of force and the inducement of wage payments in colonial currency provided labour. The work was usually to grow crops, to work in mines and the infrastructure necessary to transport the products of the plantations and the mines to the seaports. From the ports the goods could be exported to the metropoles. Conscripts were paid wages which were barely above subsistence levels. But it was enough money to enable families to pay the colonial taxes. The economy was far from being a free economy for everybody. It was the political economy of the colonial and mercantile enterprise.

African national consciousness developed in sharp reaction to the negative attitudes associated with competition and the domination of big mercantile companies. Africans did not like the fact that much of the wholesale trade was run by foreigners. Nor did they approve of the enclave industries during colonial rule.

Colonization contributed to the extension of modernization and market principles

Colonization contributed to the creation of modern political and administrative institutions as well as new economies. The development of these political and economic institutions allowed Africans to make demands and requests which were only of marginal benefit to them. Colonial powers contributed to the extension of market principles, whereby impersonal forces of world markets dominated the lives of millions of people. The colonists imposed states where none had existed before or which superseded indigenous ones. They created a mass of wage earners and peasants who were taken advantage of by the colonial system.

Between 1915 and 1945, the Africans stood against the consequences of conquest, occupation and loss of land, and demanded social amenities such as better schools, hospitals, and new forms of transportation, such as railroads and bridges. They demanded reduced taxation and the abolition of forced labour. These demands mounted fast, and gave rise to strong nationalist movements and trade unions. The trade unionists demanded equal pay for equal work, fringe benefits and family allocations as well as fair prices for farmers, and other rights to compete with European planters and traders. Populist mass movements emerged from all quarters, grouping together intellectuals, students, youth movements, market women, peasants, farmers, and trade unions. They had in mind a common goal, their emancipation, and possibly independence.

Decolonization paths and Africa's share of the world crisis

In the nationalist-reformist tradition of decolonization great emphasis is placed on the internal evolution of the new state. This was the case for Egypt, pre-Gaddafi Libya, Tunisia, Sudan, Morocco, and pre-1963 and post-Nkrumah Ghana. It was the case too for all of the African countries of French, Belgian and Italian colonial legacies. There were some exceptions: pre-1984 Guinea-Conakry, pre-1968 Mali, post-1968 Congo Brazzaville and post-1972 People's Republic of Benin. The rulers of the new African states find inspiration in the Keynesian, macro-dynamic theory. They believe in the basic tenets of efficient operation of firms, avoidance of cyclical instability combined with policies of full employment and long-term strategies of growth.

Both Ghana's former leader Kwame Nkrumah and Senegal's former leader Senghor incorporated state intervention in their decolonization model. It was based on the core model of African traditional society referring to the African experiences in relation to the presence of Islam and European Christianity.[10] Both argued that the state should determine national policies, and should manage the economy through emphasis on the export sector generating economic surplus to industrialize and modernize the countries.

Theories mildly critical of free trade and international specialization of labour were developed by Ragnar Nurske, Rosenstein Rodan, Arthur Lewis, Father Lebret and Father Fyot. These theories were used to support a certain degree of protection for investment in infrastructure, manufacturing and planning, rudimentary modernization of agriculture, education, taxation, public administration and finance.

The second model of decolonization gave special attention to the colonial period, using it to explain the lack of development of the former colonies. It assumes internal and international exploitation which exacerbated class differentiation. So development in the few African socialist countries such as Guinea and Tanzania was conceived as taking place in a society where adequate equalitarian structures have been created and where workers have been organized into a ruling class.

The African socialist development in Guinea has been changed into a liberal reformist model.[11] The Tanzanian case has lost some of its momentum because of economic deterioration.[12]

The third model, the revolutionary model of decolonization, was experienced in Algeria, the Portuguese colonies of Guinea-Bissau, Angola and Mozambique and Zimbabwe. Namibia (formerly South West Africa) is presently following this path. This third model has been the subject of the theories of Fanon and Cabral. Both Franz Fanon and Amilcar Cabral describe violent struggles from a somewhat Marxian viewpoint. They advocate means whereby nationalist struggles might develop into a social revolution of the masses. Theoretically this would result in the creation of a new humanist being who would restore and cultivate Africa's most valued cultural background.[13]

After independence, Africa's new nation-states experienced many problems of stability in nation building. Many countries without sufficient political, economic and administrative cadres or which had committed major political and economic errors were plunged into a chaotic situation, which paralyzed the bureaucratic machinery. This was the case in the former Belgian Congo in 1961, Uganda under Idi Amin, the Central African Republic under Jean Bedel Bokassa, and former Equatorial Guinea under Makias Nguema. The same situation is occurring presently in Chad.

Many explanations can be given for recurring state instability. First, at independence the state was mostly staffed by zealous colonial assistants and civil servants. The state usually controls the economic infrastructure on a constitutional basis. The parliamentarian system exists, but is deficient. The state controls the machinery of control, thanks to the single party machine and it performs an ideological function. It negotiates with foreign sources of capital, finance and investment, and it distributes and allocates the economic surplus. It regulates employment in government and business, dispenses training and education and determines social policies. The internationalist school explains the underdevelopment of these states as largely the result of colonial exploitation, thus blaming external factors more, although the new state possessed some maneuverability in terms of the limited options open to it in terms of development. It is an 'overdeveloped state' without modernized structures to match requirements of a state of such magnitude.[14]

Second, at independence there were also many problems inherent in the transition from a colonial economy to an independent economy. The African economies were characterized by the predominance of low productivity, subsistence agriculture in economic activities and the survival of traditional institutions. Cities and towns were poorly developed, as were the entrepreneurial classes. The big businesses in the wholesale trade were run to a large extent by foreign capital. The establishment of extractive industries of the enclave type were developed by transitional corporations. It would have been impossible for those African countries to aspire to economic independence after progressing for about four hundred years as partners of Western Europe. In colonial days, as now, the European countries supported most of the African currencies, subsidized their agricultural exports and trade deficits, and supported the flow of foreign aid and investment through the EEC-ACP Lome Accords.[15]

Third, there has been a fundamental problem of political leaders and bad governments. These governments' major concerns were self-preservation, rather than increasing or maintaining the standard of living of the population. This problem of long periods of presidentialism, elimination of opposition, economic stagnation, and urban inflation has meant that military officers have become the ruling political force. The military regimes, at times repressively autocratic, at times liberal under technocratic direction, proved to be easily content with the structures of liberal finance and free enterprise. These were mostly reminiscent of colonial administration.

As the crisis of recession was accentuated in the West, Africa's development experts shifted from their 1950s view of economic growth with an emphasis on modernization. At that time, growth was defined in terms of average per capita output. They changed in the 1970s and 1980s to an increasing recognition of the interdependence of agriculture and industry. The important lesson learned from the 1950s and 1960s is that technological change must be included as a central component in both the theory and practice of agricultural and rural development. In the 1970s, this resulted in broadening the development goals to include growth with equity.[16]

In the late 1970s and early 1980s the effects of the crisis due to recession in the Western world have been dramatically felt in Africa. Per capita food production has declined,[17] and there has been a sharp reduction in imports.[18] There is an endemic shortage of basic consumer goods and a soaring inflation rate. There is the omnipresence of bureaucracy in every sphere of life. Official African governments tend to blame this on skyrocketing oil prices, deteriorating terms of trade, and the world financial crisis. They also point to an uneven recovery in industrial countries, the burden of repayment of debt, adverse weather conditions, and desertification in the Sahel and elsewhere.[19]

According to the reformist-nationalist perspective, the crisis is due to extreme centralization where seventeen states are ruled by single parties, including military regimes. As a result, there is widespread dislocation of independent civilian institutions, violations of human rights, oppression, injustice and heavy-handedness. Many thousands of victims of protracted conflicts in Ethiopia, Sudan, and Southern Africa live in refugee camps. These camps are found in Somalia and in frontline states of Southern Africa, the neighbours to Apartheid South Africa.

Endogenous problems also stem from dubious agricultural collectivization schemes under the premise of internal development, state monopoly of trade, indigenization and mismanagement of public enterprises. Problems also arise from unrealistic currency exchange rates which are defined by lax monetary and price-administered policy. Then too, there is the imbalance between the private sector and public sector. States often consume the surplus of growth, exploiting the peasants. Problems show up when nonconvertible currency causes speculation on the black market and smuggling of consumer goods outside the countries. The goods flow from Guinea,

Ghana, Nigeria, Tanzania, etc. toward neighbouring countries which provide better incentives and convertible currencies to producers and traders.

The crisis, which can best be explained by the world crisis generated in the citadels of high finance, is exacerbated by the internal and external factors discussed by both schools of thought: the 'reformist-nationalist' and the 'internationist'.[20]

What is to be done?

Two documents try to answer this question: the OAU Lagos Plan for Action (LPA) and the World Bank Accelerated Development in SubSaharan Africa.[21]

The Lagos Plan for Action sets the goals of Africa's development in terms of national and collective self-reliance via a partial delinkage from the global trading system, self-sufficiency in food and regional cooperation and integration. World Bank Accelerated Development identifies the traditional goals of neoclassical development. These are emphasis on income growth versus equity distribution or regional balance; priority for small agricultural producers, and better incentives for a freer market. This approach also calls for more privatization and more export growth as well as more leverage of privatization which enables the small-scale enterprise to operate freely. This view also emphasizes decentralized decision-making at the center.

Looking at these studies, the Lagos Plan for Action has a more perceptible inward-oriented trend. Both studies agree to reduce the functional role of the state and the government corporations. Both agree that the productive capacity of the new farmers needs to be increased as a means of rural development.

The root causes of Africa's crisis, and certainly the bottom line for meaningful decolonization, is lack of sufficient production. The blame for faulty decision-making in matters affecting production can be shared equally by both former colonial metropoles and donors, as well as by the Africans themselves. The former provide aid which is not sufficient to produce self-sufficiency in the future. This aid tends to instill a taste for Western consumerism. This aid is distributed to projects aimed at assisting the donors' economies. The latter, the local Africans, are still short on practical means of generating financial clout to find alternatives to foreign aid. The issue of production, which is central to decolonization, is related to macro-economic and micro-economic considerations.

In the spirit of the late 1980s, most African countries seem to be facing the problem of self-sufficiency. They are trying to solve the problem of scarcity of financial resources. They are trying to achieve financial stability and promote a sustained rate of economic growth which depends on domestic capital formation, sound planning, pricing policy, and monetary and fiscal policy measures. Economic growth must also depend on efficient operation of public and private enterprises and resource allocation based on consistent rates of interest and exchange rates which facilitate financial intermediation, promote domestic saving and an adequate level of investment. Africa's pragmatic leaders still show some faith in a neoclassical renaissance despite the call of Africa's technocrats for self-sufficiency. Micro-economic solutions focus on the slowly but steadily declining per capita food production. Help from industrialized countries can stimulate Africa's local productive sectors, especially the rural development policy. Africa's manufacturing industry should be primarily linked to the agricultural sector. There must be some help for a plan for a water infrastructure, especially in drought-stricken countries. This stresses access to clean water. There must also be improvement in living conditions in both the cities and the rural areas. This can come about through Official Development Assistance as well as non-governmental organizations.

The extraction of raw materials must not be the main investment of industrialized countries. The foreign private sector as well as the public sector both have a role to play in Africa's development.

Conclusion

The world global order and its long-term political, economic, and strategic interests in Africa will be better served when Africa is politically stable and economically viable. The efforts of the industrialized countries will have to take into account Africa's perception toward many of the latter's involvement on the side of the South African government's policy of apartheid. These efforts must reflect the industrialized countries' commitment to promote racial justice and social change in Southern Africa. Foreign aid needs to be adapted to the driving force of change in Africa, i.e., nationalism. Aid needs to reach the productive sectors. Decolonization, which is an indispensible step in the development of formerly colonized people, must be implemented with lucidity, together with clear analysis of politics, economic conditions, business management and international relations. Otherwise it creates more problems than it can solve.

Notes

1. Yansane, Aguibou Y. (ed.). *Decolonization and Dependency: Problems of Development of African Societies.* Westport, Conn. & London: Greenwood Press, 1981. See Chapter 1; and Yansane, Aguibou Y. *Decolonization in West African States with French Colonial Legacy: comparison and contrast; Development in Guinea, the Ivory Coast and Senegal, 1945–1980.* Cambridge Mass.: Schenkman Publishing Company, Inc., 1984. See Chapters 1 and 2.
2. See Davidson, Basil. *A History of West Africa to the Nineteenth Century.* Garden City, NY: Doubleday & Company, Inc., 1966; Davidson, Basil. *A History of East and Central Africa to the Late Nineteenth Century.* Garden City, NY: Doubleday & Company, 1969; and Yansane, A. Y. 'Cultural Political and Economic Universals in West Africa'. In Asante, M. K. and K. W. Asante (eds.). *African Culture: The Rhythms of Unity.* Westport, Conn. & London: Greenwood Press, 1985, pp. 39–68.

3. Crowder, M. (ed.). *West African Resistance*. London: Longman, 1971.
4. The basis of direct and indirect rule can be the function of several factors such as the mode of production, surplus society involved in long-distance trade, centralized government. These factors were gauged to classify societies into more or less developed depending on ethnocentrism. See, for the origin of indirect rule, Lugard, F. D. *The Dual Mandate in British Tropical Africa*, 5th ed. London: Frank Cass, 1965, Chapter 7, pp. 10–13; Perham, M. *Native Administration in Nigeria*. Oxford: Oxford University Press, 1937, pp. 43–80; and Brill, M. 'Indirect Rule in Northern Nigeria, 1906–1911'. In Robinson, I. and F. Madden (eds.). *Essays in Imperial Government*. Oxford: Oxford University Press, 1965.
5. For a good fictional novel on the period of self-rule on Ghana, see Abraham, Peter. *A Wreath for Udomo*. New York: The Macmillan Company, 1971.
6. Delavignette, R. *Freedom and Authority in French West Africa*. London: Oxford University Press, 1950; and Betts, R. F. *Assimilation and Association in French Colonial Theory, 1890–1914*. New York: Columbia University Press, 1961.
7. Ryckmans, Pierre. *Dominer pour servir*. Brussels: L'Edition Universelle, 1948.
8. Axelson, E. V. *Portugal and the Scramble for Africa 1875–1891*. Johannesburg: Witwaters, 1967.
9. Nkrumah, Kwame. *Consciencism: Philosophy and Ideology for Decolonization*. New York: Monthly Review Press, 1970; and Lenghor, S. *Nation et Voie Africaine du socialisme*. Paris: Presence Africaine, 1959 (translated as *African Socialism*. New York: American Society of African Culture, 1959).
10. Lewis, Arthur W. 'Economic Development with Unlimited Supplies of Labor'. Manchester School journal, May 1954; Lewis, Arthur W. *The Theory of Economic Growth*. London: Allen and Unwin, 1961; and Nurske, Ragnar. *Problems of Capital Formation in Underdeveloped Countries*. New York: Oxford University Press, 1967.
11. Yansane, A. Y. *Decolonization in West African States,* op. cit., Chapter 3.
12. Nyere, Julius. *Ujamaa: Essays on Socialism*. London: Oxford University Press, 1968.
13. Fanon, Franz. *The Wretched of the Earth*. New York: Grove Press, 1967.
14. See Miliband, Ralph. 'Poulantzas and the capitalist state', *New Left Review*, 82, November–December 1972.
15. European Economic Community-African-Caribbean-Pacific. 'Lome Dossier.' Reprinted from *Le Courrier* 31, Special Issue, March 1975.
16. Chenery, Hollis. *Structural Change and Development Policy*. New York: Oxford University Press, 1979.
17. Agricultural production in SubSaharan Africa has been in decline since the late 1970s. See United States Department of Agriculture. *Food Problems and Prospectus in SubSaharan Africa: The Decade of the 1980s*. Washington DC: USDA, Economic Research Service Foreign Agricultural Research Report No. 166, 1981.
18. See *Africa Research Bulletin,* Economic Series Vol. 24, No. 11, 31 December 1987.
19. *Daily News*, 5 January 1988.
20. Organization of African Unity (OAU). 'The Lagos Plan for Action.' Lagos, Nigeria, 29 April 1980.
21. Brown, Robert S. and Robert J. Cummings. *The Lagos Plan for Action Versus the Berg Report: Contemporary Issues in African Economic Development*. Lawrenceville, VA: published for the African Studies and Research Program by Brunswick Publishing Company, 1984.

The State and Africa's Food Recovery

GIRMA KEBBEDE

SubSaharan Africa is in deep and persistent socio-economic, political and environmental crisis. For nearly two decades, the region's ability to feed its fast-growing population has been steadily declining. A host of factors has contributed to this deteriorating economic condition. For most African leaders, the causes are mainly externally induced, although some have recently acknowledged accountability for past failures. But most experts agree that internal socio-economic and political constraints (misappropriation of development resources, misguided policies and priorities) and external factors (deteriorating terms of trade and increasing foreign debt) are largely responsible for these perilous economic conditions.

In recent years, some African leaders have begun to address the problems that underlie poor economic performance. The Lagos Plan of Action, adopted by the Organization for African Unity in 1980, underscored the necessity of fundamental revision of African economies. The plan advocated greater self-sufficiency based on increased emphasis on domestic food production and regional cooperation. Although many countries developed national food strategies, very few of the plans were implemented. The Addis Ababa Declaration of July 1985 expressed the commitment of African leadership to take concrete actions to improve the economy in general and to rehabilitate the agricultural sector in particular. The attainment of food self-sufficiency was considered the first essential step toward recovery.

The continent-wide movement towards self-sufficiency is welcome, though the results of this commitment remain to be seen. If past experience is a guide, one has very little reason to hope. Rhetoric, promises and piecemeal solutions cannot resuscitate a moribund economy or eliminate hunger and poverty. Fundamental structural changes are needed both in economic and political spheres. Unfortunately there is no indication that the changes required in the socio-economic and political structure of Sub-Saharan Africa are likely to occur easily or soon. The fundamental changes needed directly challenge the existing political and economic power structure in these countries. It is a depressing reality that no ruling elite group is willing to redistribute political and economic power.

The exploitative nature of the existing international economic order, over which Africans cannot exercise significant influence, is another factor. African economies are deeply integrated into the international economic system in which production is determined on the basis of comparative advantage. Africans are forced to supply perpetually cheap raw materials to the industrialized economies and, in turn, to consume expensive value-added goods, which results in a chronic balance of payments crisis. As long as African economies are hooked into the international division of labour, a restructuring of production and consumption geared towards greater self-reliance and autonomy will be difficult to achieve in the immediate future.

In spite of these difficulties, certain ameliorative measures can be taken if there is a strong will and commitment on the part of the African leadership. Genuine recovery requires more measures with tangible results than those set forth in the Lagos and Addis Ababa declarations. In concrete terms, African states must adopt additional policy measures to reduce hunger and mass poverty.

Rural poverty and problems of inadequate food production cannot be addressed without explicit emphasis on the small-scale peasant sector. Publicly owned agricultural estates and collectivization schemes in Africa have not been able to induce peasant farmers to be productive. State-owned farms, which receive massive investment funds and produce mainly export commodities, have neither raised productivity nor augmented employment or wage incomes. For one thing, wages paid by state-owned farms are so low—below subsistence level in most cases—that farm workers are discouraged from becoming productive and efficient. Actual experience in many SubSaharan countries has proved that publicly-owned agricultural enterprises are inefficient and wasteful in terms of resource allocation and have failed to generate genuine rural development geared to finding solutions to the problems of food, health, and education.

Nor is the performance of collective farms better than state-operated farms. In many rural areas collectivization is resented by individual peasant farmers who prefer to work on their own holdings. Peasant farmers have shown reluctance to put maximum effort into production when told what to do, what crops to grow and at what price to sell them, which has been witnessed in African countries which pursued socialist-oriented rural development strategy. After many years of collectivized agriculture Tanzania, Ethiopia and Mozambique have not been able to break the persistent mass poverty, hunger and underdevelopment.

Large-scale capitalist enterprises have done very little to promote development that affects the majority of the rural population. Expensive and technologically sophisticated enterprises consume an excessively large proportion of available prime land by displacing small farmers; their contribution to employment is minimal as they tend to be capital-intensive; they produce cash crops for export rather than food crops for local consumption, thus further accentuating the crisis of food shortage. Because most of these enterprises are foreign-owned, most of the profit goes abroad, thus depriving the host countries of precious investment resources. Nor do such enterprises develop linkages within the country, since they depend excessively on foreign technology and technological and management expertise, whilst most of their produce is primary or semi-finished commodities. In cases of processing industries, control and ownership of production units, marketing and distribution facilities are vertically integrated. Consequently very little opportunity is provided for local entrepreneurs to benefit from such linkages.

Thus neither the state-operated agricultural schemes nor large-scale capitalist enterprises fit SubSaharan African realities. The best approach that can bring rewards and prosperity to the overwhelming majority of the population is the promotion of labour-intensive and capital-saving smallholder agricultural schemes. Small-scale farmers, if provided with appropriate yield-increasing inputs and paid fair prices for their products, can be very efficient and productive. Small, less capital-intensive holdings not only employ more people but are more productive per unit area than large-scale capitalist holdings and state-operated schemes. Even with minimum extension services, adverse market prices, and poor marketing facilities, the African small farmers have proven to be efficient, as witnessed in the Ivory Coast, Kenya, Malawi, Zimbabwe and Cameroon.

Efforts to resolve the food crisis will be futile unless the governments pay attention to the predominant role of women in African agriculture. Discrimination against women, who are of overwhelming importance to the food producing sector, is a major contributing factor to the decline of staple food production. In Africa, women produce an estimated 70 percent of subsistence food supplies. Women do between 60 and 80 percent of agricultural work and 100 percent of the domestic work. Despite their pivotal role in economic production, family support and the overall development process, they are the most neglected, dispossessed and overworked members of society. In many countries, women farmers have very little or no access to productive resources—land, technology, training, credit, extension services, marketing facilities and health services. All too often rural development projects are targeted at male farmers who usually produce cash crops and exclude females who produce food crops for domestic consumption. The failure of development decision-makers to provide assistance to women, who do most of the work, is an important factor in the disappointing performance of many of the rural development projects as well as the decline in food production. This unfair sexual distribution of resources and responsibilities must not be allowed to continue if Africa wishes to take the road to recovery and genuine development. Improving women's lot can have wider implications: it can alleviate family poverty, improve the quality of human resources and bring down population growth rates.

High population growth is often cited as a principal cause of mass poverty, food shortages, ecological deterioration and many other social problems. The SubSaharan population is growing faster than that of any other region in the world. Its growth rate has increased from about 2.5 percent in the early 1960s to more than 3 percent at the beginning of the 1980s. On the surface the link with poverty and other problems seems obvious since there are already tens of millions of starving people in Africa. Increased population means more mouths to feed, thus exacerbating the food availability crisis. There exist close connections between poverty, malnutrition and population growth. Most often these correlations are viewed as cause and effect: population growth as the cause; poverty, malnutrition and other social problems as the consequences.

In reality, however, poverty and hunger are not caused by population growth; instead, poverty and hunger provide a context for high birth rates and population growth. To increase their incomes poor families must produce more labourers. Where children are considered a financial asset, birth rates are high. Also, people who lose children to high infant mortality seek to have more in the hope that at least some will survive to adulthood. It is thus a rational economic decision for poor households to seek social and economic security in large families. The motivation to have large families declines with economic well-being, secure income, better nutrition, and improvements in health as well as education.

Efforts to balance population growth with actual economic opportunity must start with a clear understanding of the social and economic pressures that contribute to high population growth in the region. The view that high fertility rates can be controlled by the spread of modern contraceptives and other family planning methods alone is wrong. This idea is based on the mistaken assumption that people want small families and that they lack the means to control their fecundity. Kenya, for instance, has been through nearly twenty years of family planning, and yet today it has one of the highest birth rates in the world. When contraceptives were actually made available to rural households, acceptance and use rates were abysmally low.

Family planning programmes by themselves help very little to reduce fertility rates. However, the evidence that lower birth rates are linked to improvements in families' economic well-being is compelling. Fertility studies have demonstrated that improved welfare creates the desire for small family size and couples conceive fewer children when fewer of them die. Therefore, the way to curb population growth is to design and implement policies that help raise the level of economic well-being in the vast majority of families. Particularly, improvement in income, education and health of women are important prerequisites for the eventual reduction of fertility rates. Only then can family planning programmes become an effective instrument to bring fertility and mortality rates to an acceptable balance.

Many African governments intervene in the market by setting the prices of most agricultural commodities below market prices and, in extreme cases, below production cost. Such policies have reduced farmers' incentives to produce for the domestic market. This is particularly true of food production. In recent years, however, especially in the aftermath of the 1983–84 famine, some African governments have either lifted price controls or raised the price of farm products to induce farmers to produce more food for local consumption. But in many countries peasant producers are still being squeezed by low prices for their products and higher prices for consumer goods and farm inputs. Appropriate and fair pricing policies ought to be implemented to provide incentives for farmers to increase food production. Peasant farmers have proved themselves willing to work hard and sacrifice when they know that they will gain commensurate rewards. The success of Zimbabwean peasant farmers is a case in point. The government has created an environment conducive to smallholder agricultural production by providing producer incentives, extension services, credits and marketing facilities.

Agricultural research should focus on indigenous staple food crops. Particularly more attention has to be given to drought resistant crops. Current applied research policies are heavily biased in favour of cash crops, while locally consumed cereals (maize, sorghum, millet, grain legumes, etc.) and root crops (cassava, potatoes, etc.) remain seriously under-researched. Recent evidence indicates that a significant increase in crop yields can be achieved by introducing high-yield varieties. Maize-hybrids diffusion, for instance, has already increased yields in Kenya, Zambia, Malawi and Zimbabwe. Increased yield per unit area of currently cultivated land will not only solve the food problem but also reduce the pressure on grazing and forest lands.

The potential for increasing food production by more irrigation is enormous. At present, with the exception of Sudan and Madagascar, less than 5 percent of SubSaharan African arable land is irrigated compared to 31 percent for Asia. Many of the semi-arid lands could grow crops if irrigated. Much of the current irrigation is applied to large-scale cash crop producing public or private enterprises, with little attention given to small-scale food producing farmers. Most of the irrigation projects are costly in terms of initial investment and maintenance, not to mention the damage to the environment (water-logging and salinization) due to improper design and management. What is needed is not elaborate irrigation systems but small-scale projects that can reach a greater number of the peasantry. There are a vast number of inexpensive irrigation techniques that can be promoted to avoid the pitfalls of large-scale irrigation schemes.

The majority of the SubSaharan African states are too small both in terms of population and physical size to create a viable and sustainable self-sufficient economy. There is a tremendous amount of resource complementarity among SubSaharan African countries that can be exploited with the creation of regional economic cooperation schemes. Consider, for instance, agricultural complementarity. The physical landscape of the region contains several climatic regions, each with varying capacity to produce different types of staple crops. Rice, for example, can best be promoted in Guinea, the Ivory Coast, Madagascar, Nigeria, Senegal and Sierra Leone. The Sahelian countries—Senegal, Mali, Burkina Faso, Niger, Chad and Sudan—can specialize in drought-resistant crops such as sorghum and millet. Kenya, Tanzania and Uganda are suitable for maize production. Wheat, which is fast becoming a favourite imported food crop of the urban population, can be grown in Ethiopia, Kenya, Tanzania and Zimbabwe.

Cooperation in such areas as agricultural research, marketing, irrigation, transportation, energy, communication and other infrastructural facilities, resource conservation and management, weather monitoring and the development of early warning systems, disease eradication and agro-industrial enterprises would advance the efforts towards collective self-sufficiency greatly. Any endeavour towards regional cooperation and integration will also help reduce dependence upon foreign forces and provide the benefits of a wider market, economies of scale and specialization. Furthermore, cooperation lessens conflicts between African nations, creates a stable political environment and more importantly, reduces foreign intervention.

One of the most pressing problems facing SubSaharan Africa is the extensive deterioration of its environment caused mainly by unsound agricultural practices. The most widely publicized is the Sahel region where inappropriate land-use has resulted in increased aridity of the land. The process of desertification is accelerating quite extensively, and millions of hectares of arable land are being lost every year. Desertification is primarily caused by overcultivation, overgrazing, deforestation and poor irrigation practices. The degree of deforestation is so excessive that in many countries forests have virtually disappeared from the landscape.

A long-term strategy of environmental restoration is essential to reverse the recent trend of deforestation and desertification that takes enormous amounts of arable and grazing land out of production. Most rural development programmes rarely include elements that restore and preserve such vital natural resources as soils, forests, grasslands, water and wildlife habitats. Land-use capability classification studies should be done on a national scale. Land-use plans based on land capability provide clear guidelines for proper exploitation and management of natural support systems. Once the capabilities and limitations of each type of land is known, it would be much easier to adopt conservation and management measures.

Past foreign economic assistance, multilateral or bilateral, has not proved successful in promoting rural development in SubSaharan Africa. Most of the aid has been spent on highly visible large-scale, urban-biased projects (for example, highways, telecommunication, modern government buildings, huge dams, luxury hotels and conventional halls, and sophisticated hospitals) which have very little to do with promoting the basic needs of the small African peasant farmer or which cannot by any means be justified in terms of development priorities. For instance, of the more than $7 billion in aid given to the Sahelian countries in the 1970s, less than one-quarter was spent on agricultural development and less than 12 percent reached rural areas. Of the miniscule amount that reached the rural sector only a tiny fraction got to small-scale peasant farmers and cattle raisers. Much of the funds allotted for agriculture went not to improving the traditional drought-resistant staple grains like sorghum and millet, but to irrigated and rain-fed export cash crop agriculture, mainly peanuts and cotton. Even fewer funds went to improve the deteriorating ecology of the region.

Donor and recipient governments have to restructure aid programmes to benefit the agrarian sector, with particular emphasis on food production and environmental restoration. Perhaps the best method to reach people for whom aid is intended is to channel it through the private voluntary organizations of developed and developing countries. There are many non-governmental organizations in Africa that are engaged in relief and rural development activities. Donor nations and institutions should make their aid contributions through those voluntary organizations that are recognized for their effectiveness in helping the small farmer at the grassroots level.

Over the past two decades, the prices of the primary products which the region depends upon for export earnings have persistently declined relative to the prices of the manufactured products it imported. Between 1980 and 1984, the terms of trade on primary commodity exports of the region dropped an average of 15 percent, in some countries as much as 30 percent. This condition has been accentuated by the worldwide recession of the late 1970s and the early 1980s and skyrocketing oil prices which sharply reduced the region's export earnings. As a result of this chronic deterioration of terms of trade, SubSaharan Africa has lost up to 20 percent of its exports over the last decade or so. The trade deficit in 1983 alone was nearly $11 billion. In order to finance this deficit, most nations have borrowed money from Western banks and governments. This has resulted in debts that can exceed half the gross domestic product. While these debts remain, it is clear that moves towards self-sufficiency and satisfactory living conditions in the region will be seriously hampered.

In conclusion, whether SubSaharan Africa can manage to meet the basic needs of its people, eliminate poverty and take the road to genuine development depends on how it sets its priorities and development needs and how it utilizes its material and human resources and indigenous know-how. Moreover, its future success depends on fundamental changes at national, regional, and international levels. At the national level African leaders must be willing to reorientate their development strategies to meet the basic needs of their people. At the regional level, African countries must foster economic cooperation and integration to attain collective self-sufficiency. At the international level, a restructuring of the internal economic order is needed to provide better prices and greater markets for African raw and processed export commodities.

References

Bates, R. H. *Essays on the Political Economy of Rural Africa.* Cambridge and New York: Cambridge University Press, 1983.
De Wilde, J. C. *Agriculture, Marketing and Pricing in Sub-Saharan Africa.* Los Angeles: University of California, 1984.
Hansen, A. and D. E. McMillan. *Food in Sub-Saharan Africa.* Boulder, Colorado: Lynne Reinner, 1986.
Lappe, F. M. and J. Collins. *Food First: Beyond the Myth of Scarcity.* New York: Ballantine, 1979.
Michaelson, K. *And the Poor Get Children; Radical Perspectives on Population Dynamics.* New York: Monthly Review Press, 1981.
Murdoch, W. W. *The Poverty of Nations: The Political Economy of Hunger and Population.* Baltimore and London: Johns Hopkins University Press, 1983.
Rogers, B. *The Domestication of Women: Discrimination in Developing Societies.* London and New York: Tavistock Publications, 1984.
Timberlake, L. *Africa in Crisis: the Causes, Cures of Environmental Bankruptcy.* London and Washington DC: International Institute for Environment and Development, 1985.

The Third World Debt Crisis

SUSAN GEORGE

In early 1986, Third World debt passed the trillion dollar mark (a thousand billions or $1,000,000,000,000). This unprecedented financial burden has reached crisis proportions and has profound implications for relations between rich and poor countries, for citizens of both the North and the South, and for the prospects of a peaceful world. To understand these implications we need to ask:

—How such huge debts were incurred?
—How the debt is being administered and which social groups are making sacrifices to reimburse it?
—What solutions could bring an equitable end to the crisis?

How was the debt incurred?

National debt is a normal phenomenon. When borrowed money is invested productively, and helps a country to develop its economy, reimbursement should not present a serious problem. Most of the money borrowed by Third World countries during the 1970s was not, however, invested productively. Instead, it was devoted to:

—*Paying for petroleum.* Conventional explanations of the debt crisis place all the blame on the oil price increases of the 1970s. The Organization of Petroleum Exporting Countries (OPEC) raised prices twice, in 1973 and 1979, and their incomes escalated accordingly. Since OPEC countries could not absorb the sudden surge in revenues, they deposited the money in Western banks, which in turn had to find an outlet in order to pay interest to the depositors. OPEC deposits were thus recycled in Third World countries, with bankers aggressively placing loans. This explanation is true as far as it goes, but in fact higher oil prices account for less than a third of the present debt burden.

—*Weapons purchases.* Armaments are pure consumption and *never productive:* unlike investments in agriculture or industry, they do not produce

127

more wealth. Borrowing for purchases of military hardware accounts for about 20 percent of Third World debt.

—*Capital flight.* Wealthy elites and even state companies frequently sent borrowed hard currency straight back to the banks as deposits. Although it is impossible to measure precisely, Mexican capital flight alone is reliably estimated to be equivalent to Mexico's entire debt in 1987—over $100 billion! Although the borrowing country no longer has the money, it must still pay interest on the full face value of the loans. The banks, on the other hand, are paid back twice—once in flight capital deposits, again in interest on the debt shown on their books.

—*'Pharaonic' projects.* The adjective refers to ancient Egypt and to pyramid building, then as now unproductive. In the twentieth century, the 'pyramids' were huge, ecologically destructive dams, underused 'turnkey' factories, stadia, nuclear power plants and the like. Some $440 billion of debt acquired by Brazil financed nuclear plants, none of which are working; while in the Philippines, interest of $500,000 per *day* is now due on money borrowed for another nuclear plant, also non-functioning (this is fortunate, since it was built in a volcanic zone)!

—*Current consumption.* Some countries, particularly in Latin America, borrowed money so they could import foreign goods and thus keep their own upper and middle classes happy. Chileans, for example, were able to use their pesos to buy dollars—and thus imported goods billed in dollars—at rates well under the true value of the dollar. Aside from accumulating the highest debt per capita in Latin America, Chile's own firms and factories could not compete with the imports and failed by the hundreds, leaving a legacy of massive unemployment.

—*Interest.* Interest is the cost of using someone else's money. Third World countries borrowed most of their money at *variable* rather than *fixed* interest rates, thus placing themselves at the mercy of market fluctuations. In the 1970s, interest rates were often *negative*, i.e., lower than inflation (price increases). If the interest rate is 10 percent, but inflation is 12 percent, the real interest rate is −2 percent and countries would be foolish *not* to borrow. In the 1980s, however, inflation dropped dramatically and real interest rates rose, so countries were obliged to pay far more for their borrowed money.

Why are interest rates so high? US budget deficits, largely caused by military spending, are the chief reason. The United States is the world's largest borrower: its public debt in 1987 was $2 trillion, or double that of the entire Third World. Because the United States spends more than it earns, it must borrow capital from its own citizens and from foreigners who invest in Treasury bonds. To retain foreign capital, the US must offer high rates of return. The Third World's debt burden is thus directly connected to the US defense budget: to pay for military expansion, the government borrows heavily and pays high interest; most Third World debt is payable in dollars and the US rate largely determines the world interest rate.

—*Export orientation.* Even when loans were not spirited northwards in flight capital; spent on military hardware, current consumption, unproductive projects; or devoted to paying the higher cost of oil or of money; still the money was all too often invested in producing for export. Third World countries were encouraged to direct their economies towards world markets, not towards satisfying the needs of their own people. Indeed, exports were supposed to earn the hard currency needed to pay back their loans. Meanwhile, in the poor countries, local agriculture and industries geared to internal demand foundered for want of investment and unemployment became chronic.

As the debt crisis shows, all these factors add up to a costly and unsustainable development model. When 'development' is based on excessive military and police establishments, prestige projects, outward-looking economies and the enrichment of a small elite at the top of society to the detriment of everyone else, the logical consequences are continuing hunger, disease and poverty for the majority.

How is the debt being administered? Which social groups are making sacrifices to reimburse it?

When a country is in dire financial straits and can no longer pay the interest on its debt, it must borrow to bridge the gap. The only credit source in such cases is the International Monetary Fund (IMF) which loans to countries to cover *balance of payments* deficits. Such deficits occur when export revenues do not cover imports, plus debt service; i.e., when a country is living beyond its means. IMF loans, however, come with conditions—and the worse the finances of the country, the tougher the conditions. Governments must sign on for IMF 'adjustment' or 'stabilization' programs (often called 'austerity' programs) and must comply with its advice, because the IMF seal of approval is vital. Without it, no public or private financial source in the world will give them further credit.

The prime objective of the IMF's adjustment plans is to force the debtor country to earn more than it spends, or, in IMF language: 'to restore a positive balance of payments'. Payments deficits can only be wiped out when the country exports more, and at the same time reduces expenditures. Such counsel would be wise enough if only a few countries were receiving it. Unfortunately, over 40 countries are under IMF tutelage, and they are all being told the same thing. Dozens of countries at once are trying to earn hard cash by exporting. Moreover, Third World exports fit a rather narrow range: mineral and agricultural raw materials or; in the case of slightly more sophisticated economies, textiles, apparel, microprocessors, light electronic goods and the like.

The result of too many goods competing with each other on saturated world markets is glut. Glut simply means too much supply, not enough demand, and in 1987 prices for Third World raw material exports hit their lowest levels in 60 years. To compound the problem, protectionism is rampant as Northern countries try to protect their ailing industries through tariffs and other barriers. If the rich creditor countries want to be paid interest on their loans, they must open their markets and *import* from the debtors. Countries which refuse to do so are in effect refusing to be paid.

Besides insisting that countries export more, the IMF also obliges them to slash public spending. Budgets for health, education and welfare are the first to suffer, while prices for essential services like electricity, water and public transport invariably rise dramatically. Food subsidies are always an early target—with the result that prices for staple foods on which the poor most depend—foods like bread, tortillas or cooking oil—may double overnight. However, not a single IMF program has called for deep cuts in military or police expenditures, possibly because 'IMF riots' over escalating prices have become commonplace. When riots occur, people are gunned down: hundreds of lives have already been claimed in countries as different as Jamaica, the Dominican Republic, Morocco and Brazil.

Meanwhile, as the cost of life's basic necessities inexorably rises, caps are placed on wages, though price controls are abolished. Bank credit also becomes much more expensive, so local firms find it hard to expand or even stay afloat. Governments may also sack thousands of their own employees—civil servants, teachers, health workers, etc. The IMF calls this 'reducing demand'.

Sharp devaluation of the local currency is another standard feature of IMF programs. True, many Third World currencies are grossly overvalued, but drastic devaluation means that people's savings in their own countries' currency are wiped out. Their purchasing power is thus routinely reduced by 50–90 percent. All imported goods automatically cost more after devaluation. For oil-importing countries, any item requiring transportation—which is virtually everything—will naturally cost more. Most poor countries do not produce their own medicines, fertilizers, spare parts for vehicles, etc., which they must also import at far higher prices—or do without. For want of such basic items, whole industries decline, buses stop running, patients cannot be transported to hospital—where they would find little medicine and equipment in any case.

Clearly, none of these 'technical' economic measures are neutral. Although the poorer groups derive no benefit from debt-financed projects, they are the ones called upon to make sacrifices. Poor people who were already living close to the brink may not survive at all, while the middle classes slide into poverty. Elites, however, are not particularly affected when public transport, schools and hospitals deteriorate or are closed since they can afford private ones. Upper classes need not cut back on food, whereas the number of malnourished children is increasing measurably in countries undergoing IMF treatment, as is infant mortality. The debt crisis demonstrably kills.

The accent placed on exports also has harmful consequences for ordinary people. Food crops for local consumption tend to be supplanted by saleable cash crops, although these fetch very low prices. When less food is produced internally, it too becomes more expensive. When peasants are encouraged to produce more coffee or cotton, they have less time and space for corn and beans. Natural resources are squandered, too, in the effort to sell off anything saleable. In heavily indebted countries like Brazil and Indonesia, tropical forests are being cut down so fast that at present rates none will remain in the year 2000.

The debt crisis is not merely a problem for the Third World: its effects are also deeply felt in the rich industrialized countries of the North. The South used to be a good customer for Europe, purchasing about a third of European exports. Now these countries must serve the banks first—and banks have indeed made record profits. But no funds are left for other purchases, so people in the North lose their jobs in industries that once manufactured goods for export and farms fail massively, particularly in the United States, where one acre in three is devoted to crops sold abroad.

The debt crisis has created such a drain that *the poor are now financing the rich*. Between 1982–86, the Third World remitted to the rich countries $106 billion more than it received in new loans or aid. Northern industries can also buy their raw materials from the South at rock-bottom prices—though their savings are not often passed along to the consumer.

What solutions could bring an equitable end to the crisis?

Many solutions have been suggested, but most simply tend to pile new debt on old. Some countries considered particularly important to the North have had their debts 'rescheduled'—or pushed into the future—at slightly more favourable rates; they remain in debt bondage nonetheless.

Why don't Third World countries simply stop paying and let the North worry about the problem (as Fidel Castro has proposed)? Because refusal to pay, called 'default', would make these countries financial lepers for years to come. They cannot drop out of the world trading system altogether, and must therefore maintain their access to fresh funds.

Between debt bondage and default, is there a third way? Yes, if imaginative management were applied—but a just solution to the debt crisis will not happen without plenty of political pressure from citizens of North and South. If 'creative reimbursement' or the '3-D solution'—standing for Debt,

Development, Democracy—were tried, however, debt *could* become a tool for encouraging authentic peoples' participation in their own development.

Public debt (owed to governments, the World Bank or the IMF) could be paid back in local currency, not in hard earned dollars, to be placed in a national development fund. This fund would be democratically managed, by the elected representatives of peasants, artisans, teachers, health workers, etc., with special provisions made for the fair representation of women and, where appropriate, ethnic minorities. They would work with local and national officials, and could propose their own development projects to the fund for financing. The fund could also feed revolving credit schemes for small loans (sometimes called 'peoples' banking').

Countries might also elect to reimburse part of the debt *in kind*, on the principle that their natural heritage is presently being cashed in. Governments should be rewarded for preserving their forests and soils. Each project could be assigned a monetary value and the debt would be written off by that amount each time a project was completed. The national development fund could provide wages to people engaged on projects. Some examples might be: collection and conservation of plant and animal genetic species, anti-erosion and water conservation measures, planting of 'greenbelts', improvement of building techniques with local materials, etc.

Governments could limit their debt payments to a certain percentage of export earnings (as President Alan Garcia of Peru has done) or refuse to pay in today's commodity dollars. For example, copper sold for twice as much a decade ago as in 1987. One should only have to sell as many pounds of copper as would have been necessary in, say, 1979, to pay back each $1000 worth of debt. Governments could also go on interest-paying strike until banks returned some of the flight capital their citizens have illegally stashed away. All these tactics, and others which could be imagined, would be far more feasible if Southern countries united around a common program. As of this writing, they are, unfortunately, negotiating individually against united creditors.

It would be in the North's commercial interest to encourage 'creative reimbursement' and '3-D'. It is the only way to keep poor countries as players in the world game. Only healthier economies in the Third World can reduce endemic unemployment and keep economies humming in the North. There is also a political interest. Creative reimbursement could be the ultimate weapon in the conflict between democracy and totalitarianism in which the West pretends to have such a deep stake. No people who were ever granted basic freedoms to manage their own affairs have ever willingly given them up. If we are serious about democracy, the debt crisis affords the chance of the century to prove it.

PART 5

The Contribution of Feminism to the Understanding of Peace

Contemporary analyses of peace and security incorporate important insights from feminism. This section describes the ways in which feminist contributions to understanding peace and security differ from those described in the first section of the book. The writers describe various aspects of feminist analysis which challenge traditional ideas. For example, how can a nation be at peace if millions of its female citizens are badly beaten up by their husbands? How can national security be achieved if human security is not taken into consideration? The poem and three chapters provide a basis for developing the holistic and human concepts of peace and security developed from feminist theories.

Poem*

PEGGY ANTROBUS

We've come a long way baby
But, the best is yet to come.
We are still the poorest of the poor,
The most powerless of the powerless,
The least understood of those without a voice,
The most excluded from the benefits of our toil.
But we have strengths, sisters,
And a unique knowledge of what is real:
The pain and beauty of reproduction,
Of nurturing the next generation—
An essential share in the work of creation
And we can use these strengths,
And insights,
And unique experience of the life force,
To end the wars,
To change the world,
To build our societies into places
Where people can find purpose and peace.
But first, we must believe—
That we are rich in our experience of life,
Powerful in our personhood
And hold the keys
To the relationships and systems
Which keep the best at bay.

* From *Geography of Gender* by Janet Monsen and Janet Townsend, Century Hutchinson
Publishing Group Ltd., London. Reproduced with permission.

Feminist Concepts of Peace and Security

BETTY REARDON

Feminism and positive peace

The following essay has been drafted to provoke discussion and inquiry into vital issues of peace and justice. It is not neutral because it has been written by a feminist. It is not objective because there is a core argument made both implicitly and explicitly. Serious students will seek out other arguments and alternative views in order to assess the validity of the arguments upon which this all too brief treatment of the vast subject of the relationship between women and peace is based.

Over the past several years, feminist scholarship has brought to light significant questions and important new knowledge about human history and the possibilities for the future. Among the areas of human concern which are being most profoundly affected by these questions and this new knowledge is that of world peace and security. Feminist theories and proposals about these, the most important problems currently facing all the people of the world, are often in sharp contrast with prevailing ideas and policies which are currently pursued by most governments. They are also even more challenging than many of the proposals offered by the peace movements which frequently stand in opposition to official government peace and security policies.

Feminist positions on these issues are both authentically radical and truly conservative. They are radical in their insistence on going to the roots of conflict, violence and war. And they are conservative in their primary goals and methods in that they seek to protect human life and society; to preserve the human achievements and the natural environment on which the future depends; and to maintain, extend, and nurture the networks of personal and social relations which constitute human communities.

As we begin to explore these feminist concepts and theories of peace and global security, we need to be clear about the meanings of these terms. The terms *feminism* and *feminist* have almost as many varied interpretations as does peace. Feminism as a social movement and a way of looking at the

136

world manifests many cultural and political forms. There is no monolithic, single-minded worldwide feminist movement and no one particular school of feminist thought. Feminists disagree on many issues and policies. They also differ in their scholarly interpretations as do most other researchers. So feminism is a rich and varied phenomenon. There is probably only one basic tenet common to all schools and forms of feminism. That is that men and women are of equal human value and this equality should be recognized by all societies. This does not mean that women and men are the same nor should they always be treated the same. But it does mean that no one should suffer discrimination on the basis of sex.

The other virtually universal agreement among feminists is that women throughout the world suffer sex-based discrimination. This discrimination has resulted in women, women's experience, and women's perspectives being excluded from public affairs such as politics, economics, and conflict, and from the development of the formally acquired and transmitted knowledge of history and other areas of scholarship. Feminist scholarship seeks to remedy this exclusion by uncovering women's rightful place in history and integrating women's experience and perspectives into other areas of knowledge development. Until recently, we have looked at, studied and interpreted the world primarily through masculine eyes. Feminist scholarship has shown us that the world—past, present and future—looked quite different through feminine eyes. Essentially, this is what we mean by feminist scholarship: looking at the world, gathering and interpreting through feminine eyes.

When viewed through feminine eyes, peace and security look very different than they do from the masculine perspective that has determined the general public perceptions and governmental policies in regard to the defense of the national interest and of the people of the nation. From the masculine perspective, peace for the most part has meant the absence of war and the prevention of armed conflict. This is what peace researchers now refer to as negative peace. Security is thus to be found in protection from aggression and defense against armed conflict. Since the advent of nuclear weapons, security has been sought within a framework of the deterrence theory, based on the argument that a nation can best defend itself by deterring an attack through the possession of weapons of sufficient numbers and destructive capacity to inflict a devastating retaliatory blow against the attacker. Consequently, the nuclear powers have engaged in an arms race to assure that their weaponry is more numerous and destructive than their opponents' and recently through the Strategic Defense Initiative (SDI), known as 'Star Wars', to assure the capacity to destroy or deflect attacking weapons before and during an attack. Non-nuclear countries depending on so-called conventional weapons engage in similar arms races for technological and numerical superiority. Most in the peace movements, feminists among them, argue that this method of pursuing national security is too dangerous and costly, and that we must seek other means to achieve peace and maintain security.

Many feminists also argue that peace and security need to be redefined. Most tend to hold a notion of peace akin to what peace researchers call positive peace, generally described as conditions of social justice, economic equity and ecological balance. Such conditions would be more truly peaceful because they would be more life-affirming and less likely to produce the types of conflicts which lead to armed violence and war. While peace does not mean the absence of conflict, it does mean a situation in which violence is less likely, even when there are disputes and conflicts. Feminists tend to see peace as a condition of social justice and equality; equality between women and men as the foundation for equality among all peoples, an end, for example, to racism as well as sexism, and a condition in which the Universal Declaration of Human Rights is accepted and applied on a worldwide basis. Human rights are a fundamental component of a feminist concept of peace. Security is to be found in the assurance that human rights will be protected. Under such conditions of positive peace, freedom from oppression and discrimination would be as essential a basis for human society as order. Many readers will recognize that these notions of peace are now widely embraced by many; that they are not exclusively or distinctly feminist. We need them to look further at those notions of peace and security that bear a distinctly feminine cast.

Feminist concepts of security

Recent scholarship has posited that women, as a result of a different experience and differences in education, think differently from men. These differences, however, are not inborn, and both men and women are capable of what might be termed masculine and feminine thinking. Both forms of thinking are useful and should be part of a broad human repertoire of modes of thinking.

A masculine view of the world tends to emphasize institutions and organizations, such as corporations, universities, political parties, nation-states, international organizations, and how they can be run to maximize the interests of a particular group, a country, a transnational corporation, a religion or political ideology. A feminine view, however, emphasizes human relationships and how people behave to fulfill their human needs. The model of human relationships most applied by the masculine mode of thinking is that of a hierarchical organization such as the nation-state, the church and the like. The feminine mode is based on a kinship model of less structured organization designed for the fulfillment of the needs of those in the kinship networks. The values of such a mode tend to be familial, nurturant and inclusive. Whereas, the masculine values are more organizational, competitive and exclusive.

When each of these modes of thinking becomes excessive and excludes the other, there is a barrier to developing a fuller, more human range of possibilities for security or for any other human need. In their extremes, these two different ways of looking at the world, which some scholars have called the dominator (masculine) and the partnership (feminine) modes or models, lead to very different concepts of security.

Human security is generally perceived as based on two major factors; protection from attack, and the fulfillment of fundamental needs. The peace movements around the world argue that present national security policies are based almost exclusively on the first of these. Thus, they argue, military security pursued through excessive public expenditure on preparation for war reduces national capacities to meet fundamental needs for adequate housing, nutrition, health care and education for all. While some peace activists acknowledge the need for sufficient military force for national defense, military expenditures, they claim, are far in excess of these needs, so that the most fundamental bases of national security—the lives and well-being of the citizens—are placed in jeopardy. These arms expenditures, and the many dangers inherent in the arms race, make people and nations less rather than more secure. Feminists in the peace movement assert that this emphasis on military over other forms of security results from these matters being determined almost entirely by men.

Some peace groups, including both men and women, argue for the adoption of an alternative security system to replace the present arms-dependent system. Various proposals have been made for such alternatives, such as common security, placing more emphasis on international peace-keeping or strengthening the United Nations, or establishing some sort of world government. There are a variety of such proposals, and some of them are endorsed by feminists. Few proposals, however, are as comprehensive as a feminist perspective on security would demand. Among the characteristics which distinguish the feminine from the masculine modes of viewing the world, the factors of inclusivity and holism are probably the most significant.

Inclusivity is related both to the question of who must be involved in a security system and to the factors and dimensions which should be included in what the system comprises as security concerns. Feminist concepts of security tend toward a truly global scope. A feminist world security system would attempt to include all peoples and all nations based on a notion of extended kinship including the entire human family. Such a system would also reflect the belief rapidly gaining support among those who study security issues that any system to be effective must be fully global, that no nation can fully assure its own security, as the security of each is best assured by the security of all.

In a feminist framework, security would have a broad, holistic definition to assure that all interrelated and relevant factors affecting world security are taken into consideration. It would aim to protect life and to enhance its quality providing equal attention to both fundamental requirements of human security. There are thus two central questions upon which feminists base their inquiries into alternatives to the arms race and war. What are the fundamental threats to human life? And, how can we overcome these threats in a life enhancing manner? Another way of positing the question might be, how can we achieve negative peace while building the conditions for positive peace?

When the inquiry into ways to achieve greater universal human security are posed in this way, war and injustice are seen as equally significant threats to human survival and a decent quality of life. But they are not the only threats to be overcome. This kind of inquiry in its radical character looks to the most fundamental roots of life and survival. Those roots are embedded in the health and well-being of the planet on which we live. While there is much speculation, even serious research and experimentation regarding the possibilities for human settlements on other planets, it is not very likely that the majority of the human family will survive over the next generations, and perhaps centuries, if planet Earth cannot sustain life. Changes in the most basic life-giving capacity of the Earth, such as the reduction of the oxygen supply and soil erosion due to deforestation, the pollution of natural bodies of water, and the destruction of the ozone layer as a consequence of air pollution, severely threaten the health and well-being of our planet. Thus, the maintenance of ecological balance is viewed as a major security need, and problems such as the loss of our oxygen-producing rain forests are seen as threats to human security.

As the lives of all are endangered by the devastation of the planet, the lives of many, in some areas of the world the majority, are threatened by the excessive deprivation of extreme poverty. Individuals, families, nations cannot be secure if they lack the basic necessities of life. Millions in the developing world suffer from lack of clean water sufficient to the needs of basic health and hygiene. Only a small percent of the world's children receive secondary education, and millions remain illiterate, deprived of even a primary education. The world's cities are populated by millions of homeless, among them abandoned street children, some of them in the most heavily 'defended' countries in the world. Famine stalks the planet. The fundamental security of the human family is severely undermined by these conditions.

Philosophers and political scientists have often described the relationship between people and their governments as a social contract. The government, in return for the support and loyalty of citizens, promises to protect them from harm by outsiders and to assure conditions within the country which will enable the people to meet their needs whether this is done by means of a free market economy, i.e., capitalism, or by a centrally planned economy, i.e., socialism, or a bit of both; the government, i.e., the nation-state, is expected to assure order and provide the laws and circumstances necessary to enable the nation to produce the goods and services required to meet the needs of the people. Even in competitive societies, it is argued that this can and should be done fairly, that the government should not enact policies that are harmful to any of its citizens. The security of a nation depends on a government's commitment to the welfare of its people. Yet the ever increasing costs of the present military security system are so high that social and economic needs suffer badly. The arms race is as much a spending race as a weapons race. Military expenditures are constantly on the rise; even in those years when arms control agreements were reached, there was no reduction in spending. The 1986 total of $900 billion is expected soon to reach $1 trillion. This is almost equal to the total debt of developing countries. This debt now threatens the entire world economy. A significant portion of it was accumulated through arms spending. The world is spending away its economic security as violence and conflict become more extreme.

Thus, within a feminist framework, the military-dependent present world security system itself is seen as a major threat to human security. In fact, within this framework the security dimension which dominates the present system, protection from aggression or harm from other nations is viewed as the least severe. While there are severe international tensions and conflicts, most of the warfare today takes place within nations, much of it brought on as a reaction to deprivation. Feminists believe that national security policy is being formulated on the basis of the wrong questions. And they assert there is an urgent need for women to be involved in the policy-making process. They also argue that there are significant links between war and discrimination against women. These links they assert must be recognized so that two significant obstacles to both negative and positive peace, militarism and sexism, can be overcome. If we are to get to the roots of war and to be enabled to create the foundations of a just and stable peace, then we must raise some essential questions about the links between the two problems, both of which are major forms of violence.

The radical questions: the links between sexism and militarism

The radical questions also can be seen to arise from feminist concepts of security, beginning with the notion of security as protection from attack and harm by others. Feminist research has revealed that women the world over are subject to excessive violence. Wife beating is common in many countries, sometimes causing death, and 'dowry death' or 'bride burning' has occurred so frequently as to shock the entire worldwide women's movements. Thousands of women are enslaved to enforced prostitution or physically damaging working conditions, and millions stay in their homes or go abroad with anxiety because of the ever present threat of rape. Feminists, noting that violence against women is often more severe in more militarized countries, ask, is the mistreatment of women related to the willingness to kill that is required in warfare? It has also become more widely recognized through popular films as well as research that combat training often includes the use of language and comparisons that insult women and reflect hostility toward them. Feminists inquire into the possibility that the willingness to kill requires people to repress their feminine, caring characteristics, characteristics which are natural to both men and women.

Militarism and war can be maintained only in a hierarchical organization in which some give orders and others must follow them. While we do have the principle of individual responsibility not to follow an illegal order that was established at Nuremburg after the Second World War, combat does not generally allow for questioning and independence. The military system is one which depends on superior and inferior relationships between certain members. In that the essential social relationships between men and women are also superior-inferior, feminists raise the question of the significance of this relationship in socializing most people to believe in both the necessity and the inevitability of hierarchy and war.

Feminist educators and child development specialists have noted that girl children are encouraged to be cooperative, to avoid conflict and to reject using force against others, to develop their feminine characteristics. Boy children are encouraged to be competitive, to confront those who challenge them, and to exert superior strength to achieve their goals, to emphasize what are seen as masculine characteristics. The question thus arises as to whether peace requires more emphasis on the feminine. Does it in fact, as noted that many feminists assert, require the participation of more women in politics and diplomacy?

These are but a few of the radical questions raised as feminists seek to get to the roots of the causes of war and the conditions of peace and security.

The conservative questions: maintaining authentic global security

A feminist concept of global security has been outlined as four fundamental dimensions. Authentic or true security can only be achieved by adequate attention to all four, and by recognizing that we have come to a stage of human history in which the whole of the human family becomes the group of concern. If we continue to put the concerns of one group, no matter how large (even a whole region of the world or a whole sex), above the interests of the rest, we will maintain a competitive, potentially conflictual global society which runs the risk of destroying itself; if not by nuclear war, then by ecological or economic collapse. Feminist concepts of security call for new questions to be raised as we struggle to formulate policies to lead us from violence and discrimination to peace and justice, to the preservation of the Earth and the survival of humanity.

The necessity to maintain the health and life of planet Earth leads feminists to explore the ecological consequences of all security policy proposals, military and others. What, they ask, will be the impact of this proposal on the immediate environment in which it is to be carried out, and all related environments in the global ecological system? What will be its consequences in the present and in both the near and distant future? How will it affect the security of this generation and generations to come?

Security seen as the fulfillment of fundamental human needs brings forth questions related to the economic and social consequences of security policies. Within a framework which emphasizes the feminine ethic of care, they start with inquiring into the consequences to the most vulnerable of the human family. How, it will be asked, will this policy affect the poor, the sick and infirm, children and the aged and the women who must care for them?

The notion of security as a social contract in which the true security of all citizens is the major concern of the government will encourage questions about equity, fairness and discrimination. Every security policy must be measured against a standard of fairness as well as efficacy. Who will bear the burden? Will it fall more heavily on one group of citizens, or one area of the country than another? Will the costs be left to a future generation to pay? Are the real interests of the citizens to be well served by this policy?

And finally, the notion of security as protection from harm raised within a feminist framework will ask questions providing a whole new approach to defense. Rather than asking will this policy help us to be strong enough to prevent attack or defeat an attacker, the central issue will be how can we dissuade others from wanting or needing to attack us? How can we resolve conflicts nonviolently and justly? How can we change relationships from hostility and competition to amicability and cooperation? How can we extend and strengthen the network of care, interdependence and authentic security so that it may encompass the globe and embrace the whole human family? How can we conserve and develop that family?

Each of these major radical and conservative questions will lead to many other questions through which we can study the specific problems of conflict and violence and through which we may learn to achieve peace and justice.

Feminist Perspectives on Peace

BIRGIT BROCK-UTNE

What is peace for women?

In the publication *Breaching the Peace* (1983), a collection of articles by radical feminists, women's involvement in the contemporary peace movement is heavily criticized. In the Introduction there is the following statement: 'We see the women's peace movement as a symptom of the loss of feminist principles and processes—radical analysis, criticism and consciousness raising.' The authors maintain that 'women are always having a war waged upon us' (see, e.g., 1983: 9). The same thoughts are voiced by the Canadian feminist researcher Barbara Roberts. In an article she concludes that there is a war against women going on in the privacy of the home and 'so long as men are at war against women, peace for all humankind cannot exist, and there is no safe place on earth for any of us' (Roberts, 1983: 22). In the same article she points out that it is estimated that each year over 1.8 million US wives are badly beaten up by their husbands. When asked if there had ever been physical violence in their relationship, 28 percent of couples in one survey said 'yes', but the researchers believe that the true rate for wives 'ever' being battered in the life of a relationship is closer to 50 percent for all US couples.

Frankie Green (1983) in an angry article called 'Not Weaving but Frowning' maintains that because violence against women is so widespread,

> it is not seen as a war by many of the victims and certainly not defined as such by those who do the naming—the war makers. It's the very fragmented and personalized nature of the war against women that allows it to be so normal as to render it invisible. . . . As far as I am concerned the ultimate act of male violence happens every day. And when I am walking around thinking of this and I hear phrases like 'women for life on earth' and 'women for peace', I feel completely bemused. What on earth do they mean? What peace? (Green, 1983: 9)

Yes, what peace are women thinking of when they engage themselves in

144

organizations like 'Women for Peace' or they go to Greenham Common to stop the deployment of Cruise Missiles? The feminists analyzing women's involvement in the peace movement keep reminding us of the many times in history where women have stopped their own struggle against the oppression of women to fight alongside the men, for a cause which is deemed more important, the winning of a war or a revolution, for instance. Statistics gathered for the UN Decade Conference in Copenhagen in 1980 states that women do two-thirds of the work in the world, receive ten percent of the salaries and own one percent of the property. If women help some of the men who own the 99 percent to win against some of the other men, is there any guarantee that women shall own more than one percent afterwards? Before both the First and Second World Wars there were strong women's movements which suffered serious set-backs during the war when women either joined the men in violent fights to win the war or tried through reconciliation and arbitration to put an end to it. After the war the brave women heroes from the wartime tended to be forgotten, women in great numbers were taken out of their jobs and sent back home so that men could have their paid jobs. And at the same time the women's movement had been severely set back. Both within the anti-slavery movement and the civil rights movement women discovered that they were doing more of the work, the fundraising, the sewing and selling of badges, the collection of signatures, while the men wanted to give the public speeches and, in the days of television, appear in that medium. Also within the contemporary mixed-sex peace movement there is considerable sexism (see, e.g., Brock-Utne, 1985: 66–69).

How do women define peace?

What would be the logical conclusion to draw on the basis of the knowledge women have of the sexism of the mixed-sex peace movement, of the set-backs of the women's liberation movement during periods of wars, revolutions and crises? Would the logical conclusion be that women should not engage themselves in the peace movement but rather concentrate on the women's liberation struggle? Those who design and construct new weapons, manufacture them and make profits on them, deploy them and use them as threats are largely men. Should women not insist that men clean up their own mess! Why should women clean up after them like mothers clean up the toys after their sons, often having their daughters help clean up too? The radical feminists writing in *Breaching the Peace* do not see why women should help men clean up their mess. Women have to use their own resources to struggle for their own liberation. And in that struggle women have to rely on each other. There seems to be little help to be expected from men when it comes to the liberation of women. This, unfortunately, seems to be rather true. Somehow men on the far right of the political spectrum seem to have a better analysis of the relationship between feminism and the type of society they would like to see come about than men to the left of the political spectrum have. The men to the right know that if they want to have the type of society they adhere to, they have to combat feminism and the liberation of women. One of the first things Hitler did when he seized power in Germany was to crush the feminist movement and get women under the control of their husbands (*Kinder, Kuche*) and the authority of the church. But men on the left often do not see that if they want to create the type of society they are adhering to, they have to support feminism and the liberation of women.

My own conclusion, and I also consider myself a radical feminist, is that women should help men clean up the mess some men have made out of this world. We as women have to engage ourselves in the peace movement with our own solutions and insights, work from our own premises. But it is naive to think that women shall not encounter sexism in the peace movement as everywhere else in patriarchal societies. This sexism women shall have to point out and analyze when they encounter it. Women shall also have to insist that the absence of violence against women is included in the peace concept itself. In an analysis of the development of the peace concepts through the three UN Women Decade Conferences, the one in Mexico in 1975, the one in Copenhagen in 1980 and the one in Nairobi in 1985, I have shown that the only one of the final documents which stresses the feminist insight that there is no peace as long as women are being beaten and mutilated is the Nairobi document (Brock-Utne, 1986). Here it says in paragraph 258:

> Violence against women exists in various forms in everyday life in all societies. Women are being beaten, mutilated, burned, sexually abused and raped. Such violence is a major obstacle to the achievement of peace . . .

And in paragraph 257 we find the following sentences:

> The question of women and peace and the meaning of peace for women cannot be separated from the broader question of relationships between women and men in all spheres of life and in the family. Discriminatory practices and negative attitudes towards women should be eliminated and traditional gender norms changed to enhance women's participation in peace.

These two paragraphs are very important as they point to an understanding of the interconnectedness of all violence. This interconnectedness has to be understood both by the people in the peace movement fighting for disarmament and by women struggling for the liberation of women. All women are part of the same struggle, a struggle against all types of violence, for an equal distribution of resources, for the right to express oneself freely.

The peace concept has gradually been widened as the peace researchers and the international governmental communities have been confronted by new groups wanting a redefinition of the concept to include their concerns. When we from the industrialized countries talk about peace at a conference where people from the Third World are present, like at the Nairobi conference in 1985, the Third World participants rightly exclaim: 'You talk about a nuclear war which may or may not come to your territory, we see our children dying today. They are starved to death through the politics you in the industrialized countries lead.'

This type of violence where people are malnourished and starved to death also kills like wars do, only more slowly. The violence is of a more indirect kind. It is built into the structures and therefore often called structural violence. This structural violence can be found in the relationship between the industrialized countries and the Third World, but also within a country where structures have been built so that some people get richer at the expense of others. Structural violence seems to hit women worse than men. When difficult choices have to be made of what child to feed, boys tend to get fed rather than girls (see Brock-Utne, 1985: 4–9). Women and girls feel the pinch of lack of food first. This is also the case when there is structural violence within a country. The feminization of poverty, especially within the United States, seems to be a well-established fact.

In a discussion of the widening of the peace concept I have divided the concept into negative and positive peace. Negative peace exists when there is absence of personal, physical and direct violence while positive peace

TABLE 1.

	Negative peace	*Positive* peace	
	Absence of personal, physical and direct violence.	Absence of indirect violence shortening life span.	Absence of indirect violence reducing the quality of life.
Unorganized	(1) E.g., wife batterings, rapes, child abuse, street killings.	(3) Inequalities in micro structures leading to unequal life chances.	(5) Repression in micro structures leading to less freedom of choice and fulfillment.
Organized	(2) E.g., war.	(4) Economic structures built up within a country or between countries so that the life chances of some are reduced or effect of damage on nature by pollution, radiation, etc.	(6) Repression in a country of free speech, the right to organize, etc.

exists where there is absence of indirect or structural violence. This division can often be found in peace research (see, e.g., Galtung, 1969; and Wiberg, 1981). I have made a further division within the positive peace category between indirect violence leading to a shortened life span and indirect violence which reduces the quality of life. Both positive and negative peace is viewed at the micro-level where the violence is of a mere unorganized kind and at the macro-level what I term organized violence (Brock-Utne, 1987). Table 1 summarizes my discussion.

Feminist perspectives

The word 'perspective' comes from the Latin word *perspectus*, which again derives from *perspicere*, meaning 'look through, look into, see thoroughly, try out, investigate'. A perspective may be defined as that which helps us see aspects of reality. All thought processes start by seeing. We all apply various perspectives when we interpret reality around us. The perspectives help us make sense out of what we see and give direction and guidance to our focusing. Much research seems to have been conducted from a male perspective without researchers being aware of that fact. What to them has looked as gender neutrality may, through feminist analysis, be revealed as male-bias. It should not be surprising at all that a research field like peace studies which cuts across several male-biased disciplines will also be male-biased. Multidisciplinarity in itself is no guarantee that the studies will include feminist understanding.

Using a feminist perspective as an analytical tool—any feminist perspective—means insisting that women matter: the way women live, think, organize matters. It means looking at the world through the eyes of women. It means adding to and using the knowledge women and men have of the way women think and live. This body of knowledge is not just an additional knowledge to be tacked on to the curriculum. It is, instead, perspective transforming and should transform the existing curriculum from within.

Often when authors maintain that they write from a feminist perspective, they are using a radical feminist perspective which can be said to be the most perspective transforming of all perspectives. While liberal feminists want women to get a bigger, preferably equal share of the pie and Marxist feminists want the pie to be taken from private capitalists and given to the state, radical feminists want to change the basic recipe of the pie. Radical feminists do not want to assimilate to society as it is, but to change it. Those feminists are not so much concerned with equality as with liberation from patriarchal and capitalist structures. Radical feminists are not struggling for equality on men's premises, but are always asking the question: equal to do what? When the state Council for Equality in Norway for instance held a conference together with the Ministry of Defence to discuss the equal status of women in the armed forces, radical feminists asked the question: equal to kill? It is more important to change existing institutions and academic subjects than to get more women into them. If women just get trained in male thoughts and get assimilated to the existing structures, a potential for change is gone. While feminists concerned with equality and no discrimination will try to increase the number of women in the study of physics when they see that so few women opt for that subject, radical feminists will rather pose the question: what is wrong with the teaching and study of physics since so few women opt for it?

In previous studies, I have outlined six different feminist perspectives and tried to relate them to the study of peace (Brock-Utne, 1986b and 1987). I have drawn up a biological determinist perspective where the greater aggressivity of men is said to be part of their biological make-up; a liberal feminist perspective with concepts like no discrimination and equality; and a Marxist feminist perspective where the ownership of the means of production is central.

These three perspectives predate the next three which include the radical feminist perspective with its analysis of patriarchy, its insistence that the personal is political and its analysis of power; and the socialist feminist perspective which builds on the Marxist perspective but uses the analysis of patriarchy developed by radical feminists. The sixth perspective—the women of colour perspective—is still under development and may end up as a combination of some of the other perspectives. Indian feminists claim that for them it is not enough to take gender, class and colour into account. They also have to consider caste since the caste one belongs to is all-decisive in Indian society and, just like being a member of the one sex, it is something you are born into and cannot be changed.

It is possible to conduct peace studies from any of these six feminist perspectives or from a combination of them. I have found the radical feminist perspective combined with elements from a socialist feminist perspective as the most fruitful to work with (Brock-Utne, 1987). It is theoretically possible to apply any of the six perspectives to any of the six cells constituting my peace concept, allowing for 36 combinations in all.

References

Bellow, Linda, et al. *Breaching the Peace: A Collection of Radical Feminist Papers*. London: Only Women Press Ltd., 1983.
Brock-Utne, Birgit. *Education for Peace. A Feminist Perspective*. New York: Pergamon Press, 1985. (A Korean and a Norwegian edition have appeared in 1987, an Italian edition will appear soon. The Norwegian edition is published by Folkereisning mot Krigs forlag, the Italian edition by Edizione Gruppo Abele. The English edition was reprinted in 1987.)
Brock-Utne, Birgit. 'The peace concepts through three UN Women Decade Conferences', *PRIO-Working Paper 1/86*. Oslo: International Peace Research Institute of Oslo, 1986a. (Will also be published in proceedings from the 11th IPRA General Conference.)
Brock-Utne, Birgit. 'Feminist perspectives on peace research', *PRIO-Report 17/86*. Oslo: International Peace Research Institute of Oslo, 1986.

150   Birgit Brock-Utne

Brock-Utne, Birgit. *Feminist perspectives on peace and peace education*. Oslo: The Institute of Educational Research, 1987.
Galtung, Johan. 'Violence, Peace and Peace Research'. *Journal of Peace Research* (3) 167–91.
Green, Frankie. 'Not Weaving but Frowning'. In *Breaching the Peace*, op. cit., 1983.
Roberts, Barbara. 'No Safe Place. The War against Women'. *Our Generation* 15 (4): 7–26.
Wiberg, Håkan. 'Journal of Peace Research 1964–1980—What have We learnt about Peace?' *Journal of Peace Research* 18 (2): 111–148.

Third World Women: Organizing for Change

JULIE SPENCER-ROBINSON and JILL GAY

In many Third World countries people are fighting for what the United Nations terms 'basic human rights'. Human rights fall into two general categories: civil and political rights, such as the right to freedom of association, freedom of speech, freedom of the press, the right to vote and to hold elected office; and economic, social and cultural rights such as the right to an adequate standard of living—including food, clothing, housing, and medical care—and the right to an education, to work and to rest, and to culture and the arts.

Third World women enjoy the fewest human rights of anyone in the world: they work the longest hours and receive the lowest pay for that work; they are the most likely to live in poverty and without adequate shelter. Yet they are a powerful source for change.

Women in the Third World have never been more active than they are today, organizing themselves around a myriad of issues, striving to create more just societies in the countries where they live. The struggle of Third World women is a difficult one. Living in developing regions, they are faced daily with the conditions typical of underdevelopment: poverty, malnourishment, inadequate health care and housing, a lack of education. And as women, they often live under conditions of discrimination as well: women are, in many cases, denied the same social, political and economic rights that men enjoy—even though, for men, those rights may be limited.

A clear manifestation of this discrimination is that Third World women are generally responsible for the complete care of the family in addition to working outside the home in order to supplement the family's income, as most women are forced to do. Today, one-third of all households in the Third World are headed by women, which means that in those cases, women are both the sole breadwinner and the sole caretaker. Needless to say, most of these women and their families live below the poverty level.

Despite these obstacles—or perhaps because of them—Third World women have taken all kinds of action in order to change these conditions of

151

underdevelopment and discrimination, and they have been able to effect critical change on many different levels throughout society. Perhaps the best-known instances in recent times where women in the Third World have organized themselves for social change have been situations where women have lived or continue to live under dictatorships. Latin America, for example, underwent a transformation in the first part of this decade, when the governments of many countries which were controlled by repressive military regimes were turned over to civilian authorities. And women played key roles throughout this historic process.

In 1979, the dictator of Nicaragua, Anastasio Somoza, was overthrown by the Sandinista National Liberation Front (FSLN). At the time of the revolution, women constituted 25 percent of the armed forces. Since then, women have been an indispensable part of the making of a new society. Before the revolution, women—and men—had very few rights. There were no rights to free speech or association; women could not own land, they were not allowed to divorce, and they were discriminated against in schools and in the labor market.

Today women are guaranteed, by the constitution, equal access to all of these rights. 70 percent of all university students and 50 percent of all medical school students are women. Children are entitled to equal parental care, and if a father abandons his family, child-support payments will be deducted from his salary by the government once paternity is established. All prenatal medical care, including medicine, is free (Dr Gina Watson, Nicaraguan Ministry of Health, interview, 29 June 1987).

In 1977 the FSLN established a women's organization called AMNLAE, or Asociación de Mujeres Nicaraguenses Amanda Luisa Espinosa. This organization—as well as the women's office of the government—ensures that Nicaragua's laws do not discriminate against women and that women play an active role in the development of the nation. Women's role in Nicaraguan society has, indeed, undergone a radical transformation: 31 percent of all government positions are occupied by women; women represent 25 percent of the agricultural workforce and 41 percent of the urban economically active population; 42 percent of health and education workers are women; and women constitute 44 percent of total cooperative membership (Marta Munguía, Secretary of Executive Board of AMNLAE, interview, 2 July 1987).

Perhaps the most difficult struggle that Nicaraguan women face within their society is against machismo, or the sexism of Nicaraguan men. But they recognize that this struggle, too, entails the restructuring of society, and the re-education of all Nicaraguans. As women continue to take on positions of leadership—the director of police, the minister of health, the vice president of the National Assembly and the ambassador to the United Nations are all women—the redefinition of gender roles becomes easier.

Argentina, like Nicaragua, is a country that was ruled for years by dictators. From 1976 until 1983, the Argentine population was subject to arbitrary arrest, torture, murder and 'disappearance' by the military government. A 'disappearance' occurs when a person is apprehended by the state security forces—often at night, and usually accompanied by beatings and rape—and the whereabouts of that person are not disclosed. More than 30,000 disappeared in Argentina throughout the period of military rule.

In April 1977, at the height of government-sponsored repression, fourteen women began to demonstrate every Thursday outside the offices of the country's president, to protest about the human rights abuses of the military regime. All of these women were mothers whose children had disappeared. The courageous action taken by the women who came to be known as the Madres de Plaza de Mayo, and whose numbers later swelled, called international attention to the human rights situation in Argentina. Their demonstrations eventually proved to be a catalyst for the redemocratization of their country. Today the Madres continue to be a powerful human rights organization, pressuring the civilian government to bring the members of the military responsible for human rights abuses to justice (Julie Spencer-Robinson, 'Women and Transitions from Authoritarian Regimes,' Colombia University, 1986).

There are other countries, however, which still suffer under dictatorships, and where women are still fighting for democracy. In the case of Chile, women have linked this struggle with the struggle for equality between the sexes: the call for democracy in the country and democracy in the home.

Chilean women did not begin to actively participate in politics until several years into the military dictatorship—they did not even have the right to vote until 1949, and the 1952 election was the first in which women could participate. In 1973 a military coup overthrew the elected government of socialist president, Salvador Allende. As the military dictatorship began to curtail social, political and economic rights, women began to organize themselves, basically around issues of survival. They started soup kitchens and health care centers in shanty towns, and human rights groups to deal with the situations of political prisoners and the disappeared.

These kinds of actions often lead to increased political activity on the part of the women. Despite the fact that Chile's opposition is often greatly divided along political lines, women have united together, across political and class lines, to reach consensus on the belief that no real democracy can be achieved in their country unless the oppressive conditions of women are themselves democratized. Today, women control an important political space in Chile as social and political activists (Alicia Frohmann, 'Women in Chile Today,' Institute for Policy Studies, 28 September 1977).

South Korea, too, is a country ruled by a military dictatorship—open elections have not been held there since 1971, and the military has run the government for 27 years. The Korean constitution restricts civil rights—there is no freedom of speech or press—and since 1980 human rights abuses have increased markedly. Because the economic policy of the government is export-oriented, and thus its success is largely dependent on the low wages paid to workers, labor rights especially are an issue for Koreans. They are denied the right to strike or to take any collective action and 'third party interference' (between an employer and an employee) is prohibited.

Women laborers in Korea are doubly oppressed, for Korean society is inherently sexist. Not only do Korean women suffer sexual harassment in the workplace—from their boss and the official who may handle a sexual harassment dispute—but they are also exploited economically. Working a 12 hour day, women are paid about 100,000 hwan a month (approximately $120)—with living expenses amounting to about 200,000 hwan a month (Hei Soo Shin, 'Women and Human Rights in South Korea,' Institute for Policy Studies, 16 September 1987).

Since 1984, however, women have organized around these labor issues and around more general political issues. In 1984, a committee on sexual harassment was formed, which urges the boycott of certain products as well as the news programs of the government-owned television and radio stations. Also in 1984, families of political prisoners founded the Family Council for Democracy. And in 1987, a group of women workers who had been fired from their jobs formed their own organization, in recognition of their belief that they cannot participate in the movement for democracy in their country without fighting at the same time against sexism (Hei Soo Shin, 16 September 1987). Indeed, more and more Korean women are realizing that they will have to work twice as hard as their male counterparts in the struggle for democracy, for women are also struggling toward equality between the sexes.

Third World women organize themselves not just to change their societies on a national level, but also on the local and regional levels—although these actions, too, often have national implications. In Honduras, for example, women are very much involved in agrarian reform.

Land is a serious problem in this country where 70 percent of the population lives in poverty, primarily for reasons of distribution. A small percentage of the population owns a majority of the land, and this land is generally under-utilized—used for cattle grazing or wood production—or not used at all. The eleven military bases operated by the United States in Honduras also occupy a fair amount of territory.

Although an agrarian reform law, approved by both the government and the military, is on the books, this law has not been put into effect: or at least it has not been put into effect by the government. Recently, Honduran peasants have tried to apply this law themselves with what they call land recoveries. A land recovery occurs when organizations of peasants, often led by women, begin cultivating crops of foodstuffs on ill-used land. Although these women often face—and meet with—great personal danger, they have not been deterred in their struggle for a more just, productive distribution of land in Honduras. Currently, 200 peasants are in jail for their participation in land recoveries (Elvira Alvarado, 'US Involvement in Honduras: A Peasant Women's View,' Institute for Policy Studies, 6 October 1987).

Honduran women have organized around other issues as well; particularly in response to the militarization of their country by the United States and the Honduran governments. At one of its eleven bases, the US maintains a current presence of 1200 troops, and by May 1987 almost 80,000 US troops had participated in training exercises in Honduras. Between 1980 and 1985, the size of the Honduran military doubled (Medea Benjamin, 'Honduras: The Real Loser in US War Games,' Institute for Food and Development Policy, San Francisco, Calif., 1987).

A troubling result of this militarization has been the abuse of human rights. Prior to 1980, the Honduran government did not employ a systematic policy of repression. Since then, however, there have been hundreds of cases of political assassinations, disappearances, and illegal detentions. In 1984, women helped to establish the Committee of the Families of the Disappeared-Detained of Honduras, which provides legal and personal assistance to the families of people who have disappeared or been illegally detained by the government or military forces.

Women in Honduras fight not just for their rights as Hondurans—especially the right to their own territory—but also for their rights as women. Although these women live in a very sexist society, they believe that they must fight for all of their rights alongside men. They believe that machismo is as much a part of women's behavior as it is a part of men's behavior, and that both sexes must work to change this type of behavior.

Access to land, and the resources to develop that land, are very important issues for women in Africa as well as Central America. Women are the sole breadwinners in one-quarter to one-half of the families in the world (Ruth Leger Sivard, *Women: a World Survey,* World Priorities: Washington DC, 1985). The United Nations estimate that women farmers grow at least 30 percent of the world's food, and as much as 80 percent in the rural areas of some African nations (Sivard, 1985). The post-colonial government of Tanzania made a vital mistake in its quest for economic independence: while planning a rural village, no provisions were made for the women, and women were actually deprived of legal entitlement to the crops they produced (James L. Brain, 'Less than Second Class: Women in rural resettlement schemes in Tanzania.' In Nancy Hafkin and Edna Bay (eds.), *Women in Africa: Studies in Social and Economic Change.* Stanford: Stanford University Press, 1976). Many government programs failed because they were imposed from above by officials who ignored the dynamics of the community and denied peasant women decision-making power (Sandi Metheny, 'African Women's Roles Changing, Says Journalist,' *Dominion Post*, November 1986).

Independence, however, has also brought about positive changes for women in Tanzania. A government proclamation in 1967 affirmed the rights of both men and women, making it easier for everyone to realize their potential. The development of free and compulsory education for all Tanzanian children has forced families to send both boys and girls to school which in turn has enhanced the position of women. Many urban women now occupy professional positions such as doctors, lawyers, and policymakers. And new social policies which took effect in 1975 uprooted old traditions, although changes in policies and laws have not always brought about changes in practices (Metheny, 1986).

Tanzanian women are currently using the media to change the perception of their role in society. Radio, for example, is the most effective form of communication in the country. The government-run national station has a special women's program which usually addresses child care and other conventional issues. Recently, however, journalists have been using the program to air more controversial topics such as pregnancy among schoolgirls.

Tanzanian law forces girls to leave school if they become pregnant, and once out of school, these girls are often shunned by society and left to care for themselves—many are forced into prostitution simply in order to buy food. Women journalists investigating this story discovered that 80 percent of the pregnancies were caused either by the girls' schoolteachers or by upper-class men who had given the girls rides to school. As a result of the radio program, there was a widespread awareness of the issue, and the Tanzanian parliament discussed a change in the law affecting pregnant schoolgirls.

Women in the Third World, organizing themselves, have been responsible for critical social change. Women in the developed world, too, have organized themselves around many different social and political issues, and have successfully effected change in their own countries. Certain organizations work specifically to make the issues of Third World women better known in the developed world, and they often strive to link these issues with the policies of their governments toward the Third World. War on Want in Great Britain is one example of this kind of organization; another is the Third World Women's Project of the Institute for Policy Studies in Washington DC.

The Third World Women's Project invites women from the Third World to go on tour across the United States, speaking about their lives and their work to the North American people. The project generally sponsors women from countries where US policy plays an important role. In this, people in the United States are able to hear directly from Third World women about the problems they face in their daily lives, and about the ways in which US policy affects these problems. North Americans are then moved to take action for themselves, for example by writing to congressional representatives, boycotting certain products or starting solidarity groups. Much of the information in this article, in fact, was given by women who had been invited to the United States by the Third World Women's Project.

References

Boserup, Ester. *Women's Role in Economic Development.* New York: St Martin's Press, 1970.

Bronstein, Audrey. *The Triple Struggle.* London: War on Want, 1982.

Chapkis, Wendy, and Cynthia Enloe. *Of Common Cloth: Women in the Global Textile Industry.* Amsterdam: Transnational Institute, 1983.

de Chungara, Domitila Barros, with Moema Viezzer. *Let Me Speak!* New York and London: Monthly Review Press, 1978.

Deighton, Jane, Rossana Horsbeg, Sarah Stewart and Cathy Cain. *Sweet Ramparts: Women in Revolutionary Nicaragua.* London: War on Want and Nicaragua Solidarity Campaign, 1983.

El Saadawi, Nawal. *The Hidden Face of Eve: Women in the Arab World.* London: Zed Press, 1980.

El Saadawi, Nawal. *Memoirs from the Women's Prison.* London: The Women's Press, 1983.

ISIS. *Women in Development: A Resource Guide for Organization and Action.* Philadelphia: New Society Publishers, 1984.

Rogers, Barbara. *The Domestication of Women: Discrimination in Developing Societies.* London and New York: Tavistock Publications, 1980.

Steady, Filomena Chioma. *The Black Woman Cross-Culturally.* Cambridge, Mass.: Schenkman Publishing Co., 1981.

PART 6

The Contribution of Psychology to the Understanding of Peace

Robert Hinde suggests that any discussion of the bases of human aggression must start by confronting the popularly held assumption that the problems of human violence and war are insoluble because they are 'part of our make up' or 'in our genes'. This hypothesis is often attributed to Sigmund Freud, whose 'Why War?' reply to a letter from Albert Einstein provides the opening essay of this section. While many psychologists acknowledge that we have inherited a tendency to make war from our animal ancestors, the essays by Freud, Hinde and Kemp, and the Seville Statement on Violence (to be found in the Appendix), do not support the view that war is inevitable because of human instincts. Psychologists have also contributed to the understanding of peace in other ways. Thus Dorothy Rowe asks if enemies are necessary and traces the development of enemy images from childhood experiences, and Mary Midgley considers the psychological assumptions underlying deterrence.

Why War? A Reply to a Letter from Einstein*

SIGMUND FREUD

You begin with the relation between Right and Might. There can be no doubt that that is the correct starting point for our investigation. But may I replace the word 'might' by the bolder and harsher word 'violence'? Today right and violence appear to us as antithesis. It can easily be shown, however, that the one has developed out of the other; and, if we go back to the earliest beginnings and see how that first came about, the problem is easily solved.

It is a general principle that conflicts of interest between men are settled by the use of violence. This is true of the whole animal kingdom, from which men have no business to exclude themselves. To begin with, in a small human group, it was superior muscular strength which decided who owned things or whose will should prevail. Muscular strength was soon supplemented and replaced by the use of tools; the winner was the one who had the better weapons or who used them more skilfully. From the moment at which weapons were introduced, intellectual superiority already began to replace brute muscular strength; but the final purpose of the fight remained the same—one side or the other was to be compelled to abandon his claim or his objection by the damage inflicted on him and by the crippling of his strength. That purpose was most completely achieved if the victor's violence eliminated his opponent permanently—that is to say, killed him. Such, then, was the original state of things: domination by whoever had the greater might—domination by brute violence or by violence supported by intellect. As we know, this regime was altered in the course of evolution. There was a path that led from violence to right or law. What was that path? It is my belief that there was only one: the path which led by way of the fact that the superior strength of a single individual could be rivalled by the union of several weak

---

* From *Collected Papers*, Vol. 5, by Sigmund Freud, edited by James Strachey. Published by Basic Books, Inc. by arrangement with The Hogarth Press Ltd. and The Institute of Psycho-Analysis, London. Reprinted with permission.

ones. 'L'union fait la force.' Violence could be broken by union, and the power of those who were united now represented law in contrast to the violence of the single individual. Thus we see that right is the might of a community. It is still violence, ready to be directed against any individual who resists it; it works by the same methods and follows the same purposes. The only real difference lies in the fact that what prevails is no longer the violence of an individual but that of a community. But in order that the transition from violence to this new right or justice may be effected, one psychological condition must be fulfilled. The union of the majority must be a stable and lasting one. If it were only brought about for the purpose of combating a single dominant individual and were dissolved after his defeat, nothing would have been accomplished. The community must be maintained permanently, must be organized, must draw up regulations to anticipate the risk of rebellion and must institute authorities to see that those regulations—the laws—are respected and to superintend the execution of legal acts of violence. The recognition of a community of interests such as these leads to the growth of emotional ties between the members of a united group of people—communal feelings which are the true source of its strength.

From that time forward there are two factors at work in the community which are sources of unrest over matters of law but tend at the same time to a further growth of law. First, attempts are made by certain of the rulers to set themselves above the prohibitions which apply to everyone—they seek, that is, to go back from a dominion of law to a dominion of violence. Secondly, the oppressed members of the group make constant efforts to obtain more power and to have any changes that are brought about in that direction recognized in the laws—they press forward that is from unequal justice to equal justice for all. This second tendency becomes especially important if a real shift of power occurs within a community, as may happen as a result of a number of historical factors. In that case right may gradually adapt itself to the new distribution of power; or, as is more frequent, the ruling class is unwilling to recognize the change, and rebellion and civil war follow, with a temporary suspension of law and new attempts at a solution by violence, ending in the establishment of a fresh rule of law. There is yet another source from which modifications of law may arise, and one of which expression is invariably peaceful: it lies in the cultural transformation of the members of the community. This, however, belongs properly in another connection and must be considered later.

Thus we see that the violent solution of conflicts is not avoided even inside a community. However, the everyday necessities and common concerns of a community will tend to bring such struggles to a swift conclusion and create an increasing probability that peaceful solutions will be found. Yet a glance at the history of the human race reveals an endless series of conflicts between one community and another or several others, between larger and smaller units—between cities, provinces, races, nations, empires—which have always been settled by force of arms. Wars of this kind end either in the spoliation or in the complete overthrow and conquest of one of the parties. It is impossible to make any sweeping judgement upon wars of conquest. Some have brought nothing but evil. Others, on the contrary, have contributed to the transformation of violence into law by establishing larger units within which the use of violence was made impossible and in which a fresh system of law led to the solution of conflicts. In this way the conquests of the Romans gave the countries round the Mediterranean the priceless Pax Romana. Paradoxical as it may sound, it must be admitted that war might be a far from inappropriate means of establishing the eagerly desired reign of 'everlasting' peace, since it is in a position to create the large units within which a powerful central government makes further wars impossible. Nevertheless it fails in this purpose, for the results of conquest are as a rule short-lived: the newly created units fall apart once again, usually owing to a lack of cohesion between the portions that have been united by violence. Hitherto, more-over, such unifications have only been partial, and the conflicts between these have called out more than ever for a violent solution. Thus the result of all these warlike efforts has only been that the human race has exchanged numerous, and indeed unending, minor wars for wars on a grand scale that are rare but all the more destructive.

If we turn to our own times, we arrive at the following conclusion. Wars will only be prevented if mankind unites in setting up a central authority to which the right of giving judgement upon all conflicts of interest shall be handed over. There are clearly two separate requirements involved in this: the creation of a supreme agency and its endowment with the necessary power. One without the other would be quite useless. The League of Nations is designed as an agency of this kind, but the second condition has not been fulfilled: the League of Nations has no power of its own and can only acquire it if the members of the new union, the separate States, are ready to resign it. And at the moment there seems very little prospect of this.

I can now proceed to discuss another of your remarks. You express astonishment at the fact that it is so easy to make men enthusiastic about a war and add your suspicions that there is something at work in them—an instinct for hatred and destruction—which goes halfway to meet the efforts of the warmongers. Once again, I can only express my entire agreement.

According to our hypothesis human instincts are of only two kinds: those which seek to preserve and unite—which we call 'erotic' exactly in the same sense in which Plato uses the word 'Eros' in his *Symposium* or 'sexual', with a deliberate extension of the popular conception of sexuality—and those which seek to destroy and kill and which we group together as the aggressive or destructive instinct. Neither of these instincts is any less essential than the other; the phenomena of life arise from the mutually opposing actions of both. Now it seems as though an instinct of the one sort can scarcely ever operate in isolation; it is always accompanied—or, as we say, alloyed—with a certain quota from the other side, which modifies its aim or is, in some cases, what enables it to achieve that aim. It is very rarely that an action is the work of a single instinctual impulse. In order to make an action possible there must be as a rule a combination of compounded motives.

I should like to linger for a moment over our destructive instinct whose popularity is by no means equal to its importance. As a result of a little speculation, we have come to suppose that this instinct is at work in every living creature and is striving to bring it to ruin and to reduce life to its original condition of inanimate matter. Thus it quite seriously deserves to be called a death instinct, while the erotic instincts represent the effort to live. The death instinct turns into the destructive instinct when it is directed outwards on to objects. Some portion of the death instinct, however, remains operative within the organism, and we have sought to trace quite a number of phenomena to this internalization of the destructive instinct. You will notice that it is by no means a trivial matter if this process is carried too far: it is positively unhealthy. On the other hand if these forces are turned to destruction in the external world, the organism will be relieved and the effect must be beneficial. This would serve as a biological justification for all the ugly and dangerous impulses against which we are struggling.

For our immediate purposes, then, this much follows from what has been said: there is no use in trying to get rid of men's aggressive inclination. We are told that in certain happy regions of the earth, where nature provides in abundance everything that man requires, there are races whose life is passed in tranquility and who know neither coercion nor aggression. I can scarcely believe it and I should be glad to know more of these fortunate beings. In any case, as you yourself have remarked, there is no question of getting rid entirely of human aggressive impulses; it is enough to try to divert them to such an extent that they need not find expression in war.

Our mythological theory of instincts makes it easy for us to find a formula for indirect methods of combating war. If willingness to engage in war is an effect of the destructive instinct, the most obvious plan will be to bring Eros, its antagonist, into play against it. Anything that encourages the growth of emotional ties between men must operate against war. These ties may be of two kinds. In the first place they may be relations resembling those towards a loved object, though without having a sexual aim. There is no need for psycho-analysis to be ashamed to speak of love in this connection, for religion itself uses the same words: 'thou shalt love thy neighbour as thyself.' This, however is more easily said than done. The second kind of emotional tie is by means of identification. Whatever leads men to share important interests produces this community of feeling, these identifications. And the structure of human society is to a large extent based on them.

I should like to offer another suggestion for the indirect combating of the propensity to war. One instance of the innate and ineradicable inequality of men is their tendency to fall into the two classes of leaders and followers. The latter constitute the vast majority; they stand in need of an authority which will make decisions for them and to which for the most part they offer an unqualified submission. This suggests that more care should be taken than hitherto to educate an upper stratum of men with independent minds, not open to intimidation and eager in the pursuit of truth, whose business it would be to give direction to the dependent masses. It goes without saying that the encroachments made by the executive power of the State and the prohibition laid by the Church upon freedom of thought are far from propitious for the production of a class of this kind. The ideal condition of things would of course be a community of men who had subordinated their instinctual life to the dictatorship of reason. Nothing else could unite men so completely and so tenaciously, even if there were no emotional ties between them. But in all probability that is a Utopian expectation. No doubt the other indirect methods of preventing war are more practicable, though they promise no rapid success. An unpleasant picture comes to one's mind of mills that grind so slowly that people may starve before they get their flour.

I should like, finally, to discuss one more question which specially interests me. Why do you and I and so many other people rebel so violently against war? Why do we not accept it as another of the many painful calamities of life? After all, it seems to be quite a natural thing, to have a good biological basis and in practice to be scarcely avoidable. There is no need to be shocked at my raising this question. For the purpose of an investigation such as this, one may perhaps be allowed to wear a mask of assumed detachment. The answer to my question will be that we react to war in this way because everyone has a right to his own life, because war puts an end to human lives that are full of hope, because it destroys precious material objects which have been produced by the labours of humanity. It is my opinion that the main reason why we rebel against war is that we cannot help doing so. We are pacifists because we are obliged to be so for organic reasons. And we find no difficulty in producing arguments to justify our attitude.

No doubt this requires some explanation. My belief is this. For incalculable ages mankind has been passing through a process of evolution of culture. We owe to that process the best of what we have become, as well as a good part of what we suffer from. Though its causes and beginnings are obscure and its outcome uncertain, some of its characteristics are easy to perceive. The psychical modifications that go along with the process of civilization are striking and unambiguous. They consist in a progressive displacement of instinctual aims and a restriction of instinctual impulses. Sensations which were pleasurable to our ancestors have become indifferent or even intolerable to ourselves; there are organic grounds for the changes in our ethical and aesthetic ideals. Of the psychological characteristics of civilization two appear to be the most important: a strengthening of the intellect, which is beginning to govern instinctual life, and an internalization of the aggressive impulses, with all its consequent advantages and perils. Now war is in the crassest opposition to the psychical attitude imposed on us by the process of civilization, and for that reason we are bound to rebel against it; we simply cannot any longer put up with it. This is not merely an intellectual and emotional repudiation; we pacifists have a constitutional intolerance of war, an idiosyncrasy magnified, as it were, to the highest degree. It seems indeed as though the lowering of aesthetic standards in war plays a scarcely smaller part in our rebellion than do its cruelties.

And how long shall we have to wait before the rest of mankind become pacifists too? There is no telling. But it may not be Utopian to hope that these two factors, the cultural attitude and the justified dread of the consequences of a future war, may result within a measurable time in putting an end to the waging of war. By what paths or by what side tracks this will come about we cannot guess. But one thing we can say: whatever fosters the growth of civilization works at the same time against war.

Are Enemies Necessary?

DOROTHY ROWE

Do you have enemies? If so, who are they?

Many people, certainly many of the people who would read this book, would say that they had no enemies. They feel that being aggressive and having enemies is quite wrong. They themselves are friendly with everyone and totally unaggressive.

Many more people, certainly the kind of people who would *not* read this book, would say that they did have enemies. These enemies could be Communists or Capitalists, Arabs or Jews, Protestants or Catholics, Sikhs or Hindus, blacks or whites and so on. They would say that they themselves were not aggressive, but their enemies were aggressive and dangerous too, and so they have to defend themselves against their enemies.

A few people would say that they felt quite secure so at the moment they have no enemies and feel quite unaggressive. However they know that that could change. If someone should threaten their lives or the lives of their loved one, if they were unfairly dismissed from their jobs, or were cheated out of what was rightly theirs, or if someone near to them was treacherous and disloyal and betrayed their trust, then they would become aggressive and, seeing the person who had harmed them as an enemy, would seek to defend themselves. In such a situation, they would say, 'you know who your friends are'.

The first group of people are nice, kind, well-meaning people who are fooling themselves. We can no more give up aggression than we can give up breathing, and I know this only too well, when at the end of every lecture where I have talked about how enemies are necessary, these people advance upon me menacingly, demanding, 'How dare you say I'm aggressive?'

The second group, the largest group, are those people who have never questioned the way they were brought up and the way their society is organized. All their lives they have felt much pain and the anger of a life frustrated, and they relieve their pain and anger, and so survive, by taking their bad feelings out on the people they have been taught to see as their enemies. Without such enemies their pain and anger would be unendurable.

The third group are the people who have actually confronted the perennial problem that we need our anger and aggression to survive in a dangerous world, to carry our lives forward and to be creative. They have seen that we can express our aggression in a multitude of ways, from the firmness of saying, 'I find your behaviour unacceptable' to the violence of killing. They know that it is vitally important to learn how to distinguish those people who are actually intending to harm us from those who are simply the unwitting bearers of our aggressive fantasies. They know that the enemies in our heads are a greater danger to us than our enemies in reality.

The enemies in our heads are not mere random fantasies, derived from our watching of television violence. They are an essential part of the necessary process whereby we learned to live and work with others.

To understand this we need to understand the basic nature of how we function as human beings.

How we perceive and know

When we look about us in our ordinary lives, we see a world which looks solid and real. In fact, the world looks like that because we are a certain size and possess sense organs which function in a certain way. If we were much smaller or much bigger, or if we could borrow, say, a fly's eyes or a dog's ears, we would perceive the world in a totally different way. We would have no difficulty then understanding that while there is probably some kind of real reality, some constantly shifting, changing something, we can never know what it is. All we can ever know are the structures we create in order to live within something we can never know.

The structures we create are what we see, hear, touch, smell, feel, think and speak. Whether we see a world full of colour depends on whether we have the necessary equipment in our eyes: how we perceive and evaluate the world we live in depends on which language we have learned to speak.

If you speak or have ever tried to learn a second langauge, you will know that different languages are not just different sets of labels stuck on to the objects in one reality. Languages are different attempts at dividing up an amorphous changing something-or-other to create a structure which the speakers of that language call reality. It is language which creates reality, not reality which creates language.

So, what we call reality is, in fact, a set of structures which we have created.

The creation of such structures can begin in only one way.

The nature of our sense organs is such that we can perceive only when we can identify some contrast or differential. If we lived in a world of perpetual light with no shadows, we would not have a concept of light. To know light there must be dark. If we lived in a world where nothing ever died, we would not know that we were alive. To know life there must be death. If we lived in a world where everything was perfect, we would not know perfection. To know perfection there must be imperfection. If we lived in a world where everyone was unfailingly kind and friendly, we would not know friendship. To know friends there must be enemies.

Thus we define the group we belong to in terms of those who are excluded from our group.

These are the basic conditions by which we perceive and know. (If you would like to read further on this see the first three chapters of my book *Choosing, Not Losing*.)

If every moment of our lives we were consciously aware that what we were seeing and acting on were mere structures that we had created, we would be unable to act. We have to put from our consciousness this knowledge and act as if the world was the way we see it, solid and real. Whenever something happens to remind us the reality is not what we think it is, we feel fear, and to survive and overcome the fear we feel anger and to carry our anger and to hammer our structures back into place and to insist that reality is what we say it is, we feel aggression. Without aggression we are lost.

However, while anger and aggression are essential to maintain us as individuals, they create great problems for us when we try to fulfil one of our basic needs and that is other people.

Being a member of a group

We cannot live alone. Babies that are fed and kept warm but are never held in the enclosing circle of another person's arms go grey and die. Adults put in solitary confinement for an indefinite period go mad. So babies cry to be picked up and hostages, in the way that we will eat anything when we are starving, make friends with their captors.

We need other people in order to survive, but it is other people who threaten and try to destroy our structures. Trees don't tell us we have got our structures wrong. Other people do that, and they always will, because each of us creates our own individual world of meaning and no two worlds are the same.

Thus, to maintain the structure which we call 'myself and the way I see things' we have to be aggressive. Sometimes we are aggressive in a purely defensive way, saying, 'I'll see it my way and you see it yours', and other times we defend our structures by trying to get other people to relinquish their structures and accept ours. We can do this by persuasion or by threat. Power is essentially the ability to get other people to accept your definition of reality.

As developmental psychologists have been showing over the last few years, we are born with the ability to distinguish human faces and voices from all other shapes and noises and in the first days of life to identify our mother's face and voice from all other faces and voices.

When we are born we know that we need other people, and so we love the person who mothers us. We want to please her and, later, those people we have learned to call 'my family'. We discover that, much as our family loves us, we are not good enough. If we want to be accepted into the family group we have to give up being ourselves.

Babies are born greedy, angry, spontaneous and selfish. If they were not they would not survive. A baby who is not greedy will not suck. A baby who is not angry cannot react to clear an obstruction to his breathing. A baby who cannot respond spontaneously to the pressures in his body cannot relieve these pressures by urinating, defecating and vomiting. A baby who is not selfish will not cry in protest when he feels in some way endangered.

Within weeks of our birth our family begins teaching us that our characteristics of greed, anger, spontaneity and selfishness are unacceptable. If we want to become a member of the family group we have to give up such characteristics.

We are taught that we cannot expect to be fed when we wish. We have to eat when and what our family decrees. We are taught that anger is wicked: some of us are taught that no one in our family ever gets angry, while others are taught that adults can get angry with children, but not children with adults. We are taught to see spontaneity as dirtiness and irresponsibility, and so we become clean and responsible. We are taught that it is wrong to be concerned with our own needs. We must always consider other people's interests before our own, especially the needs of our parents and members of our family.

We learn all this in the first five years of our life and we are taught it in ways which involve threats of abandonment, physical pain and humiliation. If we do not learn it, or if we protest, we are told that we are 'spoilt' and need 'a damn good hiding'. (Adults who, as children, learned to conform envy those children and adolescents who refuse to conform, and such envy is murderous.)

Some of you reading this will be remembering a few of the painful events of your childhood and saying, 'Yes, this is so.' Others of you will be saying, 'My childhood was not like that. My parents were wonderful', and thus obeying the rule which Alice Miller calls 'Thou shalt not be aware'. You must forget what your parents did to you. Thus in adult life, whenever you say something critical about your parents you immediately feel guilty and say, 'But really my parents are wonderful. They would do anything for me.'

The reason we as children agree to follow the rule 'Thou shalt not be aware' is that we want our parents to be perfect. A few people reading this will be saying to themselves, 'My parents weren't wonderful. They didn't care about me at all, and I hate them.' Such people, like the ones who claim their parents were wonderful, are still clinging to the desire to have the security of parents who are perfect. They are not prepared to accept the insecurity of having parents who are simply human.

In the process whereby we, as children, are taught to conform to the rules of our family (and thus the rules of our family's race, religion, nationality, class, and sexes) we are taught that the unacceptable characteristics we have are the characteristics of those people who are excluded from our family and from the groups to which our family belongs. As a child I was taught that these despicable characteristics were possessed by the children of Happy Valley (people unemployed in the Depression of the 1930s lived in shacks in Happy Valley in Newcastle, Australia), by the Aborigines, Catholics, Chinese and, during the war, the Germans, Italians and Japanese. You might like to make a similar list from your childhood.

In our childhood such enemies of the group to which we belong help us to survive as persons. When the pain our parents and teachers inflict on us threatens to overwhelm us and wipe us out, annihilate us as a person, we can defend ourselves by, in fantasy, taking those characteristics for which we are being punished and projecting them on to our group's enemies. We say to ourselves, 'I am not dirty and irresponsible, like those blacks,' and, 'We are not aggressive like those Russians (or militarists and politicians).'

Thus, to survive as persons and members of a group we create our enemies in the head.

Since all children in all cultures are socialized in the same way, all children grow up with enemies in their head. Hence the enemies in our heads can also be our enemies in reality. Distinguishing the enemies in our heads from the enemies who are really threatening us can be difficult.

The people who find this task relatively easy are people who grew up in families which did not insist on conformity to rigid standards of goodness, who inflicted little pain on the children and who accepted the children *as themselves*. Thus these children could grow up accepting their own anger, aggressiveness, greed and envy.

But there are not many such families. More frequently the people who can distinguish the two kinds of enemy and react appropriately are those who have undertaken the painful task of reviewing their childhood, coming to terms with it and accepting that we are all simply human.

References

Miller, Alice. *For Your Own Good: The Hidden Roots of Violence.* London: Virago, 1987.
Miller, Alice. *Thou Shalt Not Be Aware.* London: Virago, 1987.
Rowe, Dorothy. *Living with the Bomb: Can We Live Without Enemies?* London: Routledge, 1984.
Rowe, Dorothy. *Beyond Fear.* London: Fontana, 1987.
Rowe, Dorothy. *Choosing, Not Losing.* London: Fontana, 1988.

Human Aggression: Biological Propensities and Social Forces

ROBERT A. HINDE

Introduction: natural selection and human behaviour

Any discussion of the bases of human aggression must start by confronting a popularly held but erroneous assumption. It is often claimed that the problems of human violence and war are insoluble because they are 'part of our make-up' or 'in our genes'. There is no scientific foundation for this view. Humans are certainly capable of aggression, but it is not inevitable that they should be aggressive. In the course of evolution, natural selection has ensured that individuals are born with *potentials* to behave not only aggressively, but also cooperatively, acquisitively, assertively, altruistically and in many other ways. But the extent to which individuals actually behave in any of these ways, and the short-term goals to which their behaviour is directed, are strongly influenced by social experience.

Now biologists have shown that the behaviour of animals is by and large adaptive—that is, that individuals behave in ways that increase the probability that they (or their close relatives) will survive and reproduce. For behaviour to be adaptive, it must be adjusted to the current situation. For example, the individuals in a group of animals can usually be arranged in a dominance hierarchy—A can boss B, B can boss C, and so on down to the bottom animal. It pays to be at the top of the hierarchy, because the top individual has priority of access to scarce resources. But for an individual who is not, it may be better to adopt other strategies, rather than to fight against hopeless odds. One possible strategy would be to cooperate with a peer to overthrow the despot. Another would be to employ stealth or cunning to get the resources.

Similar principles apply to some aspects of human behaviour. In general, individuals are endowed with propensities that will enable them to survive and reproduce. There are strong grounds for believing that these basic propensities are part of our biological heritage, and have been influenced by natural selection over the course of evolution. Consider for instance the circumstances in which individuals behave unselfishly to others. Amongst animals, evolutionary theory would suggest that such behaviour might pay (a) when it was likely to be reciprocated, and (b) when the recipient is a close relative. In the former case the behaviour is hardly unselfish: dividends are expected in the long run. The second case, help to relatives, has a rather different basis. Natural selection has operated through the survival of genes. If an individual acts so as to increase the chances of survival of others with genes similar to his or her own, even at some risk to himself, such behaviour could be selected for. Much (though, as we shall see, not all) apparently unselfish human behaviour falls into one or other of these categories. For example, individuals are especially likely to do a good turn to others when they are later likely to be rewarded for doing so in some way, and they are more likely to help relatives than non-relatives.

As this example implies, survival and reproduction are long-term issues, and we must pursue many shorter-term consequences along the way: natural selection has favoured individuals who help others when they are likely to be reciprocated only because, in the long run, such individuals are more likely to reproduce successfully. Often, however, these shorter-term goals become dissociated from their longer-term consequences, and are pursued in their own right. As an obvious example, much human courtship behaviour is quite unrelated to any conscious desire or intention to reproduce. Indeed as we shall see, much human behaviour, especially in industrialized societies, is directed towards goals that are either unrelated or even inimical to reproductive success.

Individual aggression

Now let us focus on the question of human aggression. Much aggressive behaviour occurs in situations where it brings the aggressor access to resources he or she covets, or enhanced status amongst peers. Consider two schoolboys fighting over the possession of a toy. Each boy is acquisitive and attempts to gain the object. As a means to that end, each is aggressive and attempts to hurt the other. Each may also be assertive and hope to enhance his own status by overcoming his rival.

This example illustrates another issue—namely that the motivation of human aggression is seldom simple. In this case, the primary motivation is acquisitiveness, and aggressiveness is employed as a tool, with assertiveness entering in, perhaps as a consequence of the situation.

Aggression as a means of acquisitiveness tends to become less common as children get older and find other, more acceptable, ways of getting what they want. But some children's aggression seems to have no tangible goal. In 'teasing aggression' one individual behaves aggressively towards another

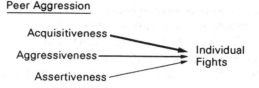

Peer Aggression

FIG 1.

even though no object is in dispute, and even though his or her status will not be increased. The evidence suggests that this teasing aggression is less likely to decrease with age, and that it may be the forerunner of behaviour problems in adolescence. It probably often stems from unsatisfactory social relationships in early childhood, especially within the family. Perhaps we should often also regard it as based on assertiveness, involving an attempt to gain status in the actor's own eyes. It may not be adaptive, in a biological sense at all.

This very simple case of two boys in dispute over a toy illustrates three ways in which we can try to reduce the level of violence in the world. First, much violence involves attempts to gain resources. One route, therefore, is to try to ensure that everyone's basic needs are met, and that the world's resources are more equally distributed than is at present the case. Of course it is difficult to define which needs are basic, but individuals tend to define their needs in terms of what they see others to have. So long as competitiveness is held up as a primary human virtue, individuals will use violent means to acquire things that others have. And so long as the world's scarce resources are distributed inequitably, people will compete for them.

Second, some individuals are more likely to resort to violence than others. Whilst genetic factors may be involved in some cases, the main issues here concern the environment of upbringing. Recent studies show that aggressiveness in boys is associated with homes in which parental control has been authoritarian, unpredictable and unaccompanied by warmth, or with permissive homes, in which parental discipline has been virtually absent. The least aggressive children tend to come from homes where the parents exercised reasonable and reasoned control in the context of a warm and loving relationship. The second route, therefore, must be to try to foster this sort of atmosphere in families. The task is not an easy one, since effects are transmitted across generations: unstable parents are likely to have inadequate relationships with their children, who in turn grow up to be unstable. However, the effects of an inadequate childhood can be ameliorated in other ways—for instance by a happy marriage to a supportive spouse. There is, therefore, a large scope for the educationalist and the social worker.

A third issue here is that individuals' behaviour is strongly influenced by the culture in which they grow up. If aggressive behaviour is rewarded, if individuals who behave aggressively are held up as models, if the use of violent means to gain ends is condoned in the media, children are more likely to develop into aggressive individuals.

We have seen that the initial sources of the human capacity for aggression lie in the motivational propensities with which man has been endowed by natural selection, though the strengths of these propensities, and the precise goals towards which they are directed, are also much affected by experience. This means that aggression is not inevitable: we can reduce its incidence by trying to build a more caring world where more emphasis is placed on cooperation and trust, and less on competition and self-assertiveness. We have also seen that the motivation of most aggression is far from simple. We have also touched on another potent factor in human aggression—the examples set by, and the values acquired from, other individuals in the society. We must now turn to a closely related issue—institutionalized violence.

Human institutions

Let us digress for a moment to consider the nature of institutions. In our own culture we have many institutions, each with its associated roles — for instance, marriage (with the roles of husband and wife), or Parliament (with the roles of Prime Minister, the Members, the voting public and so on). For each institution there are generally accepted norms and values as to the proper way for the incumbents of each role to behave. Now the behaviour of a married person clearly depends upon specific propensities of individuals—to behave sexually and parentally; assertiveness, involving entering into a special status; and in many cultures acquisitiveness. However, the institutionally imposed rights and duties of the incumbents as recognized by the society are at least as important as their individual propensities in influencing their behaviour. They are required to behave in ways that, though differing between cultures, are deemed to be appropriate to their new status. This may involve new residence, special ways of dressing, a reorientation of their sexuality, and so on. In other words, motivation of the behaviour of marriage partners is again not simple, but affected by basic human propensities as shaped by the dictates of the social institution of marriage.

This interweaving of different influences in shaping our behaviour is ubiquitous. Consider another example. Young children have a tendency to be afraid of snakes. Their response depends on the behaviour of their caregiver—if they see their mother show fear, their initial nervousness may be much enhanced. In a few cases, a snake phobia develops. Now snakes play an important part in the mythology of our culture, where they not only represent something to be feared, but also symbolize evil. Those two aspects come together in the legend of the Garden of Eden and in the Rubens paintings showing snakes gnawing at the genitals of lost souls cast down into hell. Thus snakes have become incorporated into the symbolism of what was one of the most important institutions in our society—the Church: an institution which still has an important influence in shaping the values of a secular society. It seems improbable that individuals would develop snake phobias if the initial potential for fear of snakes were not present in most individuals, and likely that their occurrence is accentuated by the myths of our culture. Nevertheless those myths themselves depend in part on the initial susceptibility to fear snakes, though involving religious beliefs and much else that capitalizes on many human propensities.

War

Let us now return to the question of aggression and consider village warfare in groups that have only recently been touched by civilization. This involves relatively small groups of individuals. The leaders take part in the combat, and each participant stands to gain—in living space, booty, wives or what have you, as well as in prestige. The fighting is accompanied by a great deal of threat and bombast, but the number of people killed is not large. Aggressiveness no doubt plays a not unimportant part, but so also do acquisitiveness and assertiveness. But institutions also often play a role. Individuals may be encouraged to fight bravely, even to sacrifice themselves, by religious leaders who inculcate beliefs about rewards in another life for those who die in battle, the approval of ancestors, and so on.

   Now consider modern warfare. Large armies are directed by leaders who occupy relatively safe positions remote from the fighting (though no one, combatant or non-combatant, is in fact safe from artillery, air attack or missiles). The relations between the motivations of the individual participants and the combat, direct in the case of the schoolboys and apparent in tribal warfare, is of a quite different nature in modern warfare. Modern war

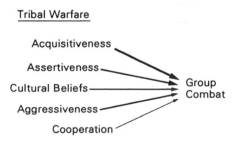

Tribal Warfare

Acquisitiveness
Assertiveness
Cultural Beliefs
Aggressiveness
Cooperation

Group Combat

FIG 2.

is properly considered as a human institution in which the individuals have specific roles, each with its attendant rights and duties.

The leaders may see it as their duty to impose war on the country, and their motivation is likely to include also fear of disapproval by supporters, self-assertiveness, and so on. But it is the institution of war that determines their rights and duties.

Amongst the combatants, aggressiveness plays only a very small part, as ex-soldiers will testify. Propensities to cooperate with others and to obey superiors, potentiated by feelings of nationalism, are certainly crucial. They may also hope for individual rewards at the end of the war. Primarily, however, they fight because of *their beliefs*. They *believe* that by so doing they can avoid a worse fate and protect their loved ones and the values they hold dear. They may even go more readily into battle because they believe it will lead them to a better afterlife. These beliefs and values, true in various degrees, are inherent in their culture and accentuated by governmental propaganda as part of the institution of war.

Civilians in arms factories, scientists and other backroom workers are influenced by the need to earn money, by personal ambition, and so on, but for them also cultural values accentuated or distorted by propaganda accompanying the institution of war are of major importance.

The institution of war exploits the propensities of soldiers and workers to cooperate with each other and to obey their superiors. It results in a distortion of everyday values to justify otherwise unthinkable actions. To the small extent that aggressiveness does enter into the behaviour of the individual combatant, it is induced either by fear or by a hostile and dehumanized image of the enemy and by a nationalism inculcated by institution-based propaganda. The propaganda must be seen as a tool used by the leaders (though perhaps with the best intentions) to stabilize the

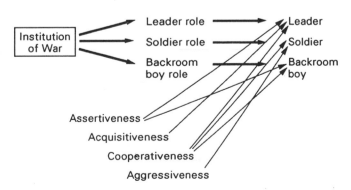

Modern Warfare

FIG 3.

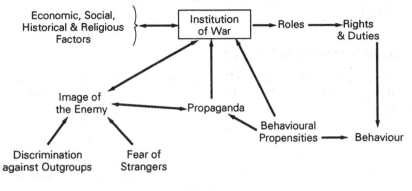

FIG 4.

institution of war, to confirm individuals in their roles as combatants, munitions workers in their jobs, and so on.

We must therefore ask, what are the bases of institutionalized war? These of course vary to some extent between societies and with the occasion, but some generalizations are possible. A partial (though not unimportant) answer is that the institution of war itself gains support from images that have their bases in the aggressive, acquisitive and defensive sides of human nature. The speeches of the leaders and the propaganda use aggressive images, and exploit egoistic propensities in individuals. Because individuals identify with their nation, the goals of national power and prestige are accepted as individual goals—though history shows that this is often a delusion, even for the survivors. Such goals are of course even more effective under conditions where individuals are deprived, and see resources in another country which are not available to themselves, or see another country as a threat to their own resources. Indeed the propaganda often uses fear as an incentive.

But whilst the institution of war depends upon human aggressiveness and self-interest it is supported also from many other sources. Religions have played a major part in many wars. Codes of honour and blood feuds have had a similar role. National pride, so often a constructive force, can also serve to bolster the institution of war. The propaganda even plays upon what we see as the highest parts of human nature: the British were invoked to 'Defend brave little Belgium' (in the First World War) or to 'Protect your heritage' (in the Second). Thereby the institution of war, like that of marriage, acquires a moral force, lending great strength to its directives. The ability of individuals to see the situation in a detached manner is negated. Thus to understand how individuals are recruited into a modern war we must come to terms with two sets of processes—the establishment and maintenance of the institution, and the impact of the institution on the behaviour of individuals.

Undermining the institution of war

Few will regard the institution of war as a desirable one—war is a poor way to solve problems, and with nuclear weapons could lead to the annihilation of the human race. We must therefore seek to undermine the institution itself. Our most powerful tool here is surely understanding. Once individuals understand the nature of the institution, they will be less likely to allow themselves to be used by it. Consider, for example, the creation of the enemy stereotype. In times of impending or actual war, an image of the enemy as inhuman and evil is promulgated in subtle and less subtle ways by the propaganda machines, and used to bolster the institution of war. What are the sources of its effectiveness?

A primary source is probably fear of the strange, the unknown. In the environment in which our species evolved, it was probably adaptive to fear strangers from infancy onwards. Fear of strangers appears, to a varying degree, in children during the second six months of life, and forms one basis of the mistrust of strangers that colours many of our feelings in adult life.

A second source, perhaps equally important, stems from the fact that every person seeks to define him or herself as an individual. In part, this involves identifying with groups—we see ourselves as male or female, of a certain generation, of a certain profession, of a certain political party, nationality, and so on. Along with identification with one group, we seek to devalue others. This is a major source of social and national stereotypes.

In time of war or impending war these tendencies are used by the political leaders to create an image of the enemy that is strange and therefore fear-inducing. A situation is then created, in which individuals can gain in status amongst their peers by denigrating the enemy—and certainly lose status by regarding them as fellow human beings.

If the psychological mechanisms at work in the creation of the enemy are unmasked, and the so-called enemy can be seen as composed of individuals just like ourselves, part of the power of the institution of war will have gone.

This process will be made easier by promoting knowledge of other peoples, and facilitating increased contact between individuals of different nations. The emphasis here must be on respecting other people's values, not on adopting them. In the modern world a variety of forces can combine towards producing cultural uniformity—well-intentioned projects involving education or religious teaching, or attempts to raise local living standards, as well as more dubious efforts by business enterprises to find new outlets for their products or new sources of raw materials, and deliberate attempts to suppress local cultures by various forms of political coercion. In any case, whilst increased contact between cultures can be enriching, its effects are often drab and alienating. Indeed the production of a crude fast-food culture by increased contact between nations can be fiercely resented by the peoples whose traditional values are suddenly shattered. The violent upsurge of nationalist movements in developed countries and of Islamic fundamentalism demonstrate the power of such forces, which can be a major cause of strife. Even if we deplore the violence and instability, we can sometimes sympathize with the motives of those involved. Thus we must seek to enhance understanding without imposing uniformity.

Another route towards undermining the institution of war involves the historical perspective. The institution of war did not arise overnight—it is a product of most nations' histories. Policies that are seen to work in one generation are transmitted to the next. As a consequence, rulers and governed alike may do risky things that bear no relation to a rational calculation of current costs and benefits. The historical processes that favoured warlike behaviour did not look into the future, and now operate in conditions to which they no longer apply. The institution of war will lose much of its force if people become aware of the ways in which our current behaviour is influenced by past events, so that we no longer adopt policies that make no sense whatsoever in a nuclear age. And of course we must see that other traditions are possible—there are nations, such as Switzerland, which have learned that a non-combatant tradition works better; and the example of Sweden shows that a previously militaristic nation can change its orientation.

The modern institution of war is also fed by a desire to respect those who placed a higher value on the 'good' of their companions than on their own lives. History gives war an honourable status. Furthermore much of the history that is taught is the history of wars—and usually from the perspective of the victors whose cause is seen as right and just. But the course of history is not preordained: individuals must strive to determine the world's destiny.

Conclusion

This chapter has concentrated on the causes of aggression and violence, and on the ways of removing them. But it is important that we should have aims more positive than the mere removal of current threats. We must seek to build a world in which the causes of civilization's discontents are minimized, and the potential of individuals to live fulfilled lives is more fully achieved. Even though this sounds like a Utopian dream, even though a degree of conflict and dissatisfaction may continue to arise, we must not abandon this aim. For there is real hope for progress. We now have the means to limit populations, we now realize the urgency of conserving the world's resources, we can now see how a generation's self-centredness can contaminate the globe. The nuclear threat has provided a new impetus to reaching an understanding of these worldwide problems, and the will to do so is increasing. Over the last 150 years there has been a real expansion of social conscience in the Western World. From a situation in which a starving pauper could obtain assistance only from the parish in which he was born, we have reached a situation in which individuals and governments despatch aid to those caught up in famine or disaster half a globe away. We must accelerate this process.

The essence of this argument lies in the need to understand ourselves. Humans need not be aggressive, and can work together and for each other with enormous effectiveness. Unfortunately, such cooperation can be directed against as well as for fellow human beings, but we can seek to build a world in which true cooperation predominates. In the past the benefits of risking life in organized conflict may often have outweighed the costs. Now that our technology has made warlike behaviour not only risky but suicidal, we have to find ways of controlling it. The way to start that process is to maximize the likelihood that all humans will be treated as allies in what has become the real struggle for survival. Cooperation requires mutual confidence. It follows that a major political and educational effort should be made to augment prosocial behaviour and to generate trust. That is surely an essential step towards the proper management of ourselves and our planet.

References

Groebel, J., and R. A. Hinde. *Violence and War.* Cambridge: Cambridge University Press (in press).

Hinde, R. A., and D. Parry. *Education for Peace* (in preparation).

Olweus, D., J. Block, and M. Radke-Yarrow. *Development of Antisocial and Prosocial Behavior.* Orlando, Florida: Academic Press, 1986.

Zahn-Waxler, C., E. M. Cumming, and R. Iannotti. *Altruism and Aggression.* Cambridge: Cambridge University Press, 1986.

The Art of War

GRAHAM KEMP

Clearly in the twentieth century the most common, dangerous, horrifying and difficult-to-explain acts of aggression are not those of a lone individual against another . . . (to some degree) we understand them. . . . What is less easy to understand is aggression on a massive scale in the context of modern warfare (John Sabini, Psychologist, 1978).[1]

Richardson in his *Statistics of Deadly Quarrels* calculated that from 1820 to 1946, 9.7 million people were killed by individual acts of homicide.[2] Acts we could understand as expressions of social deprivation, mental imbalance and stress, or a result of a criminal antisocial mentality. But he adds, 49.3 million people were killed in wartime. That is by ordinary people who become, en masse, organized to kill. People, who in their normal lives would rarely seek to seriously harm others. Yet under the cover of war, they appear to desire the brutal murder of others (even ones they know and socialize with as in a civil war). Sabini comments, if we must understand aggression, '. . . it is much more important to understand the aggression of people with (normally) no desire to harm anyone'.[3]

But such initial 'institutional aggression', as psychology terms it, seems to defy any rationale or reason, even when the consequences of it are appreciated, and there is an active campaign against it. Let us take one historical example, the Great War of 1914–18.

Europe in the early twentieth century established a policy of peace alliances or military agreements. An attack on one nation would be an attack on many. This alliance policy was backed up by large-scale arms and military preparation. As one British military writer wrote in 1916, 'the best defence is to be fully prepared for war'. The effect of this was fully examined. For example, Barbara Tuchman refers to the exhaustive work of Ivan Bloch on the future of the European War, written in 1899:

> Because conscription could call on a pool of the entire nation, he saw wars of the future absorbing the total energies and resources of the combatant states, who, unable to achieve decisive victory on the battlefield, would fight to exhaustion until they had brought each other down to total ruin.[4]

The Russian ambassador to Turkey in 1913 commented,

> I do not think any monarch in Europe would dare risk such an adventure. Do you not think, too, that the fevered armaments which are being multiplied on every hand are the best guarantee that we have entered into a long period of peace.[5]

The period between the 1890s and 1914 saw the development of strong popular peace movements. Many people, both nationally and internationally were organizing peace campaigns. Prominent among these were the socialists who believed that a growing educated and organized working class would lead workers of Europe to unite against any war caused by their imperial and capitalist masters. Not only was August 1914 to prove a disillusion of such a hope, but also many socialists joined the national fervour for war. Merely days after talk of international revolts for peace, socialists were declaring their support for war. This led the Kaiser of Germany to declare: 'Henceforth I know no parties, I only know Germans', and the French President of the Chamber of Deputies to declare in the Chamber: 'There are no more adversaries here, there are only Frenchmen'. As Barbara Tuchman adds, 'No socialist in either parliament disputed these statements of primary loyalty'. August 1914 saw the beginning of a malaise, called 'war fever', and when the European nations caught it opposition doubts to war withered away.[6] It is historical pointers like this that can explain many people's modern day pessimism about future wars, nuclear weapons or not. Wars seem to happen, ordinary people seem powerless to stop them. Even when the cost is so high and the gains suspect, they are still prepared to continue to fight.

For people, Count Ciano, foreign minister to Mussolini, reveals a strong desire among Italians of all strata to avoid war in 1939–40, and certainly a war in alliance with Germany. The only one who actively desired such a war was Mussolini himself. Yet for three years, 1940–43, Italians fought Mussolini's war, before overthrowing him and effectively changing sides. And the sacrifice is great, not just death, but the risk of terrible pain and mutilation, and famine and disease upon your families. A clandestine survey of public opinion in early 1939 revealed only a minority of Germans supported the idea of war.[7] Yet Germany as a nation fought to a bitter and terrible end. When the atom bombs were dropped on Japan in 1945, with their unspeakable horror, it took the authority of the Emperor to bring Japan to sue for peace. For many ordinary soldiers and civilians it was difficult to contemplate such an action.

Why? What makes us do it? War seems an irrational process. This article tries to examine that process, to give some light on how people can gain the reason and the power to stop wars. And wars, even today, dominate the lives of millions, directly or indirectly. Many people appear to give up basic rights of food, health, education, in order to allow expenditures on military arms in case of war. And as 1914 showed, military preparedness, stockpiles of the latest arms, do not prevent wars.

A popular approach, particularly with Western traditions, is to postulate some unconscious aggressive urge for killing which at times of war is unleashed. War may be seen as the breakdown of civilization, civilization being the process where our aggressive urges are kept in check. Once war breaks out, man pursues an orgy of destruction to fulfill an unconscious desire for savagery. The evidence for this is very thin (see the Seville Statement in the Appendix to this book). Some commentators suggest we possess our savage aggressive instinct as a result of our animal past. But biology has shown that aggression in animals is predominantly nonlethal, and, particularly in mammals, avoids the possibility of physical harm to conspecifics. Predation, it is argued, is not equatable with aggression.

Firstly, predation is inter-species (between members of the same species) and is about killing for food, or the avoidance of being eaten. Aggression, 'in the proper and narrow sense of the word',[8] as defined by biology, is rivalry over resources. And rivalry for the same resource tends to be intra-species (between members of different species). This is necessarily true where the rivalry is over resources such as breeding partners or breeding space. Thus aggression is perceived as conflict between members of the same species. Here, there can be seen no requirement to kill.

> The survival function is to space out individuals (or pairs or groups) over the available habitats to ensure the most favourable exploitation of a region and the food sources it contains.[9]

In other words, it ensures some individuals of the species gain sufficient resources to survive. Animal species that have adopted this strategy have survived better to the extent that such aggressive behaviour is predominant in the majority of animal life. As the ethologist Konrad Lorenz writes,

> The danger of too dense a population of an animal species settling in one part of the available biotype and exhausting all its resources of nutrition and so starving can be obviated by a *mutual repulsion* acting on the animals of the same species effecting their spacing out [my emphasis].[10]

And as the popular writer Robert Ardrey states: 'Man is a predator whose natural instinct is to kill with a weapon'.[11] But as already mentioned, biological studies of animals do not see a correlation between predation and the ability to kill or inflict harm on fellow species members. Many herbivore mammals demonstrate far more intra-species aggression than predators such as the wolf. Often the behaviour is very different. For instance, rattlesnakes while using their poisoned fangs for predation, in conflict with other rattlesnakes entwine their bodies and engage in a form of body wrestling until one admits defeat. While ungulates, such as deer, have horns that can prove physically dangerous to the flank of a predator, they themselves engage in intra-species aggression head to head, which aids in minimizing injury.[12] Aggression amongst members of the same species becomes

> a harmless contest in which movements do not aim to injure and weapons, if potentially harmful, are used harmlessly (and this), preserves the adaptiveness of aggression by producing a winner without harming either winner or loser . . .[13]

Predation and the ability to kill one's own kind do not correspond. And in fact man's elevation above other animals has been more to do with his ability to cultivate plants than to hunt prey which he himself can barely outrun.

A third idea is to link our early history to the development of savage impulses. Bertrand Russell, in his 1948 Reith Lectures, spoke of

> our largely unconscious primitive ferocity . . . the old instincts that have come down to us from our tribal ancestors—all kinds of aggressive impulses inherited from the long generations.[14]

There is in fact very little evidence of our ancestral past. The little evidence obtainable mainly from bone finds offers only conflicting evidence on what early man was like. But the anthropologist Ashley Montagu writes,

> Everything points to the non-violence of the greater part of man's early life, to the contribution made by increasing development of co-operative activities—the very social process of hunting itself, the invention of speech, the development of food-getting and the like.[15]

And what is a savage tribal ancestor? Europeans have often described other tribal cultures, particularly in the past, as savages, labelling them often as cannibals. The social anthropologist, Professor Arens, examining evidence of cannibalism could find no primary (firsthand) evidence of culturally organized cannibalism.[16] Only cases of survival cannibalism, as in the case of shipwrecks and aircrashes, could be verified. He puts forward the suggestion that Europeans labelled others as cannibals to lower their status as human beings, to justify the superiority of the European, and the right of Europeans to take, exploit and enslave other races. It is interesting to note that the so-called 'Fierce People', the Yananamo of the Amazon, see themselves as people because they are non-cannibals, while the rest of us are.[17]

The suggestion that war is explainable in terms of some deep-seated urge among humanity for destruction of others has really little support. But it has popular roots, probably because of long held religious ideas such as the concept of original sin, and the story of Cain and Abel. One social scientist, Leopold Szondi (1969), termed that aggressive urge 'the Cain tendency'.

The value of the idea is that it is comforting, in the sense that war is to do with human nature, not human culture. Thus there is little we can do about our actions. Arendt, addressing this in *Eichmann in Jerusalem* (1963), argued that the workings of the Nazi death machine cannot be explained as merely the

> consequence of some titanic force that desired to spread suffering and death, but the banal and simple consequence of thousands, even millions, of ordinary people doing their jobs with total disregard to its content.[18]

Which suggests there is something we can do, but what? First abandon the idea that war is due to our biology. War is a cultural, organized event and is carried out for the supposed benefit of individual cultures and societies. Despite the peace campaigns, the military deterrence, the awareness of the danger of war, European nations prior to 1914 maintained war as a legitimate means of national advancement, a belief which was maintained by the fascists of the 1930s. And war for national advancement was not officially declared against international law until after 1945. So how do culture, societies, organize their people to kill and sacrifice themselves?

First there is considerable evidence to indicate that the human species like most of animal life has strong inhibition processes that prevent us from inflicting physical harm on fellow human beings. Therefore to carry out war one must first dehumanize the enemy: indicate that the enemy has no status to be treated as a human being. It may be noted that war propaganda concentrates at least half its efforts in such dehumanizing of the enemy. If one is going to war to kill it is not described in terms of killing fellow human beings like yourself. Words are used which help one to conceive the enemy as things not beings. Thus one goes to war to kill the 'hun', 'commies', 'argies', 'imperialists' and so on. Such propaganda can seek to change the nature of the conflict, where the inhibitions against killing are far less.

> . . . man engaged in war, or other forms of intra-specific killing, seems to be able to fuse these different motivations into one super-motivation: the enemy is to the warrior not merely another human being, he is at the same time a dangerous predator, a parasite . . .[19]

Terminology such as 'hunter-killer', 'wolf pack', 'the Russian bear' underline this point. Many warrior groups take on predator names. The Aztec warriors, for instance, dressed as jaguars or eagles. War could be seen as a hunting exercise, or a defence against a predator, not about killing between equals. In the same way, war is described in neutral impersonal terms, which convey little of its horrific realities. Such terms as 'collateral damage' (civilian casualties), 'free fire zones' (indiscriminate killing allowed), and 'fallout', which the Japanese, possibly more accurately, term 'death dust'. 'Casualties were sustained' is another phrase, not 'people were killed or wounded'. But such neutral language is for home consumption. On the field of battle, soldiers, warriors, do come face to face with their human enemy. Here the atrocities of killing that can occur help to deny the human status of the victim, and thus sustain the act. This may be the case for some, but as

Eibl-Eibesfeldt points out, for many the inhibitions against intra-species aggression, inflicting and risking harm, are as strong as in the rest of animal life. He refers to an age old military problem,

> the readiness to form a bond with one's fellow man is so great that there is always a danger that two hostile groups may fraternize if they face one another for long enough and at close quarters.[20]

The history of war is littered with examples of such soldier camaraderie and fraternization with the enemy. Bruce Caton, for example, in his description of the siege of Richmond during the American Civil War, refers to enemy pickets fishing from opposite banks of the same stream, conversing and trading with each other, while at the same time they organized lookouts for patrolling officers. One of the most famous examples is the event of Christmas 1914 on the Western Front. Here, the developing fraternization of opposing infantry in the frontlines gave way to a spontaneous ceasefire to celebrate Christmas. Troops from opposing trenches walked out into no-man's-land to exchange Christmas greetings. And even impromptu football matches were reported to occur.

This fellow feeling could also be an attempt to indicate that the killing is nothing personal, particularly in respect to humane treatment of enemy wounded and dead. But as Eibl-Eibesfeldt also suggests, it reflects not just inhibitions, but a positive strong urge in humanity to socialize. As he writes: 'The great significance attached to war propaganda shows how strongly men, left to themselves, incline towards peaceful contact.'[21] Humanity may be described as the most social of animals. Social cooperation and organization have been recognized by anthropology, sociology and social psychology as the means by which humanity survives, and the medium in which we structure our life. If one considers what one owes through social interaction, learning, status, identity particularly in terms of political and religious beliefs, the importance of social interaction with others may be gauged. Also the extent of our sociability may be understood when one considers the number of peaceful and even social interactions we have in a day with complete strangers, e.g., in a supermarket, theatre, or on holiday. And if one considers that there are 4000 million inhabitants on the planet and how many such social interactions take place a day—how many of these really are violent? How many other animals can socialize, show altruistic feelings towards not only strangers but to other species? But if that social urge is so strong, why do we still persist in killing?

One answer is the weapons we use. The most useful killing machines are ones that minimize contact between human beings. A gun is too quick and has a range which makes it hard to make contact. Artillery, the real killer in the 1914–18 war, allows a distance that makes killing almost completely unseen. You are hitting a point on a map, not mutilating human beings. Weapon technology this century has reached a point where you can make ordinary people pour petrol over even women and children and set fire to them. How is it done? You place your 'killer' in a bomber at 50,000 feet with a napalm payload. At My Lai, in the Vietnam War, a young American officer had civilians killed in cold blood. This was described as a war crime. But at the same time bomber crews were indiscriminantly killing men, women and children civilians consistently throughout the war. But the contact was not there, which may be why My Lai was a crime. It may be added, that bombing and artillery fire do not form effective killing machines in terms of accuracy and expenditure of resources, as the 1914–18 war and Vietnam showed. But they kill over consistent periods without the killers needing to see the consequences. Thus one need not face the social consequences of one's actions. They are also indiscriminate, bringing a sense of mistrust and fear between opposing forces. It was the indiscriminate use of artillery that destroyed much of the fraternization on the Western Front.

The second answer is to make war not an act of aggression, but an expression of social solidarity: to utilize that strong social urge in people to conform and be part of a social group. Send people to war, not to kill, but to defend their homes, families, friends, religion, beliefs and 'way of life'. Allow them to express a social solidarity and answer the call to defend their particular social world they live in. Not to fight is to betray your friends, your fellow humanity—possibly the ultimate crime in such a social animal. The removal of all opposition and dissension in wartime (including the isolation of conscientious objectors) is essential so that no individual may feel that in breaking ranks he has social support. If dissent is allowed to develop, then the will to wage war declines.

To make war a social act rather than an aggressive one has its applications in producing elite fighting forces. The best fighting units are ones which are socially most closeknit. The regimental system is probably successful, in that through tradition, rituals, and an organization which bonds people together without the allowance of dissension, you produce an effective killing machine. And if they kill, it is not murder, for murder is an antisocial act. Killing in war is portrayed as a supreme act of love for your comrades, country or regiment. The paradox that killing in war is about social emotions not aggressive ones. As the psychologist Seymour Feshbach recently commented, 'Patriotism and Nationalism. . . . They are among the noblest and the most destructive of human impulses.'[22]

So what can one conclude from this? The killing of 49.3 million people in war was about human expressions of social solidarity, and a consequence of seeing the enemy not as a fellow human. War is always possible when we are prepared to see others as less than human. Second, we must keep in mind the consequences of our weapon technology, and avoid the temptation they give of keeping anonymous the suffering of our actions. Arendt argues that it is such temptation by ordinary citizens that made the Nazi death machine work. Here, the great value of peace literature may be understood in keeping the consequences of the impact of, for example, nuclear weapons as an issue in the minds of ordinary citizens.

Finally, war must no longer be held to be regarded as a theatre of the supreme social sacrifice. We no longer think just in terms of the misused biblical quote: 'No greater love hath man, who lays down his life for his friends.' As Darwin argued, what love we learn and possess for our friends, we must extend to all, as we have slowly done, from tribal groups to nations, and now hopefully to the species.[23] We should socially organize for peace. And here is probably the real value of popular peace campaigns (and peace education), irrespective of whether their specific aims are carried out or agreed with; they do create social solidarity in the cause of peace. Also famine appeals, such as Band Aid or Sport Aid, give us the means to express social solidarity with all humanity. We honour our war dead, irrespective of creed, religion and race. Surely, we should honour more the ordinary peace campaigner, the famine relief worker. After all, they are not the victims of a tragic man-made disaster. No greater love hath man, who through his love of his friends, seeks to promote life for all.

Notes

1. Sabini, John. 'Aggression in Laboratory', in Kutash, Irwin, et al (eds.), *Violence, Perspectives on Murder and Aggression.* London: Jossey-Bass, 1978.
2. Richardson, Lewis. *Statistics of Deadly Quarrels.* Pittsburgh: Boxword Press, 1960.
3. Sabini, John. 'Aggression in Laboratory'.
4. Tuchman, Barbara. *The Proud Tower.* London: Macmillan, 1966.
5. Author anonymous and given as '*****'. *The Near East From Within.* London: Cassell, 1915.
6. See Tuchman, *The Proud Tower*, Chapter 8.
7. The survey was carried out by Geoffrey Pyke. See David Lampe, *Pyke—The Unknown Genius.* London: Evan Bros., 1959.
8. Lorenz, Konrad. *On Aggression.* Translated by M. Latzke, foreword by Sir Julian Huxley. London: Methuen, 1966.
9. Nisbitt, A. *Konrad Lorenz.* London: Methuen, 1975.
10. Lorenz, Konrad. *On Aggression.*
11. Ardrey, Robert. *The Territorial Imperative.* New York: Atheneum, 1966.
12. Eibl-Eibesfeldt, I. *Ethology—The Biology of Behaviour.* Translated by K. Klinghammer, 2nd ed. New York: Holt, Rinehart and Winston, 1975.
13. Schuster, Richard. 'The Ethological Theories of Aggression', in Kutash, Irwin, et al (eds.), *Violence: Perspectives on Murder and Aggression.* London: Jossey-Bass, 1978.
14. Quoted by Lewis J. and B. Towers in *Naked Ape or Homo Sapiens.* London: Garnstone Press, 1969.
15. Montagu, Ashley. *The Nature of Human Aggression.* Oxford: Oxford University Press, 1978.
16. *Antenna*, BBC2, 30 September 1987.
17. Lizot, Jacques. *Tales of Yanomami.* Translated by E. Simon. Cambridge: Cambridge University Press, 1985.
18. Sabini, John. 'Aggression in the Laboratory'.
19. Tinbergen, Niko. 'Ethology in a Changing World', in Bateson, P. and R. A. Hinde (eds.), *Growing Points in Ethology.* Cambridge: Cambridge University Press, 1976.
20. Eibl-Eibesfeldt, I. *Love and Hate.*
21. Ibid.

22. Feshbach, Seymour. 'Individual Aggression, National Attachment, and the Search for Peace', Presidential Address to the 7th World Meeting of International Society for Research on Aggression, Chicago, 1986. In *Aggressive Behaviour* 13 (1987), pp. 315–25.
23. Darwin, Charles. *The Origin of the Species*. London: Murray, 1859.

Supportive Reference Material

The following books have been used in the preparation of this article. They are included here, as reference books easily obtainable from most libraries.

Biology

Eibl-Eibesfeldt, I. *Love and Hate*. Methuen, 1971.
Tinbergen, N. *The Animal in its World: Explorations of an Ethologist. 1932–72,* Vol. 2. Allen and Unwin, 1973.

Anthropology

Montagu, A. *The Nature of Human Aggression*. Oxford University Press, 1978.
Montagu, A. *Learning Nonaggression*. Oxford University Press.
Dentan, R. K. *The Semai—A Nonviolent People*. Holt, Rinehart and Winston, 1968.

History

Tuchman, B. *The Proud Tower*. Macmillan, 1966.
Richardson, L. F. *The Statistics of Deadly Quarrels*. Boxword Press, 1960.

Not so easy to locate, but highly recommended is:

Ramirez, J. Martin, R. A. Hinde and Jo Groebel (eds.). *Essays On Violence*. Publicaciones de La Universidad de Sevilla, 1987.

Deterrence and Provocation*

MARY MIDGLEY

Past confusions

Understanding deterrence is a complex skill, not at all like falling off a log. This emerges from every discussion of the arms problem today, and it is one faintly cheering feature of such discussions that they do not admit this complexity. Professor Laurence Martin's Reith Lectures were doubly cheering in this respect. Firstly, Professor Martin took the problem very seriously, admitting freely that he thought its difficulties crushing, and that it scared him still—a prime qualification, surely, for discussing the subject at all. Secondly, he pointed out how much of this difficulty was political and psychological, yet how crudely those aspects of it had been handled by the earlier architects of modern weaponry. He shows how casually, in the early years, it was assumed that atomic weapons should be designed for 'city busting', merely because no other use for them had yet occurred to anybody. 'There was,' he remarks, 'certainly no psycho-political analysis of what it takes to deter.'[1] Larger and larger bombs were therefore provided, and this fairly unconsidered habit of mind was rationalized into the explicit policy of 'mutually assured destruction' (MAD), to be provided by building up the superpowers' capacity to demolish each other's cities instantly. This policy was cheerfully accepted as making a positive virtue of the weapons' destructiveness, and, as he explains, the West made deliberate efforts to convert the Russians to that idea, which they viewed with some alarm.

Inevitably, however, attempts were soon made to refine this hopelessly crude deterrence arrangement by technological advances. 'Flexible response' was developed and the supposedly simple, reliable deterrent was lost for ever. 'The early architects of deterrence,' remarks Professor Martin, 'seem to have been so much preoccupied with staving off massive nuclear

* A fuller version of this paper appeared in Blake and Pole (eds.), *Dangers of Deterrence*, Associated Book Publishers (UK) Ltd., 1983. Used with permission.

attack that they gave little thought to why it might occur.'[2] That is, they neglected the whole political context and in particular the fact that most disputes are small. They provided no means of nutcracking except a steam-hammer. When the mass of nut-sized disputes on hand became obvious, they supplemented this with a variety of steam-powered nutcrackers, certain to smash crockery and likely to set the steam-hammer itself going as well. Hence we have, at present, problems of appalling intricacy for which Professor Martin provided an impressive set of very subtle, but by no means confident, diagnoses. (His refusal to dogmatize is another of his virtues.) He concludes that, while it is a great pity that we ever got into this mess, and while we should do all we can to bring about arms control, we probably need for deterrence most of the weapons currently on hand or on offer, and a good few more conventional ones as well. If we say we don't much like this, he replies (not offensively but sympathetically) in the words of Bruce Bairnsfather's Old Bill, 'Well, if you knows of a better 'ole, then go to it.'[3]

To say that I find this approach relatively cheering, and an improvement on some earlier ones, is obviously to start from a fairly depressed position. I have in mind two ways in particular in which reliance on weapons used to be defended. The first is the mindless, all-purpose Empire-day patriotism which prevailed in my childhood, and which was recently revived under the name of the Falklands Spirit. The second is the complacent certainty that—given the right aims—the current policy for implementing them must be right, the extraordinary confidence in military judgement about means which prevailed for some time after the Second World War. (It prevailed, in fact, at the very time when the mistakes which Professor Martin now nails were being made.) This is what has brought us to what he justly calls our present 'miserably dangerous situation'. That kind of complacency is scarcely possible now because the solid simple orthodoxy of belief in MAD has given way. In its place, those who are most expert and professional in these matters are now deeply divided, propounding a range of different ideas on how to deter. Among them are quite a few very distinguished people (such as ex-ambassador George Kennan and Field Marshal Lord Carver), who say that one thing we need badly is fewer nuclear weapons. Professor Martin himself makes an interesting point in noting that George Kennan himself, when he gave the Reith Lectures in 1957, poured scorn on this way of thinking. But the crucial thing is the direction of change. That was in the age of complacency.

Certainly we have to face realistically the problems of how to attempt reduction. If the Angel Gabriel were to persuade all existing governments tomorrow that they had better get rid of the things, there would still be grave problems about how to do it. But that does not mean that these ideas should be swept away. Professor Martin, when he considers them, is discouraged to the point of despair by the difficulty of getting reliable agreements and inspection procedures. That is a psychological problem, concerning the motivation of all concerned. And to this general type of problem I now return, asking in a general way, firstly, what is deterrence?

The psychology of deterrence and provocation

The motivation of deterrence links the threatener's hardware to the motivation of the person threatened in a very simple way. It treats the threat merely as producing fear, and so discouraging action. Threats, however, do not only frighten; they can also provoke. The proportion of discouragement to provocation varies greatly in different situations, and always needs attention. This snag is well-known over deterrent punishment, which is the main sphere in which the idea of deterrence has so far been used outside warfare. The case of penal deterrence compares interestingly with international deterrence.

Someone who has been punished for one offence and is contemplating another does not necessarily see his former punishment, and the threat of a further one, simply as natural phenomena. He can see them also as hostile acts. He does not have to respond in a prudential manner, assessing the warning and the danger as he might when predicting renewed attacks of gout or indigestion. If he resents the punishment and the threat, he may see them instead as expressive gestures by which the punishing authority rejects him, and shows him that it is idle to try to come to terms with it—he will never be fully accepted by that authority. In this case, threats of stronger action will only intensify his defiance. The effectiveness of penal deterrence is limited by this tendency of punishment to turn many people into 'hardened criminals'—even if they have no particular views beforehand about the punishing authority. If they do—if they belong already to a group which feels alien to the authorities—it is even less effective. It is less so still where (as in Northern Ireland) long-standing political feuds underlie the rejection. In that sort of situation, even very heavy penalties fail to deter. This continually surprises judges, who often respond by giving heavier and heavier sentences in the hope that they can somehow get through to the next lot of offenders. But deterrence does not seem to work like this, in a way proportional to the expected penalty. It apparently depends far more on the community with which one identifies. It can even be counterproductive, causing bystanders to join the threatened community and reject the threatening one. Those of us who are thoroughly integrated into the communities which do the punishing are indeed easy to deter, because we mind about the disgrace of offending that community. Such disgrace seems to be far more feared than the mere pain or nuisance of punishment. (The fact that judges and legislators are usually members of this group, and offenders often are not, accounts for a good deal of mutual misunderstanding.) But for people who have no reputation to lose, or who belong to a distinct community in which punishment won't affect their reputation, this danger is removed. In this situation, the mere basic prudence which is adjusted to the size of the penalty is often extraordinarily weak. And judicial reproofs commonly cut no ice at all.

Without fellowship, communication fails

Penal deterrence depends, then, far more than seems to have been noticed on the inclusion of deterrer and deterred within the same moral and emotional community. Where this fails, not only is the motivation presupposed by deterrence undermined, but its credibility also becomes much harder to establish. A normal law-abiding citizen tends to think that, if he offended, he would not get away with it. He expects on the whole that his fellow citizens would catch him and punish him, because on the whole he thinks they ought to, and thinks they will share his view. He sees them as an externalized extension of his own conscience. But to someone who feels detached from that community, things look quite different. For him, the question is one of objective probabilities, as it would be over dangers from disease or weather. And this calculation is often quite uncertain, because the data are scanty. It tends to appear as a gamble. He may well get away with it. And the less he grasps the reasoning of those who may punish him, the less certain it will seem whether they will actually do what they threaten. If he cannot see why they would be strong-willed, he will have less reason to be sure that they will be strong-willed. Even heavy punishments, in such circumstances, tend to have little effect against a strong immediate motive for offending.

This is what made it possible for even quite prosperous eighteenth-century thieves to continue their business in spite of regularly seeing large numbers of their colleagues hanged for doing it. They took the physical risk, as fishermen risk drowning and car-drivers risk accidents, because it was occupational and they had indeed become hardened to it. They were not taking any emotional risk, because thieving was their tribal business, and they would have been despised for leaving it. All this is doubtless very imprudent. What it shows is that the human imagination is rather an unreliable device for producing prudence, because it has innumerable other functions to fulfill as well. And it is particularly unreliable in dealings with alien tribes. This is something which needs to be thought about whenever we are planning to rely on penal deterrence.

Now of course the penal situation is very different from the international one, and I am not trying to draw any simple parallel between them. But I think that the comparison can give us some light—the interesting thing is to see how far it will shine. In the first place I think there is real reason to suppose that between nations too intelligible and useful deterrence can only work within the context of some sense of fellowship resting on shared basic aims, which—in spite of very wide local differences—makes it possible to understand and sympathize with the motives of one's opponent. Without it, effective deterrence becomes impossible, because the basis of reliable communication is undermined. We will understand what others say if we fail to grasp why they are saying it. Complete aliens are in principle unintelligible, and therefore unpredictable. Consequently their threats lack credibility. In saying this, I am not being utopian about what a sense of shared aims can achieve. I am not ignoring the endless cases of successful international blackmail and oppression. Athens wiped out Melos. The Holy Roman Empire bullied its client states into suppressing the Protestant Reformation. And so on. But these are transactions between a dominant state and a much weaker one which is already well within its power. They do not help us to a model of deterrence between independent sovereign states of approximately equal standing.

Pursuing for a moment the case of equal and independent nations, we can put the question why, when they disagree, wars do not continually break out between them? (The question is an odd one, and I put it in this form only because it seems to be the question implicitly addressed by people who say that peace has been produced over the last few decades simply by the presence of nuclear weapons.) The most obvious way to answer this does not begin by listing the armies and the hardware, but by asking why it should. Nations have other ways of settling their disputes, and those disputes do not take place in a social vacuum. Nations are not sealed boxes, isolated from each other except for the conduct of disputes. Their boundaries are often arbitrary and inconvenient for current purposes; all sorts of activities go on across them. Unless deliberately prevented, citizens of different states tend strongly to travel and trade together, and to engage in all sorts of activities, ranging from sport to religion, which ignore political frontiers. Both personally and economically, much advantage is drawn from these habits. When therefore a cause of dispute arises, it has to be weighed against the drawbacks of breaking them. Even to threaten violently is something of a gamble; one may drive lasting friendship away elsewhere. Accordingly, though armed forces and the power of using them are a regular element in such disputes, the threat of using them forms only one part in a whole complex web of bonds, propositions, offers, half-offers, threats and promises, out of which, as a rule, some sort of tolerable understanding emerges. Other sorts of threat, for instance concerned with trade, are of a much commoner coin.

Notes

1. Martin, Lawrence. *The Listener,* 15 November 1981, p. 597.
2. *Ibid.,* p. 598.
3. Martin, Lawrence. *The Listener,* 12 November 1981, p. 565.

References

Prins, Gwyn (ed.). *Defended to Death: A Study of the Nuclear Arms Race.* Harmondsworth: Penguin, 1983.

Lifton, Robert Jay, and Richark Falk. *Indefensible Weapons: The Political and Psychological Case against Nuclearism.* New York: Basic Books, 1982.

Miall, Hugh. *Nuclear Weapons: Who's in Charge.* London: Macmillan, 1987.

PART 7

The Alternative of Nonviolence

The final section of the book provides a brief introduction to the ideas of nonviolence. Two aspects of nonviolence are explored by the authors. The first is the use of nonviolent techniques for 'fighting' conflicts or confronting an opponent. Rex Ambler discusses the use of direct action, non-cooperation and civil disobedience as examples, and both he and April Carter discuss important differences between violent and nonviolent conflict. The second aspect of nonviolence explored by the authors concerns nonviolence as a way of life, as a basis for social organization. A nonviolent society for these authors would avoid social hierarchies and discrimination, political and economic oppression and war. Geoffrey Ostergaard describes such an ideal society, the Sarvodaya society, and its resemblance to historical utopias and peaceful societies.

Gandhian Peacemaking

REX AMBLER

The Gandhian approach to conflict and peace is inspired by Indian ideas that may be very strange to those of us who do not share an Indian background. I want to try and make those ideas intelligible in our own context so that we can consider how this distinctive approach to peace might be applicable to us. Let us consider four elements in the process of making peace.

Understanding the conflict

Our response to a conflict, whether we are directly involved or not, is partly determined by our understanding or perception of it. I think it is fair to say that we tend to see conflicts as a clash of interests, and that we therefore see the resolution of conflict as a struggle for power which must result in either one side winning or the two coming to some compromise agreement. This attitude is particularly prevalent in the 'realistic' and almost cynical atmosphere of the West today. The Gandhian approach is very different from this. It does not accept conflicts at face value, but regards them as in some respects rooted in illusion. This is not to say that conflicts are illusory, but that they are instigated and maintained by illusions, among other things. The racist attitude that prompted the struggle in South Africa in the 1890s was, according to Gandhi, based on the 'error' that Indians were intrinsically inferior to Europeans. The British attitude in India was grounded in a similarly false perception of human beings. So in each case the struggle against oppression took the form of an assertion of truth, i.e. an attempt to dispel the illusion that supported oppression. Gandhi chose a word for this kind of struggle which expressed the point precisely, although sadly its significance has been ignored. It was *satyagraha*, which in Sanskrit means 'adherence to truth' or 'commitment to truth'; it could also mean—read in a different way—'truth-force', a striking alternative to brute physical force. Gandhi wrote in 1922: 'The struggle on behalf of the people mostly consists in opposing error in the shape of unjust laws.'[1]

It could be said that 'errors' such as these simply masked the self-serving interests of those in power. That may be so, and Gandhi was not resistant to the idea that false ideas were rooted in selfishness. Indeed this is the essence of the Indian doctrine of *maya* which Gandhi imbibed. But selfishness in its turn is rooted in illusion. In this case the ultimate illusion is that each individual (or group) is separate from everything and everyone else and has to look after its own interests first at the expense of others. The truth is that we are not ultimately separate, but profoundly tied together in the unity of life. And it was this overriding truth which Gandhi devoted his life to realizing. So in any specific conflict in which he became involved he found it necessary both to dispel the illusion, or layers of illusion, and to reveal the underlying truth of the unity between human beings.

Confronting the opponent

The process of making peace includes two activities which may seem contradictory, and which are certainly difficult to undertake simultaneously. One is the active and persistent rejection of the falsehoods imposed by the other side. The other is a positive affirmation of the opponent as in truth a fellow human being. Gandhi resisted British imperialism very strongly, of course, but he also said, 'we [Indians] must resolutely refuse to think of our opponents [the British] as enemies of the country'.[2] And again, 'Whilst we may attack measures and systems, we may not, must not attack men. Imperfect ourselves, we must be tender towards others and slow to impute motives.'[3]

The immediate application of this principle is to rely on persuasion in the attempt to win the opponent over, rather than on force or other coercive tactics. To give the opponent every chance of a decent response the case should be set out as clearly as possible with all the relevant facts and claims. But if petitioning, argument, discussion all fail then, and only then, should we resort to direct action: to non-cooperation, fasts, civil disobedience, and such like. (These three forms of direct action comprise almost all the actions undertaken by Gandhi himself.) In situations where deep self-interest was at stake this was nearly always necessary. 'Never has anything been done on earth without direct action,' Gandhi said rather emphatically.[4] Even then the intention is to persuade, not to coerce, although in practice it may be very difficult to make this distinction clear or to prevent a persuasive tactic from becoming coercive in fact. The opponent has to be helped to read our actions by generous explanation and by the general tone of a campaign. But also, and most importantly, the actions themselves have to be expressive of the truth they are witness to. The most effective actions in which Gandhi engaged had a high degree of symbolism, and of a sort that spoke directly to the hearts of those involved. Not many people, whether British or Indian, could have missed the symbolic point of a boycott of imported British cloth and a simultaneous use of the old Indian spinning wheel. And the dramatic march to Dandi beach across 240 miles, climaxing with Gandhi picking up salt, had a communicative power which galvanized the whole nation and made the British think again about Indian independence. In both these actions, a refusal to cooperate with injustice was combined symbolically with a positive affirmation of the alternative.

Fasting is perhaps for us the most obscure form of action. It is however part of the Indian tradition to deny oneself food both to purify oneself and to convince others of one's sincerity.[5] If we ever had such a tradition in the West it has been largely forgotten. When Gandhi fasted it was understood by his fellow Indians that he was taking the suffering of the conflict upon himself in an attempt to overcome his own self-interest in the conflict (self-purification) and to reassure his followers and friends that the truth they were fighting for was above anyone's immediate self-interest. He did not however fast 'against' his opponents, for in his view such action would have been coercive. On one occasion when his fast was taken to be coercive by his opponent—the mill-strike of 1918—Gandhi reckoned he had made a big mistake. It is not clear, however, that Gandhi always took account of the unintended impact of his actions. It may be that his own purity prevented him appreciating the real ambiguity of direct action. This is an issue we still have to work through. But one way or another, as Gandhi said. 'reason has to be strengthened by suffering, and suffering opens the eyes of understanding.'[6]

There are surely resources in the Western tradition for making sense of that insight. I am thinking especially, of course, of the suffering of Christ.

Closely allied with self-suffering is the refusal to cause suffering to others, i.e. the discipline of nonviolence. Gandhi fused these two disciplines in his own practice, although it is helpful analytically to distinguish them. In the Indian tradition in fact *ahimsa* (nonviolence or noninjury) is quite distinct from *tapasya* (self-suffering),[7] and both as well are to be distinguished from the Christian idea of love as a service which Gandhi also took on. But in bringing these three together he put each of them to new use, transferring them from merely individual quests for truth to social and political action. Nonviolence became an active engagement in conflict, without inflicting violence on others, whilst self-suffering became a willingness to accept violence from others, which in itself of course further emphasized the nonviolence of the direct action. And both were made socially creative by being harnessed to actions that positively supported the interests of opponents.

Nonviolent action in Gandhi's campaign was often a dramatization of opposites (a point highlighted by the feature film, *Gandhi*). Violence was met with nonviolence, unreason with reason, injustice with justice, inhumanity with humanity. It exemplified the fundamental strategy of Gandhian peacemaking, which was to embody the goals to be struggled for in the conduct of the struggle itself. In any event the way the struggle was conducted would affect the outcome far more than any stated aims, as can be seen in the destabilizing effect of any violent campaign. Gandhi would never accept that the end justified the means, and for the shrewd reason that a bad means would produce a bad end. This indeed was his strongest argument against the use of violence. Violence might be effective in the short term, but it alienates an opponent and makes dialogue impossible. Nonviolence on the other hand 'softens' the opponent and creates the conditions of dialogue, which, as Vinoba Bhave says,[8] is the whole point of the exercise. Being soft on the opponent and hard on oneself is no easy option, though nonviolent action is often treated as if it were. Gandhi himself had problems in convincing people of this. It got confused with 'passive resistance', for example, which was partly Gandhi's own fault since he had used the phrase himself to describe his campaigns in South Africa. He meant, of course, that resistance was not to be violent or forceful. It was taken instead to mean that it was not to be active and assertive. But, he said: 'Yours . . . should be an active thing which will carry the war into the enemy's camp.'[9]

Confronting oneself

This, we might think, is the last consideration in a situation of conflict. We need to be sure of ourselves and strong in the presentation of our case. How can we stand up to injustice if we do not assert ourselves? But Gandhi has some unusual advice: 'A person who claims to be a *satyagrahi* (a practitioner of *satyagraha*) always tries by close and prayerful self-introspection and self-analysis to find out whether he is himself completely free from the taint of anger, ill-will and other such human infirmities, whether he is not himself capable of those very evils against which he is out to lead a crusade. In self-purification and penance lies half the victory of a *satyagrahi*.'[10]

Gandhi is describing here a psychological process which we have come to know as 'projection', but which is all too rarely taken account of in situations of conflict. It has, however, been taken up recently in a psychological study of the arms race. Jeremy Holmes writes: 'Each of the superpowers sees in its opponent an image of its own ambition, expansionism and desire for absolute superiority. This terrifying vision of the enemy then fuels the race for more fearsome deterrents on each side. In this atmosphere of mutual projection it is impossible for each side realistically to assess the threat which the other poses.'[11] They are caught up in a process of illusion-in-the-making, deceiving both themselves and others as to the reality of the situation. This in turn leads to further polarization in which each side sees the other as its diametric opposite, containing all that is bad, while seeing itself as wholly good and pure. The only way out of this dilemma, short of destructive conflict, is the Gandhian way: that each side measure itself honestly and searchingly by the standards it applies to the opponent. More positively, that each side regard the confrontation as a unique occasion for self-discovery and self-change. This will encourage the other side also to examine itself, and without showing 'weakness' or losing 'face'. It would defuse the need to be defensive.

Gandhi himself was remarkably, even disturbingly, frank about his own inadequacies and those of his fellow Indians, even while trying to convince the British of theirs. But the effect of this apparently counterproductive exercise in humility was that the British were made to believe that Gandhi was genuinely trying to be fair. In this context he could afford to assert himself and his (and Indians') rights because he was manifestly appealing to a universal sense of justice and not to his own self interest. And to create and maintain that shared sense of justice is surely necessary in any peacemaking process.

Building confidence

To be aware of truth or justice is one thing. To believe that we or our opponents can put it into practice is quite another. An awareness of our own inadequacy and/or a projection of that inadequacy on to our opponents can undermine our confidence in achieving something together. Moreover, the damaging and exaggerated criticisms that are hurled both ways in a heated conflict can have a deeper effect than we like to admit: they can undermine all our self-confidence. This can also happen if we suffer oppression for a very long time, for we tend to 'introject' the false idea of our basic inferiority. In either case we are left grasping at some other illusory self-image to compensate for our inner despair; and in desperately asserting that self-image to convince our opponents we may do the very same thing to them. The confidence between us is then virtually destroyed. In this dark confusion we need to find ways of building confidence both in ourselves and in our relations with others.

The Gandhian approach therefore includes within and alongside the confrontation itself a parallel activity of confidence-building. An obvious example of this would be supporting the other side in an enterprise quite unconnected with the issue at stake, as when Gandhi organized an ambulance unit during the Zulu War in South Africa. Perhaps less obvious, but equally effective, are the following.

Making a study of the other's point of view

This may require a big imaginative leap, and perhaps some experience of what it is like to be in their situation. Gandhi cultivated friendships for this purpose, listening intently to other people's stories. Certainly, for us to understand the protagonists in Northern Ireland or the officials in the Kremlin we need more than a TV eye view of them. We have somehow to listen to what they are saying. But '. . . immediately we begin to think of things as our opponents think of them we shall be able to do them full justice.

I know that this requires a detached state of mind, and is a state very difficult to reach. Nevertheless, for a *satyagraha* it is absolutely essential. Three fourths of all the miseries and misunderstandings in the world will disappear, if we step into the shoes of our adversaries and understand their viewpoint.'[12]

Refusing to embarrass the opponent

'It is often forgotten,' Gandhi wrote, 'that it is never the intention of the *satyagrahi* to embarrass the wrong-doer. The appeal is never to his fear; it is, it must be, always to his heart. The *satyagrahi*'s object is to convert, not to coerce, the wrong-doer.'[13] This is a far cry from contemporary British politics where the main electoral weapon (sic) is a convincing (illusory) 'image', and where the most effective counter-attack is to break the image by 'embarrassing' the politicians concerned.

Accepting compromise so as not to inflict defeat

This does not mean accepting defeat either. But in either case the point is not to win, but to achieve some justice and peace. Gandhian compromise has at least the positive value that it enables the opponent to save face. And a sense of mutual satisfaction in a compromise settlement can lay the ground for further dialogue. This in itself requires a certain 'detached state of mind' because we easily become attached to winning.

Winning at a pace that all can follow

Gandhi's own leadership may seem a bit autocratic to us. But he was always concerned to take the people with him. If a nonviolent campaign became violent he called it off, perhaps retiring for years till the people were ready. If the British were at war he held back his demands until they were in a decent position to negotiate. This is no strategy for leaders who want justice now. But it is worth reflecting on the price that has been paid by modern revolutions that could not wait for the people to catch up.

Becoming more independent in practice

The best antidote to a feeling of inferiority or dependency is to learn to look after yourself. The best way out of economic and political oppression is to provide for yourself in the basic necessities of life. This was Gandhi's simple prescription for India and the poor nations of the world. In this respect he was very realistic about the conflict with Britain which, in his view, was rooted in Britain's expansive economy and its exploitation of India's labour, resources and markets. But his answer to the problem was not first of all to get rid of the British, but to get India to look after itself so that it no longer needed others to provide for it or feared others who might dominate it. He therefore devoted much, if not most, of his time to what he called 'constructive work' at the grassroots level. From a position of basic self-sufficiency it would then be possible not only to achieve real independence but also to have relations with other countries which were genuinely just and peaceful. Part of the work of peace is away from the point of conflict in the creation of conditions that are conducive to peace. Is this perhaps the most important part?

Notes

1. An article in *Young India*, 1922, cited in Duncan, R. (ed.). *Selected Writings of Mahatma Gandhi*. London: Fontana, 1971, p. 65.
2. *Young India*, 29 September 1921.
3. *Young India*, 25 May 1921.
4. Bose, N. K. (ed.). *Selections from Gandhi*. Navajivan: Ahmedabad, 1948, p. 159.
5. For details, see Bashan, A. L. 'Traditional influences on the thoughts of Mahatma Gandhi'. In Kumar, K. (ed.). *Essays on Gandhian Politics*. Oxford: OUP, 1971, pp. 28–39.
6. *Young India,* 19 March 1925.
7. Cf. Saxena, S. K. 'The fabric of self-suffering: a study in Gandhi', *Religious Studies,* 12 June 1976, pp. 239–247.
8. Bhane, Vinoba. *Vinoba on Gandhi*. Serva Sava Sangh Prakashan: Varanasi, 1973, e.g., p. 52: 'The essence of *satyagraha* is to have only good intentions and to persuade the opponent to see your point, to carry on a dialogue patiently and to discover your own faults in the process. Often it happens that the opponent, because of imaginary self-interest or because of anger, attachment or other passions, is not ready to listen. This provides the occasion for enduring suffering and for the other disciplines of non-violence. But this provokes thinking in its turn and what follows is solely [in] the sphere of thought. So the chief characteristic of *satyagraha* is constantly to apply thought and to develop it and to be ever ready to understand the thought of the opponent.'
9. Bose, N. K. *Selection from Gandhi*, p. 159.
10. *Collected Works of Mahatma Gandhi*, Vol. 41. New Delhi: Ministry of Information, 1950, p. 203.
11. In a collection of essays edited by Ian Fenton, *The Psychology of Nuclear Conflict*, Shaftesbury, Dorset: Conventure, 1986.
12. *Collected Works*, Vol. 26, p. 271.
13. *Collected Works,* Vol. 69, p. 69. I owe this and some other quotations cited to an unpublished paper by Stephen Bay on 'The non-relevance and relevance of Gandhi's goals and procedure to the US-Soviet Union embroilment,' delivered to the International Gandhi Colloquium at Claremont, California, in 1983.

A Gandhian Perspective on Development*

GEOFFREY OSTERGAARD

In Gandhi's view, the colonial policies of Western states were a product of their industrialism. Political domination of the colonized countries facilitated their economic exploitation. The colonies were treated as the source of raw materials for factories in the imperial countries where they were made into finished goods mainly for sale in colonial markets. In the process, the traditional local, largely self-sufficient economies of colonized countries were either destroyed or seriously disrupted. India provided a glaring example. Its once flourishing cottage industry of hand-made textiles, second only in importance to agriculture, had been virtually destroyed. As a consequence, unemployment and poverty had increased, village economies had been thrown off balance, and the communities based on them undermined. The solution to the problems could not, however, be found by India becoming an industrial state on the Western model. That would still leave the villages—'the real India'—exploited by the cities, even if they were Indian rather than British ones. And it would mean India itself joining the ranks of the exploiting nations. The solution was to be found, not in mass production located in cities with dehumanized workers using machines owned by others, but in production by the masses in the villages, with people using machines they themselves owned and controlled. In short the solution was to be found in the spinning wheel, the *charkha*. Not, of course, in the instrument itself, but in all it symbolized for Gandhi.

For him it symbolized many things. Village industries and crafts that could provide work for unemployed villagers, making their migration to the cities unnecessary. There was also the simplicity in living, not to be identified with poverty, which was a great scourge that had to be, and could be, eliminated. For as Gandhi put it, 'There is enough in the world for man's need but not for his greed.' The *charkha* also symbolized the importance of 'bread labour'—

---

* Abridged from the original paper by Geoffrey Ostergaard which appeared in G. Chester and A. Rigby (eds.), *Articles of Peace*, Bridport, Dorset: Prism Press, 1986, pp. 142–168.

the idea that everybody, in earning their daily sustenance, should at least work part of the time with their hands, thus overcoming the age-old division between mental and manual labour. Further, it symbolized an economy based on the principle of *swadeshi*. Originally this meant the boycott of foreign-made goods; but Gandhi extended his meaning to embrace self-reliance and self-sufficiency. Self-sufficiency did not imply complete economic independence. Interdependence was an inescapable and also welcome fact of life. But it did imply that each local, as well as national, community should be capable of meeting its basic material needs. Beyond the economic, *swadeshi* implied a way of serving the world through serving one's local community: 'it is the spirit in us which restricts us to the use and service of our immediate surroundings to the exclusion of the more remote.' Again the *charkha* symbolized the need for creative self-expression, and the satisfaction that comes from making objects of real use to people. And, not least of all, the *charkha* symbolized a non-exploitative technology.

Gandhi's condemnation of the machine—his term for technology—was open to misinterpretation. In *Hind Swaraj*, a booklet written in 1909 while he was still in South Africa, Gandhi emphasized the exploitative and enslaving nature of industrialism. Later, he expanded on this theme: 'There should be no place for machines that concentrate power in a few hands and turn the masses into mere machine-minders, if indeed they do not make them unemployed . . . there would be no objection to villagers using even the most modern machines and tools they can make and afford to use.'[1] It was not technology as such that Gandhi objected to, but industrialism. Industrialism had been the product of capitalism, but, again, capitalism as such was not the root of the problem. Hence, simply replacing capitalism with socialism would not solve it. Perceptively, he observed, 'Pandit Nehru wants industrialization because he thinks that if it is socialized, it would be free from the evils of capitalism. My view is that the evils are inherent in industrialism and no amount of socialism can eradicate them.'[2]

The promotion of *khadi* (handspun, handwoven cloth) became the best known item in Gandhi's Constructive Programme. This comprised 18 items but the list was open-ended, and one item, economic equality, was described as 'the master key to nonviolent independence'.[3] The underlying purpose of the Programme was the rehabilitation of Indian society, without which, in Gandhi's view, *swaraj* (self-government) could not be attained or have real meaning. In present parlance, it was his practical programme for development. It reflected also the positive face of nonviolence. Nonviolent resistance to the British, though necessary, reflected the negative face. He believed, indeed, that if workers made a success of the Programme, independence could be achieved without civil disobedience. However, towards the end of his life Gandhi confessed that he had got his priorities wrong: fearing to estrange co-workers, he had placed civil disobedience before constructive work. The nonviolence displayed in the independence struggle, he concluded, had been largely that of the weak, not the strong. 'Nonviolence of the weak' was Gandhi's phrase for 'pragmatic' as distinct from 'principled' nonviolence—adopted because violent weapons are not available or because their use, in a particular struggle, is judged inexpedient. Although his own nonviolence was 'principled', he had promoted nonviolence as a 'policy' rather than as a 'creed' in the belief that it would be effective as a policy, but also in the hope that its adoption as a policy would lead to its acceptance as a creed. In the event, his hopes were largely dashed, and at his death he left unresolved the vexing issue of the relationship between pragmatic and principled nonviolence.

It is clear, however, that Gandhi did not regard nonviolent action merely as a political technique. 'Technique' suggests a framework of thought in which means are separable from ends. This framework has become dominant in the West in modern times but it is not Gandhi's framework. He saw human action as a continuous process in which ends and means are distinguishable temporally but not morally. This implies that means are never merely instrumental; they are also always expressive of values: ends-in-the-making. The relationship between the two is not technical, but, like seed and tree, organic. And, since one can never be sure of attaining one's ends, one should concentrate on means, which are within one's control. Then, if the means are pure, the end-result will coincide with the end-goal.

Because the Constructive Programme represented Gandhi's positive means, it prefigured his end-goal: the *sarvodaya* society—a society dedicated to 'the raising up and the welfare of all'. Since the state is 'violence in a concentrated form',[4] *sarvodaya* is a stateless society in which all political and legal authority have been abrogated, relations between people being governed only by moral authority. Structurally, it is 'a great society of small communities', each autonomous and self-governing but linked with others in a non-hierarchical network—part of an 'oceanic circle', to use Gandhi's more vivid image. Internally, such community is a participatory democracy, taking decisions by consensus, so that individual and collective self-government coincide. Each community is self-sufficient in meeting its basic needs for food, clothing and shelter. Agriculture is the main occupation, but there are various other small-scale industries, organized cooperatively and using a technology that serves human needs. Any large-scale industry that may be necessary is organized on a federal basis. Private property in the capitalist sense and public property in the state socialist sense do not exist. Instead, the principle of trusteeship prevails: all property, however 'owned', including the natural talents of individuals, is held on trust for the service of all. Economic equality, interpreted to mean distribution according to needs, is the rule, and the society is classless. But equality is combined with respect for freedom of the individual—the person at the centre of the 'oceanic circle'.

The *sarvodaya* society is, of course, an ideal society and, like all ideals, it may never be fully realized. But it indicates the direction in which, so Gandhians believe, Indian society and, eventually, societies throughout the world should move. The *sarvodaya* society, it should be noted, resembles that visualized by libertarian socialists, such as the Owenite cooperators, the Russian populists, and Kropotkinian anarchist-communists. It is located squarely in the tradition of 'village communism' which contrasts sharply with Bolshevik Communism. 'Communism which is imposed on people,' wrote Gandhi, 'would be repugnant to India. I believe in nonviolent Communism . . . If Communism comes without any violence it would be most welcome.'[5]

'Without any violence' implied in Gandhi's view that development should proceed from below and not be directed from above by the state. Hence, on the eve of his assassination, 30 January 1948, he proposed that the Congress, having attained political independence, should disband as a political party and become a constructive work organization with the task of achieving 'real *swaraj*' for India's villages. The proposal was rejected and, instead, the Congress, with Nehru waving the banner of democratic socialism, sought to develop India as a modern, industrialized nation-state. It was left to a few thousand constructive workers, led by Vinoba Bhave and Jayaprakash Narayan, to pursue Gandhi's strategy. This they did through campaigns for *Bhoodan* (landgifts) and, later, *Gramdan* (voluntary villagization of land), the emphasis, until 1947, being heavily on constructive rather than resistive nonviolence. As a result of the campaigns, in the course of which they elaborated Gandhi's concept of nonviolent revolution, half a million landless labourers were given land and a few thousand *Gramdan* villages have begun to develop in the Gandhian way. But the overall impact on the wider society has been limited and today Gandhi's vision of an India of village republics remains largely a dream.[6]

Notes

1. Gandhi, M. K. *Village Swaraj.* Ahmedabad: Navajivan, 1963, p. 14.
2. Ibid.
3. Gandhi, M. K. *The Constructive Programme,* rev. edn. Ahmedabad: Navajivan, 1945. Among the items is achieving equality of status and opportunity for women.
4. Bose, N. K. *Selections from Gandhi.* Ahmedabad: Navajivan, 1957, p. 41.
5. Quoted in Bideleux, R. *Communism and Development.* New York: Methuen, 1985, p. 48.
6. For an account of the movement, see my *Nonviolent Revolution in India.* Gandhi Peace Foundation: New Delhi/Housmans: London, 1985.

Nonviolence as a Strategy for Change

APRIL CARTER

The history of how people have tried to change society is often presented as the history of wars and violent revolutions. But there is a significant if less visible tradition of nonviolent resistance. Religious believers have upheld and practised their faith despite state suppression and at the cost of martyrdom—this was true of the early Christians and of persecuted Christians since. Conquered nations like the Poles have kept alive over long periods their language, culture, history and hope of political independence. The campaign to extend democratic rights has often depended on illegal pamphleteering, meetings and mass demonstrations, while the labour movement has won many victories through strikes and boycotts. Even revolutions have often begun with popular demonstrations, strikes and appeals to the military to defect, as in February 1917 in Russia.

Nonviolence, like violence, can be interpreted narrowly or given a much wider meaning. Violence may simply mean inflicting physical hurt or damage, but is often extended to cover inflicting psychological hurt and to denote repressive social institutions and practices. When Franz Fanon, a theorist of the Algerian revolution against the French, denounced colonialism as an expression of violence he meant a system of oppression and racial denigration which denied dignity and autonomy to colonized peoples, as well as a system which resorted to torture and killing of those who dared to rebel against it.[1] Similarly, nonviolence must at minimum imply refraining from taking up arms or killing or wounding people. When people adopt nonviolent methods of protest or resistance for purely tactical reasons this may be all that nonviolence means to them. But belief in nonviolence in principle does involve rejection of any use of physical violence on moral grounds and also includes a commitment to try to persuade or convert an opponent to see the justice of one's cause. The aim of a nonviolent struggle based on a philosophy of nonviolence is not victory over the other side, but mutual gain through realizing an intrinsically good end. Nonviolence may

210

also be understood as a basis for social organization: a nonviolent society would avoid social hierarchies and discrimination, political and economic oppression and war. Finally, it can be embraced as a personal way of life.

Nonviolence as a strategy for change was developed most fully by Mahatma Gandhi in his campaigns centred on the goal of independence from Britain.[2] Gandhi's campaign involved large numbers in non-cooperation and civil disobedience, but also stressed the need for nonviolent discipline and seeking a settlement recognized as just by all concerned. Gandhi was prepared to call off a campaign that turned violent and to make compromises with his opponents. The Gandhian strategy included a strong emphasis on a constructive commitment to develop economic independence for India, symbolized by spinning and weaving their own cloth, and promoting a vision of democracy based on local autonomy. Gandhi campaigned to end the injustices inherent within Indian society, in particular the caste discrimination of Hinduism and the plight of the untouchables, and the growing divisions between Hindus and Muslims. He also believed in the power of example and practised an ascetic and spiritual mode of life based on his own nonviolent community.

Gandhi fused religious values and practices, for example fasting, with political goals and a shrewd political strategy. Much of his inspiration for adopting nonviolence stemmed from religious traditions. Nonviolent principles can be found in Buddhism and in the Christian gospels, and the latter have promoted a tradition of nonviolence, first among the early Christians and later among various sects that rebelled against established churches and tried to live by Christ's teaching in the gospels. Many of these groups created before or during the Reformation withdrew as far as possible from all involvement in the state, the law and politics, not only refusing to bear arms but to hold any public office, and concentrating on spiritual salvation. But there has been a more activist and political strand of Christian pacifism, represented for example by the Quakers, which found expression in the manifesto of a small group of Americans, who came together in 1838 to found the New England Non-Resistance Society and urge active but nonviolent opposition to war and all preparations for war.[3]

The writings of Adin Ballou elaborating on the concept of non-resistance influenced Leo Tolstoy, who in later life was passionately opposed to the organized violence of the state, expressed in floggings, hangings and war and to the economic oppression resulting from a few owning large tracts of land and major industrial enterprises on which the majority of peasants and workers depended.[4] Tolstoy called for a return to the pure precepts of the gospels and argued that if the exploited peoples refused to cooperate with their political and economic masters' tyranny, colonialism and other government hierarchies would collapse and that mass refusal to serve in the armed forces would prevent further wars. Tolstoy's political essays were read by Gandhi when he was beginning to develop his own concept of nonviolent resistance and to blend a strategy of political noncooperation and challenging disobedience with a nonviolent philosophy he found in the Hindu religion, in particular the *Bhagavad-Gita.*

Gandhi's examples and ideas had a considerable influence on other movements. Nonviolent methods of noncooperation and civil disobedience were taken up by some African parties campaigning for independence from the British, by the Civil Rights Movement in the Deep South of the USA in the late 1950s and by Western peace movements to protest against military policies, in particular nuclear weapons testing and nuclear bases. Martin Luther King, Jr. was inspired by the Gandhian philosophy of nonviolence and in the civil rights campaigns he led combined nonviolent tactics with a strong emphasis on Christian values of love and forgiveness towards white racists.[5] But most of those who were directly or indirectly influenced by Gandhi's strategy focused on the possibilities of nonviolent resistance as a method of struggle.

Western theorists of nonviolent resistance have set out to translate Gandhian ideas into a more acceptable vocabulary. Gandhi used Hindu terms for his key concepts—for example *satyagraha*, literally 'holding on to truth', for his technique of nonviolent resistance— which made his thought culturally alien and could make it seem irrelevant. Western writers also related Gandhian ideas to Western psychology and Western political thought, as well as linking the method of nonviolent struggle to wider historical examples of nonviolent resistance, for example the Hungarians' struggle through noncooperation to win independence from Austria in the nineteenth century. Finally, theorists of nonviolent resistance often saw it not only as an effective and creative means of opposing social evils or foreign rule, but as a moral and political alternative to war. These themes were taken up by Richard Gregg in a now classic work *The Power of Nonviolence*, first published in 1935.[6] Gregg laid particular stress on the 'moral jiu-jitsu' achieved by nonviolent resisters who accepted imprisonment or physical injury without retaliating and demonstrated courage and willingness to suffer voluntarily for their cause, and on how nonviolent resistance could sap the morale of the opposite side and work through its persuasive power.

Gene Sharp, best known contemporary theorist of nonviolent action, has laid most emphasis on the power of noncooperation, noting how a ruler's power depends on the obedience of his subjects, and that even a regime relying largely on enforced obedience through terror relies on the willing obedience of the police and armed forces.[7] There are indeed examples of nonviolent resistance under the most repressive regimes, for example the strikes in the Vorkuta labour camps in the Soviet Union where prisoners demanded abolition of the camps very soon after the death of Stalin in 1953. Some of the most impressive examples of mass noncooperation and nonviolent resistance come from Nazi-occupied Europe during World War Two, especially the successful opposition by Norwegian teachers and other professionals to the imposition of a fascist state, and the cooperation by the Danes to save the lives of the Danish Jews. Examples of national resistance to colonial occupation, to German occupation in World War Two and to Soviet armed force in eastern Europe—in particular the initial Czechoslovak refusal to surrender the gains of the Prague Spring in the face of Soviet occupation in August 1968—have encouraged research into the possibility of a nation deterring occupation by systematic preparations for nonviolent resistance. Although defence through nonviolent methods was first proposed in the 1930s, this idea has gained in urgency and persuasiveness since the invention of nuclear weapons.[8]

There is a good deal of evidence, both from spontaneous examples of nonviolent action and from consciously nonviolent campaigns, that nonviolent resistance can be effective. There are also persuasive arguments why nonviolent methods of struggle are preferable to violent ones, both morally and politically. But there are important questions and problems to be raised about the effectiveness of nonviolent methods, their applicability in all situations, and the realism of nonviolent prescriptions.

One common objection is that nonviolence may work against a moderate opponent like the British, in a context where there was explicit support for Indian independence freely expressed within Britain itself, but it will not work against a ruthless and dictatorial regime. Civilian resistance to German occupation in the Second World War is not a wholly convincing rebuttal of this argument, since the major examples occurred in countries where Nazi rule was mildest and in a context of hope for liberation by the Allied powers. But sustained nonviolent resistance to dictatorship—especially the kind of open defiance embodied in Gandhian nonviolence—may require quite impossible levels of heroism.

It follows from this objection that nonviolent resistance may sometimes be impossible, even though in theory noncooperation could topple the regime or undermine a system of racial or economic oppression. Doubts as to whether nonviolence can necessarily overthrow foreign occupation also raises questions about the validity of a defence policy based purely on nonviolent resistance. There are other difficulties too about this particular application of nonviolent methods of struggle—defence policy is intended to deter a wide range of threats to national security and actual occupation may be a remote danger.

Proponents of nonviolence can legitimately respond that violent resistance too is often ineffective. Indeed a well-armed and ruthless regime may find it easier to quell some forms of guerrilla warfare or violent uprising than a major strike or mass noncooperation, the reprisals are often even more savage, and repression of violence is easier to justify, internally and externally, if any justification is required. The case for nonviolence rests heavily on the destruction and suffering caused by resort to violence, in particular in modern warfare. If defence of people's lives and way of life depends on weapons which could, if used, result in total destruction of that society, and if humane and civilized values are to be defended by inhumane weapons of mass destruction, there is a total disjunction between the declared ends and the means.

One central tenet in the theory of nonviolence is that there must be congruence between ends and means. Means that are ignoble or destructive, and that generate hatred, ruthlessness or intolerance among those who resort to them, will corrupt the ends. So if national independence is won by violent struggle there will be a temptation for groups who lose out politically in the new state to resort again to the gun. Or if a struggle for freedom is waged by a military organization requiring strict hierarchy and military obedience, those principles may be carried over into the organization of the independent country and there will be a temptation to crush political opponents and forget the true meaning of freedom. The belief that a just society could only be attained by good means was at the heart of Gandhi's philosophy and is maintained by later theorists of nonviolent struggle. The argument may be over-simplified (certainly use of violence or nonviolence may not be the only relevant factor affecting the outcome of a struggle and the subsequent nature of that society), but it does have considerable force.

There is however a rather different objection that can be raised, and that is the difficulty of ensuring any major campaign remains nonviolent. The historical evidence indicates that this is a real difficulty. Although a particular demonstration may remain totally nonviolent, any prolonged strike, boycott or other form of noncooperation is likely to be marked by sporadic violence if not actual riots. It must also involve psychological coercion, if not outright violence and intimidation, against blacklegs or those who refuse to join in the resistance and demonstrate solidarity in the struggle. There is also a tendency for a campaign which begins with nonviolent action to escalate into violence over time, because nonviolence is seen to be ineffective, or because even though it has gained some success it seems insufficiently radical. For example, the African National Congress in South Africa moved from nonviolent protest in the 1950s to guerrilla warfare, and the US Civil Rights Movement, despite gains in breaking down segregation in the South, gave way to the Black Power movement of the later 1960s that looked to guerrilla warfare, not to Gandhi, as a model.

There are psychological reasons for the tendency to resort to violence, which is often a natural response to anger and frustration and a way of reacting to and denying fear. There is also a deep-seated identification of the image of the warrior with courage, pride and assertiveness, and indeed with true masculinity, in Western and many other cultures. This image encourages romanticization of violent action and of the bearing of arms, and promotes distrust and dislike of nonviolence, often quite falsely characterized as 'passive' or acquiescent.

The advocate of nonviolence can respond that the incidental violence which may arise out of mass noncooperation is different in kind from deliberate resort to guerrilla warfare and does not invalidate the value of effectiveness of the method itself—though if popular violence turns into sustained rioting there may be a case for trying to end the campaign temporarily. One possible approach is to try to train people for nonviolent action so that they retain a nonviolent discipline, but this is only possible for small numbers who might undertake exemplary civil disobedience or be assigned to lead local protests. As for the continuing psychological attractions of violence, it is the aim of nonviolent action to translate courage, dignity and assertiveness into an effective form of struggle, and Gandhi stressed that nonviolence should require more, not less, bravery than violence. Now that television transmits to us directly examples of popular nonviolent resistance, for example the overthrow of President Marcos in part by demonstrations of 'people's power' in the Philippines, the image of nonviolent action may become more positive. Warlike attitudes, soldierly virtues and indeed definitions of masculinity itself are also being challenged by both peace movements and by feminism.

One final criticism of nonviolent struggle that we should note briefly here is that because it implies moderation and compromise it does not pose a radical challenge to vested economic or political interests. This is a criticism often made by Marxists. It may also be linked to specific criticisms of Gandhi—for example his acceptance of support from big businessmen—or of Martin Luther King, Jr. for trying to work through the Democratic Party and the political establishment in the USA. Since nonviolence depends in part on persuasion of opponents and does not aim at their total destruction it is less likely to achieve rapid social change than a successful violent revolution, but may avoid too the danger of creating a new form of repression.

The issues of what kind of social policies are promoted by nonviolent campaigns raises the question of what is meant by a nonviolent society. This concept does imply repudiating armed forces for external defence and reliance on a police force and repressive punishment to maintain internal order, and is also closely associated with the idea of decentralizing political and economic power. The goal of a nonviolent society is therefore closely associated with pacificist anarchism—Tolstoy represents this link between nonviolence and anarchism. But there is no consensus on whether a nonviolent society would be strictly anarchist, whether it would be rigorously egalitarian, how the means of production should be owned, and whether it would be compatible with modern technology or, as Gandhi suggested, implies emphasis on a simple and small-scale technology. The method of nonviolent struggle has been much more rigorously conceptualized than the goal of nonviolent society.

Notes

1. Fanon, Franz. *The Wretched of the Earth.* Translated by C. Farrington. London: MacGibbon and Kee, 1965.
2. Bondurant, Joan. *Conquest of Violence: The Gandhian Philosophy of Conflict.* Princeton, NJ: Princeton University Press, 1958.
3. The Society's statement of principles and Adin Ballou's definition of 'non-resistance' can be found in Peter Mayer (ed.), *The Pacifist Conscience.* Harmondsworth: Penguin, 1966.
4. Tolstoy's views were set out in a number of essays and letters. Two of the best known are 'Letter to a Non-commissioned Officer' and 'Letter to a Hindu', which can be found in Peter Mayer, op. cit.
5. See King, Martin Luther. *Stride Toward Freedom.* London: Gollancz, 1959.
6. Gregg, Richard B. *The Power of Nonviolence.* London: James Clarke, 1960.
7. Sharp, Gene. *The Politics of Nonviolent Action.* Boston, Mass.: Porter Sargent, 1973.
8. See King-Hall, Sir Stephen. *Defence in the Nuclear Age.* London: Gollancz, 1958; and Roberts, Adam (ed.). *Civil Resistance as a National Defence Policy.* Harmondsworth: Penguin, 1969.

Nonviolence and Social Change*

NIGEL YOUNG

The legacy of the twentieth century revolutions is ambiguous. Hundreds of millions have been made homeless. Others have been mutilated, maddened or imprisoned. Many have died. The connection between these historical events and the egalitarian, libertarian and humanist ideas of classic socialist thought are tenuous indeed. These ideas declined in the development of the new left which sustained a new cult of militarism in the 1960s—an obsession with armed struggle and polarization which endorses these revolutions as 'progressive', especially those in Cuba, China, Algeria and Vietnam.

Those who seek alternative routes of transforming society, non-military, decentralist, participatory but nevertheless 'revolutionary' in the comprehensiveness of the changes sought, are ridiculed and edged to the margins of the debate. Yet in places like Eastern Europe and Central America, alternatives are essential. In the process both the past, the present and thus possibilities for the future are distorted to emphasize the necessity and desirability of collective violence and coercive change. This could be seen, for example, in South Africa and in the Civil Rights Movement in the United States in the 1960s. The wing around Martin Luther King, Jr. were advocating and practising nonviolent mass actions and attempting to integrate people into civic society with equal access to institutions by peaceful, legal and electoral means. They were accused by the more militant wing around Malcolm X of working to incorporate black people into the status quo. Their Christian pacifist principles and apparent dependence on existing elites were consistently challenged.

The previous history and methods of every revolutionary movement are mirrored in the end product, the new social order. Whether we look at Bolshevik Russia, Zionist Israel or Castro's Cuba the circumstances which surround the emergence of new regimes determine their subsequent actions;

* This article is adapted from the original which appeared in the *New Internationalist* in March 1977. Used with permission.

no revolutionary power structure has yet been able to transcend the specific constellation of necessities which conditioned its development. These developments focus on the coercive apparatus of state power. To seize this apparatus of armed forces, secret police, bureaucrats, etc., a counter-monopoly of violence is needed. Thus in such 'liberation' the waystation to a dispersal of power becomes the concentration of more power; the waystation to internationalism becomes national consolidation; the means to an abolition of violence is the use of even more violence, etc. The means used, far from being compatible with the ends sought, become the exact opposite. No wonder that ostensibly 'socialist' or utopian movements become brutalized and degenerate.

The organization of violence is of itself undemocratic and inegalitarian. Vanguard revolutionary parties and terrorist groups, based on orders and obedience, have no room for political debate. Armies and police forces are amongst the least egalitarian of institutions. Authoritarianism is given a free reign. The exploitation of popular acquiescence by minority power becomes the accepted pattern, an anti-egalitarian pattern that does not disappear with 'victory'. Once the 'seizure of power' is achieved, new outrages can be justified on behalf of whatever the new elite defines as 'revolutionary'. Compulsion and uniformity become both means and ends. Radical transformation or participatory democracy are sacrificed on the altars of necessity and efficiency . . . postponed to somewhere in the hereafter.

The removal of an elite by coup no more guarantees real change of structure than the assassination of one member of that elite; too often the methods of the opponent are imitated—and its structures reproduced, even its agencies of control rehabilitated. The violent origins of any regime are reflected in its pattern of administration and the lifestyle of its ruling class, especially intolerance of opposition. This is especially marked in the use of inherited structures (for example, the bureaucracy, military elites, geopolitical boundaries—even secret police—of the previous regime). This can be seen in particular in countries in Central America and in Africa—and in Vietnam—as well as in the 'classic' revolutions—Russia, China, etc.

A tragic example of this process can be found in the history of the nationalist revolution between 1940–85 in Vietnam. The several protracted wars in Indochina led finally, not to a model of socialist progress, but instead to a centralized state soon at war against most of its neighbors, e.g. China and Kampuchea, which it soon occupied. Internal repression of ethnic Chinese and Catholics, of non-communists and unreliables in re-education camps—even of the pacifist/neutralist Buddhists—led to a mass exodus—many of them as 'boat people'—many to death and exile. Indeed the 'liberation' meant the forcible domination of the southerners by the collectivist state of the North and the rebuilding after the war was both harsh and oppressive. Even the peace or anti-war movements in the West had split between those simply wanting to end the killing and those wanting a victory by the Northern army, to become one of the largest military forces in Asia. The latter tended themselves to imitate the violence of the guerrilla NLF— isolating themselves from friends and the public at large. The movement became like its counterpart, more elitist and intolerant as it became more violent.

The destructiveness of war and mass violence has heavy human costs, and this has an important political effect as well. The loss of life, the misery, the widowing, orphaning and isolation of millions resulting in mental illness, suicide, alcoholism, disease and starvation, all make ordinary people less resistant to dictatorship, and more vulnerable to tyranny once the holocaust is over. This encourages a limited and socially negative definition of power as 'springing from the barrel of a gun'. Yet there is an alternative. By draining support and legitimacy from violent actions and coercive structures, the sources of reactionary violence are undermined. By not forming an army, by not confronting the hierarchies with others, nonviolent movements can occupy new ground, form new institutions. By not taking on the State where it is strongest, for example in collective violence, unarmed struggle can turn the opponent and refuse it self-justification of 'defence' or 'peace-keeping'.

In a limited space there is no chance to survey or amplify the wide variety of techniques and illustrations of such action available (for those who wish to pursue this further, Gene Sharp's encyclopaedic *Politics of Nonviolent Action* details 200 such methods, with hundreds of examples from scores of Western and non-Western societies). Instead it is worth noting the ways in which unarmed struggle offers the hope of transcending the self-destructive character of militarized revolution.

Violence undoes the work of fraternization, communication and education, all essential for the conversion or neutralization of opponents. As the Czech events of 1968 showed, one cannot throw a Molotov cocktail at a person and at the same time expect that person to abandon their role as defender of the status quo or maintain political communication with them. Civil resistance is open and flexible, it subverts rather than confronts the forces of control.

The creative and disruptive effects of nonviolent action are not like those of revolutionary violence. Instead they are linked to the replacement of one set of institutions by another which draws to it popular legitimacy. For example, the use of the general strike, boycott, factory occupation and trades union organizations in the revolution are essential if free trades unions and the right to strike are to be part of the aftermath of the struggle. In too many 'socialist' societies these rights have been lost.

The democratic impulses embodied in the use of popular nonviolent power must be part of the transformation process. For example, the refusal to pay taxes altogether or hold back the percentage of tax that would finance the military complex and resistance to military service as practised in many

Western and Eastern European countries, are both ways of noncooperation with the state, and lay the basis for a less centralist revolution. Conscientious objection is growing in Eastern Europe. But destructive violence would lead to the dangers of a power vacuum into which any organized elite or other state can move. But democratic popular movements lead to a spread of leadership which inhibits elitism and makes selective repression difficult.

Armed violence depersonalizes and brutalizes both the victim and the executioner. It drains humanity, egalitarianism and communicative politics from any situation—and in a revolution that can be disastrous. Even the most idealized revolutionary states have crushed decentralized tendencies in the name of national uniformity and efficiency. Nonviolence on the other hand offers the hope of a continuing dispersal of power, an obstacle to the exploitation of the periphery by the centre, and a socialist pluralism based on a degree of communal autonomy.

A yawning chasm opens up between those who argue for violence as the only means for radical change, and their proclaimed ends. There is no historical evidence which connects violent means with their goals. Moreover, although there is a superficial resemblance of these people's aims with those who endorse non-military means—from the outset the division over means implies fundamentally different visions. Those who argue that there is a difference only in technique delude themselves.

Appendix: The Seville Statement on Violence

Believing that it is our responsibility to address from our particular disciplines the most dangerous and destructive activities of our species, violence and war; recognizing that science is a human cultural product which cannot be definitive or all-encompassing; and gratefully acknowledging the support of the authorities of Seville and representatives of the Spanish UNESCO; we, the undersigned scholars from around the world and from relevant sciences, have met and arrived at the following Statement on Violence. In it, we challenge a number of alleged biological findings that have been used, even by some in our disciplines, to justify violence and war. Because the alleged findings have contributed to an atmosphere of pessimism in our time, we submit that the open, considered rejection of these misstatements can contribute significantly to the International Year of Peace.

Misuse of scientific theories and data to justify violence and war is not new but has been made since the advent of modern science. For example, the theory of evolution has been used to justify not only war, but also genocide, colonialism, and suppression of the weak.

We state our position in the form of five propositions. We are aware that there are many other issues about violence and war that could be fruitfully addressed from the standpoint of our disciplines, but we restrict ourselves here to what we consider a most important first step.

IT IS SCIENTIFICALLY INCORRECT to say that we have inherited a tendency to make war from our animal ancestors. Although fighting occurs widely throughout animal species, only a few cases of destructive intra-species fighting between organized groups have ever been reported among naturally living species, and none of these involve the use of tools designed to be weapons. Normal predatory feeding upon other species cannot be equated with intra-species violence. Warfare is a peculiarly human phenomenon and does not occur in other animals.

The fact that warfare has changed so radically over time indicates that it is a product of culture. Its biological connection is primarily through language which makes possible the coordination of groups, the transmission of

221

technology, and the use of tools. War is biologically possible, but it is not inevitable, as evidenced by its variation in occurrence and nature over time and space. There are cultures which have not engaged in war for centuries, and there are cultures which have engaged in war frequently at some times and not at others.

IT IS SCIENTIFICALLY INCORRECT to say that war or any violent behavior is genetically programed into our human nature. While genes are involved at all levels of nervous system function, they provide a developmental potential that can be actualized only in conjunction with the ecological and social environment. While individuals vary in their predispositions to be affected by their experience, it is the interaction between their genetic endowment and conditions of nurturance that determines their personalities. Except for rare pathologies, the genes do not produce individuals necessarily predisposed to violence. Neither do they determine the opposite. While genes are co-involved in establishing our behavioral capacities, they do not by themselves specify the outcome.

IT IS SCIENTIFICALLY INCORRECT to say that in the course of human evolution there has been a selection for aggressive behavior more than for other kinds of behavior. In all well-studied species, status within the group is achieved by the ability to cooperate and to fulfill social functions relevant to the structure of that group. 'Dominance' involves social bondings and affiliations; it is not simply a matter of the possession and use of superior physical power, although it does involve aggressive behaviors. Where genetic selection for aggressive behavior has been artificially instituted in animals, it has rapidly succeeded in producing hyper-aggressive individuals; this indicates that aggression was not maximally selected under natural conditions. When such experimentally-created hyper-aggressive animals are present in a social group, they either disrupt its social structure or are driven out. Violence is neither in our evolutionary legacy nor in our genes.

IT IS SCIENTIFICALLY INCORRECT to say that humans have a 'violent brain.' While we do have the neural apparatus to act violently, it is not automatically activated by internal or external stimuli. Like higher primates and unlike other animals, our higher neural processes filter such stimuli before they can be acted upon. How we act is shaped by how we have been conditioned and socialized. There is nothing in our neurophysiology that compels us to react violently.

IT IS SCIENTIFICALLY INCORRECT to say that war is caused by 'instinct' or any single motivation. The emergence of modern warfare has been a journey from the primacy of emotional and motivational factors, sometimes called 'instincts,' to the primacy of cognitive factors. Modern war involves institutional use of personal characteristics such as obedience, suggestibility, and idealism, social skills such as language, and rational considerations such as cost-calculation, planning, and information processing. The technology of modern war has exaggerated traits associated with violence both in the training of actual combatants and in the preparation of support for war in the general population. As a result of this exaggeration, such traits are often mistaken to be the causes rather than the consequences of the process.

We conclude that biology does not condemn humanity to war, and that humanity can be freed from the bondage of biological pessimism and empowered with confidence to undertake the transformative tasks needed in this International Year of Peace and in the years to come. Although these tasks are mainly institutional and collective, they also rest upon the consciousness of individual participants for whom pessimism and optimism are crucial factors. Just as 'wars begin in the minds of men,' peace also begins in our minds. The same species who invented war is capable of inventing peace. The responsibility lies with each of us.

Seville, May 16, 1986

David Adams, Psychology, Wesleyan University, Middletown, CT, USA
S. A. Barnett, Ethology, The Australian National University, Canberra, Australia
N. P. Bechtereva, Neurophysiology, Institute for Experimental Medicine of Academy of Medical Sciences of USSR, Leningrad, USSR
Bonnie Frank Carter, Psychology, Albert Einstein Medical Center, Philadelphia, PA, USA
José M. Rodríguez Delgado, Neurophysiology, Centro de Estudios Neurobiológicos, Madrid, Spain
José Luis Díaz, Ethology, Instituto Mexicano de Psiquiatría, Mexico D.F., Mexico
Andrzej Eliasz, Individual Differences Psychology, Polish Academy of Sciences, Warsaw, Poland
Santiago Genovés, Biological Anthropology, Instituto de Estudios Antropolóqicos, Mexico D.F., Mexico
Benson E. Ginsburg, Behavior Genetics, University of Connecticut, Storrs, CT, USA
Jo Groebel, Social Psychology, Erziehungswissenschaftliche Hochschule, Landau, Federal Republic of Germany
Samir-Kumar Ghosh, Sociology, Indian Institute of Human Sciences, Calcutta, India
Robert Hinde, Animal Behavior, Cambridge University, UK
Richard E. Leakey, Physical Anthropology, National Museums of Kenya, Nairobi, Kenya
Taha H. Malasi, Psychiatry, Kuwait University, Kuwait
J. Martin Ramírez, Psychobiology, Universidad de Sevilla, Spain
Federico Mayor Zaragoza, Biochemistry, Universidad Autónoma, Madrid, Spain
Diana L. Mendoza, Ethology, Universidad de Sevilla, Spain
Ashis Nandy, Political Psychology, Center for the Study of Developing Societies, Delhi, India
John Paul Scott, Animal Behavior, Bowling Green State University, Bowling Green, OH, USA
Riitta Wahlström, Psychology, University of Jyväskylä, Finland

Glossary

Acquisitive, acquiring. Valuing the possession of more and more material things.

Adaptive. Capable of fitting different conditions; adjustable.

Administered prices. Prices that are fixed outside the general market, but by an administration (e.g., the Soviet Union).

Affiliate company. Usually a company that is linked to another in some way, often through ownership. A truly 'owned' company is most often described as a subsidiary, but the broader term 'affiliate' or 'affiliate company' may be used to include those linked companies that are not controlled by parent multinational companies.

Aggression. Generally, actions intended to harm others. Since the 1930s the term has been used in international relations to refer to an unprovoked attack by one state upon another.

Arms control. Refers to the international limitation of testing, deployment or use of weapons that, at the same time, accepts the inevitability of the continued existence of national military establishments. Arms control does not prohibit weapons production, but under certain conditions it may have an inhibiting effect. According to some interpretations, it may also include international agreements that do not pertain specifically to weapons, for example, the 'Hot Line' Agreement in 1963 which created a direct link between the leaders of the USA and the USSR.

Arms limitation. The reduction and limitation of national armaments by general international agreement. The possibility of arms limitation did not come before an international assembly until The Hague conventions of 1899 and 1907, which ended in failure. In early 1970, the Strategic Arms Limitations Treaties began between the United States and the Soviet Union. Agreement about reducing nuclear arms was hampered, however, by each country's insistence on bargaining from a position of strength.

Assertive. Having or showing positive assurance.

Balance of payment. A tabulation of the credit and debit transactions of one country with other countries and international institutions. These transactions are divided into two broad groups: current account and capital account.

Capitalism. An economic system in which the means of production are privately owned, capital is concentrated and used to make and accumulate profit and the mass of the population are employees engaging in free wage labour.

Cash crop. A crop primarily for sale, as contrasted with a subsistence crop grown for the use of the grower and/or the grower's family.

Chamber of Deputies. The French parliament.

Chancellor of the Exchequer. In Britain, he is the Cabinet Minister who is responsible for the financial affairs of the country, including the collection and allocation of revenue by the government.

Civil disobedience. When constructive uplift of one's own community is bogged down and nonconfrontational efforts at educating the opponent are falling on deaf ears, it becomes necessary to offer noncooperation or civil disobedience to unjust regulations. The most important guideline for true civil disobedience is that the resister must not attempt to avoid legal penalties for such disobedience.

Civilization. Refers to those societies and cultures which have achieved a degree of historical continuity owing to the development of written language. The development of written language is a watershed in the evolution of societies because it permits the transmission of a set of cultural values and social institutions through the ages. Hence the word 'civilization' is more generally applied to denote broad historical epochs of a type of society, e.g., as in 'Greek civilization', 'Chinese civilization' or 'Western civilization'.

Codes of conduct. First called for at the United Nations Conference on Trade and Development (UNCTAD) in Santiago in 1972. It refers to the formulation of international, regional or sectorial instruments which set standards and principles for the regulation and national treatment of international business.

Collective responsibility. Refers to the principle that each member of a decision-making body holds membership on the condition of accepting full responsibility for all the group's decisions, even those the individual may not agree with. This principle is applied in the British Cabinet.

Collective self-reliance. Includes cooperation, solidarity and trade amongst the developing countries themselves.

Collectivization. The process of amalgamating privately owned farms and/or estates under state supervision and management. In the Soviet Union this was ruthlessly and forcibly carried out under Stalin in the 1930s and has been a common feature of state socialist agriculture in a number of East European states.

Colonialism. (see **Imperialism**)

Commercialization. The production of goods and services principally for exchange in the market as opposed to their production for immediate household or community needs.

Comparative advantage. A theory first developed by David Ricardo in 1817. It applies his law of comparative costs to the field of international trade. Ricardo agreed that when two countries both produce the same two commodities but the relative costs of the production of these commodities differs within each country, that both countries will be better off concentrating their productive efforts on that commodity which they can produce most cheaply, and trade with one another. Thus, in Ricardo's own celebrated example, if England produces both cloth and wine more cheaply (in terms of cost of man-hours) than Portugal, but England produces cloth more cheaply than wine, and Portugal on the other hand produces wine more cheaply than cloth, both countries will gain if England concentrates on producing the cloth and Portugal on wine and they trade the cloth and wine between them.

Comptroller (or controller). An official whose primary responsibility is to furnish an organization with accounting records and reports. A comptroller is responsible for instituting and maintaining documents and records, safeguarding assets, disclosing liabilities, presenting income and other tax information, and preparing and interpreting operating and financial reports.

Cost and performance. Refers to the balance between the price of a weapon system and its military performance.

Deforestation. Refers to the heavy destruction of trees so that a forest cannot recover. Some causes of deforestation are commercial logging, clearing forests to feed cattle and gathering firewood. Deforestation has very serious consequences including soil erosion, damage to climate, loss of wildlife habitats and the displacement or even genocide of traditional forest dwellers.

Desertification. A term used when deserts increase in area as a result of human action. Dry, but cultivated, land bordering desert is gradually transformed into desert. The United Nations Environment Programme estimates that one-third of the earth's surface is at risk of desertification, affecting the livelihood of millions of people.

Détente. From the French word meaning relaxation. Refers generally to a lessening of tension between states who may nevertheless still be in opposition. Used commonly to describe the relationship between NATO and Warsaw Pact states in the late 1960s and early 1970s. Following the Cuban Missile Crisis in 1962, the USSR and the USA were forced to recognize the danger of a nuclear war resulting from any direct conflict between them, and so took steps to avoid this. The US interpretation of détente stressed interdependence of the two states and sought to achieve this by various trade, cultural and scientific cooperation. The intention was thereby to seek to influence Soviet foreign policy by withdrawing cooperation if US interests were being damaged. The Soviet Union, on the other hand, under the philosophy of 'peaceful coexistence', continued its traditional support for national liberation and revolutionary movements whilst still pursuing mutually profitable relations with the US. Thus the two parties to détente had very different interpretations of it.

Deterrence. Based on the idea that in calculating whether or not to undertake a certain foreign policy or a certain action, a state will not act if the probable outcome involves costs that will be too high compared to the anticipated gains.

Disarmament. May be the penal destruction or reduction of the arms of a defeated country; or a bilateral or multilateral agreement applying to a specific geographical location; or disarmament may entail the abolition of all armaments.

Discrimination. The differential treatment of people ascribed to particular social categories, for example, 'black' or 'disabled'. An action is discriminatory if someone is treated differently because she or he is thought to belong to such a category, and therefore the concept entails a comparison of a particular action with others. Policies providing for more favourable treatment of members of groups otherwise discriminated against are known as 'positive discrimination'.

Dual capability. Refers to (nuclear) weapons with more than one purpose designed for them.

Economic infrastructure. The system of structures which are necessary for the operation of a country's economy, i.e., banks and other organizations which handle and control money.

Economic nationalism. Reflected in domestic economic policies such as nationalization of foreign property, statutory limitation of foreign participation in the economy, government subsidies for key industrial sectors or the protection through tariffs and other import restrictions of certain economic activities.

Engels, Friedrich (1820–1895). German social philosopher, businessman and closest collaborator of Karl Marx. He lived and worked near Manchester, England. Characteristic of Engels is his prediction of the obsolescence of war as an instrument of national policy in a world progressively unified through industrialization.

Enlightenment, The. A movement amongst European intellectuals in the seventeenth and eighteenth centuries. They endeavoured to adopt a strictly rational approach to problems of the human condition and challenged many traditional beliefs, religious as well as political. A particular characteristic was that rather than being cyclical or static, human civilization was constantly progressing and improving.

Ethnocentrism. The tendency to evaluate matters by reference to the values shared in the subject's own ethnic group as if that group were the centre of everything.

Ethology. The biological study of animal behaviour in the natural environment. This is usually done by observation, and then relating what is observed to the way the species survives.

Fascism. The characteristics of fascism are militant nationalism with a strong emphasis on the state, the glorification of an individual political leader and social control by the state using the mechanisms of the economy and culture. It differs from traditional right-wing authoritarianism in its appeal to and mobilization of the masses, and in its emphasis on state intervention. It is considered by some to be characteristic of societies made insecure by transition, especially when a rural population moves to the cities. Others have emphasized the psychological factors of a disorganized population seeking security in a strong political leader. Another interpretation considers fascism a final phase in the development of capitalism.

Feminization of poverty. A feature of capitalism in the Third World and increasingly in the US and Europe. Women are pushed into the permanent 'underclass' in larger and larger numbers, for example, in the US, two out of three poor adults are women.

Feminism. A set of beliefs and theoretical constructions about the nature of women's oppression and the part that this oppression plays within the social reality more generally.

Fichte, Johann Gottlieb (1762–1814). German philosopher and patriot. He argued that pure practical reason postulates the existence of God, but he tried to transform Kant's rational faith into speculative knowledge, on which he based both his theory of science and his ethics.

Flexible response. A strategy based on the theory of superiority by the Warsaw Pact in terms of conventional weapons. If NATO started to lose a conventional war, it would respond flexibly by employing artillery equipped with nuclear shells and by using short-range nuclear missiles such as the Lance. The theory is, therefore, that NATO could contain Warsaw Pact aggression in Europe without the full-scale use of nuclear weapons.

Gandhi, Mahatma (1869–1948). Hindu politician and philosopher. At 18 he went to London to study law and in 1893 went to South Africa to work. After his return to India, he began his work towards the liberation of India from English colonial rule and for a new social order. His main concerns were with the liberation of the caste system and a peaceful coexistence between Hindu and Moslem communities. He believed in nonviolence and *satyagraha* (see glossary entry below) and used them in his civil disobedience campaigns (e.g., he tried to convince people to take up hand-spinning in order to break free from their poverty and dependence on town-made goods). His most famous civil disobedience campaign was the Salt March in 1930 to defy the government's salt monopoly. From 1924–37 and 1940–41 he was President of the All Indian Congress Party. He was shot by a Hindu in 1948.

Gandhian. Related to the teachings of M. K. Gandhi (1869–1948). He applied religious ideas from Hinduism to practical social and political problems, most notably in South Africa and India. He was especially famous for his use of nonviolent techniques to bring to an end British rule in India.

Haganah. Clandestine Jewish organization for armed defence in Israel under the British Mandate, which eventually evolved into a people's militia and became the basis of the Israeli army.

Human rights. Fundamental to the concept of human rights is the notion that they are universal, applying to all people regardless of social, political or religious grouping. Various human rights have been outlined which define permissible behaviour between individuals and between groups, e.g., between states and individuals. The most widely known is the United Nations Universal Declaration of Human Rights. The basis of the Declaration is that all human beings are born free and equal in dignity and rights, are endowed with reason and conscience, should act towards one another in a spirit of brotherhood, and are entitled to all kinds of rights and freedoms without any kind of distinction. Everyone has the right to life, liberty and security of person. The Declaration then goes on to elaborate on this, detailing rights such as the right to work, to own property, to free expression and to social security.

Imperialism. The practice of one state extending its sovereignty over others, usually by force and for the purpose of economic exploitation and national glorification. Colonialism is a specific form of imperialism, where a distinction is made between the territories of the conquering nation and its 'colonies', and where the inhabitants of the colonies have inferior political and legal rights.

Industrial Revolution. From the second half of the eighteenth century through the first half of the nineteenth century Britain experienced a series of economic, technological, social and organizational changes which transformed it from a predominantly agrarian and small manufacturing society to the world's first factory-based machine-featuring society.

Industrialization. A process of transforming a predominantly agricultural economy into one where the manufacture of goods increasingly contributes to overall output and exports. The percentage share of people employed in agriculture declines and that in industry increases.

Infrastructure. The basic structure of a country, society or organization on which it is built, such as the facilities, services and equipment that are needed for it to function properly.

Institution. A reasonably enduring, complex, integrated pattern of behaviour by which social control is exerted and through which basic social needs or desires can be met.

International Atomic Energy Agency (IAEA). Founded in 1956 by the decision of all member states of the UNO and set up as an independent body of UNO. Its main task is the promotion of peaceful utilization of nuclear energy; it also oversees sales and purchases of fissible energy.

International division of labour. In a regional or global economy, countries may specialize in different kinds of economic activities and so be interdependent—just as occupations are in the national division of labour. In the modern world system, countries are also either in actuality or in pretension, cohesive nation-states, raising the possibility that within the international division of labour each may be a class.

International economic order. The overall global structure of international economic relations.

The term embraces both the totality of private commercial transactions spontaneously organized through the operation of the free world market, as well as economic and financial cross-border transactions occurring within multinational enterprises, and international agreements and organizations set up to regulate all these transactions.

International Monetary Fund (IMF). Set up in 1944 through the Bretton Woods Agreement and came into operation in 1947. The idea was to encourage international cooperation in the monetary field, the removal of foreign exchange restrictions, to stabilize exchange rates and to facilitate a multilateral payments system between member countries.

International Monetary System. A system of internationally agreed principles and institutions governing international financial transactions and exchange rates. The most comprehensive system was first developed in Bretton Woods in 1944 but this system broke down in 1971; since then the world has not had an international monetary system as such, but only temporary, partial, and sometimes regional agreements, e.g., the Smithsonian Agreement, the Louvre Accord and the European Monetary System.

International terrorism. The threat of use of violence for political purposes both when such action is intended to influence the attitude and behaviour of a target group wider than its immediate victims and its ramifications transcend national boundaries (as a result, for example, of the nationality or foreign ties of its perpetrators, its locale, the identity of its institutional or human victims, its declared objectives, or the mechanics of its resolution).

Inter-species. Between members of different species.

Intra-species. Between members of the same species.

Irgun Zeva'i Le'ummi **(IZL or National Military Organization).** Underground Jewish organization in Israel founded in 1931. It seceded from the *Haganah*, which engaged from 1937 in retaliatory acts on Arab attacks and later against the British Mandate authority.

Irish National Liberation Army (INLA). Thought to be formed by a merger of the People's Liberation Army and the Official Irish Republican Army. It was responsible for the assassination of the MP Airey Neave amongst other terrorist attacks. Politically, it combines socialist with nationalist ideas.

Irish Republican Army (IRA). Formed in 1919 to fight for an independent republic of all Ireland, it continues to engage in terrorist acts against the British presence in Northern Ireland. It split in 1970 into the Provisional and Official sections, with only the Provisionals now remaining active.

Jewish Agency. Zionist organization set up to advise and cooperate with the British administration in economic, social and any other matters concerning the Jewish National Home and the Jewish population in Palestine.

Joint Strategic Target Planning Staff (JSTPS). This group was created in 1960 by the US Secretary of Defense Thomas Gates. The aim is to produce an integrated plan for the use of nuclear weapons possessed by all the US military commands throughout the world and to coordinate the nuclear plan with the Western allies.

Kant, Immanuel (1724–1804). German philosopher and one of the most important thinkers of modern times. He proposed that some of the properties we ascribe to objects may be a function of our perceptions. This does not threaten, indeed it guarantees, the certainty of our knowledge, but it means that our knowledge cannot go beyond our experience. We can only know 'phenomena', not 'things in themselves'.

Keynesian economics. A general description of the school of economic thought which derives from the Cambridge economist J. M. Keynes (1883–1946). Keynes challenged the prevailing classical economists' claim that an unregulated economy will move automatically to a position of full employment. He argued that under certain conditions it was possible for equilibrium to be established at less than full employment. Any government wishing to pursue a policy of full employment should stimulate aggregate expenditure to increase national output and thereby reduce unemployment. This recommendation for government to assume responsibility for stabilization policies became part of the accepted orthodoxy in all Western economies for most of the post-World War II period. Towards the end of the 1960s the simultaneous emergence of high rates of inflation and high levels of unemployment, as well as the apparent failure of conventional policies to control them, led to disenchantment with the Keynesian diagnosis and remedies. In particular, the work by Milton Friedman and his associates emphasized the role of the money supply by reforming the pre-Keynesian quantity theory of money (monetarism).

KGB. Russian abbreviation for the Committee for State Security. Under Stalin the KGB had extensive powers of arrest, search and execution and was responsible only to Stalin himself. Since Stalin's death these powers have been severely limited and it is now under Communist Party control.

Labour emancipation. The achievement through education and struggle of rights and privileges (such as better incomes and improved working conditions) by organized labour.

Lance. A US surface-to-surface missile which can deliver a nuclear or conventional warhead over a distance of up to 80 miles maximum range. It has been in service since 1973.

Liberalism. A political philosophy in which 'freedom' is the central value and principle—to be used by governments as a method and philosophy. The history of this idea can be traced back to the Greek philosopher Socrates, but the modern form of liberalism was developed in Europe in the eighteenth and nineteenth centuries, when it absorbed many concepts from the revolutionary movements of those times. Liberal philosophers such as Rousseau and Locke maintained that men (and perhaps women) had rights rooted in natural law, and that those should be enshrined in secular law. Liberalism also stresses the self-realization of the individual, whose happiness and fulfilment is of supreme importance.

Macro rationality. A term sometimes used to describe the profit orientation of multinational economic enterprises. While rationality of economic activity normally involves precise calculation of costs and benefits of a firm's national activities, macro-rationality involves the firm's calculation of costs and benefits (i.e., profit maximization) on an international scale and embracing the activities of all its branches and subsidiaries across the globe.

Marginalization. In many successful developing countries, national economic progress is accompanied by the exclusion of large sections of the population from economic life. This is because the path of industrialization and economic development typically involves heavy reliance on imported capital-intensive, labour-saving techniques and the neglect of staple food production.

Marx, Karl (1818–1883). German philosopher and one of the most important figures in the history of socialist thinking. He was strongly influenced by the works of Georg Friedrich Hegel. In 1841 he received a doctorate from the University of Jena, Germany. Because of his political views he had to leave Germany and went into exile to Paris and Brussels. In Brussels he published the *Communist Manifesto*, a summary of his whole social philosophy. He settled in London in 1849 where he wrote his most famous work *Das Kapital*. In it he developed a theory of the capitalist system and its dynamics, with emphasis on its self-destructive tendencies. He lived in poverty all his life, being financially supported by his friend and colleague Friedrich Engels and is buried at Highgate Cemetery, London.

Metropolitan. Pertaining to the chief city or centre of a network of activities, most commonly economic activities.

Militarism. A term which emerged in the nineteenth century to describe societies with universal male conscription and large armies with professional officer corps. It now indicates a growing influence of the military on any nation's domestic or foreign affairs. It is suggested by some that such changes are the result of a culture that sees the use of organized violence in support of the existing social order as acceptable and inevitable and where there are close links between the military establishment, the state and economic elites.

Mode of production. An organizing concept developed by Marx to explain the structure and dynamics of any given society, and particularly the transition from one to another. Marxists today generally argue that this does not refer exclusively to the economy, but to the structured relationship between the means of production (raw materials, land, labour, tools, etc.) and the relations of production (the ownership of these means of production and the social relationships they entail).

Nationalism. The belief among a people that it comprises a distinctive community with special characteristics that mark it off from others, and the desire to protect and promote that distinctiveness within an autonomous state.

Nationalist movements. The demand for self-government for the nation against alien rule. A distinction should be made between the demands of those peoples amongst whom a sense of national identity is already present, and those where it is not.

Negative peace. Refers to the absence of behavioural violence, but where relations are 'unpeaceful'. Negative peace may be marked by structural violence.

Nonviolence. In Gandhian terms this means *ahimsa*, which connotes not merely the absence of the thing negated, but the positive quality which is its opposite. The term usually, and somewhat erroneously, suggests the mere absence of any force whatsoever. Gandhi believed that nonviolence is discreetly present as the active force behind the innumerable partial forms one does encounter in individuals, movements and societies.

Nonviolent resistance. There seem to be three general principles underlying successful nonviolent resistance: firstly, respect for persons, the nonviolent actor constantly distinguishes the opponent's person from the deed or attitude deemed objectionable; secondly, persuasion rather than coercion where the attempt is always to educate the opponent, to draw rather than to push; and, finally, means and ends—the nonviolent actor cannot use means incongruent with the desired nonviolent ends.

Nuclear weapons categories.

Battlefield or tactical—having a range of less than 200 km. For use in attacks on key targets such as airfields, depots and troops.

Strategic—having a range of more than 5500 km. Designed to destroy enemy society totally.

Intermediate—having a range between 200 and 5500 km. Can attack targets behind enemy lines but because of their range, they are able to reach into the USSR from Western Europe. Soviet intermediate nuclear forces (INF) can reach NATO bases in Europe but not the USA.

Overcultivation. To prepare land only for the growing of crops, and/or to plant, grow and raise (a crop) by preparing the soil, providing water, etc.

Overgrazing. The putting of so many animals on the land that the pasture or other vegetation cover is damaged, sometimes beyond recovery.

Palestine Liberation Organization (PLO). Main political and diplomatic vehicle of the Palestinian cause. It is regarded by Israel as a terrorist group but was recognized by the Arab states in 1974 as 'the sole legitimate representative of the Palestinian people'. The organization is made up of several wings with the military wing, *Fatah*, under the leadership of Yasser Arafat, being the largest. The PLO consists of about 5000 full-time fighters and is based in Iraq since Israel's bombing of the Lebanon.

Patriarchy. Refers to the institutional structure of male domination and the social arrangements within which women's oppression is elaborated.

Peaceful coexistence. A phrase coined by Lenin in 1917 and used subsequently by Krushchev. It means that a war between capitalism and communism is not 'fatally inevitable' and that confrontation should be replaced by peaceful, competitive coexistence in non-military spheres; especially with an increase in trade and cultural exchange.

People's imperialism. A term concerned to capture the improvements in living and working conditions enjoyed by ordinary people (both workers and consumers) in the advanced countries as a consequence of the exploitative economic relationships existing between advanced and less developed countries which have resulted from colonialism and imperialism.

Pershing 1A. A US and West German mobile ballistic missile armed with a W50 nuclear warhead with yield options of 60, 200 and 400 kilotons. It has a maximum range of 460 miles.

Pershing 2. The first missile with a range of over 1000 miles employing terminal guidance, thus representing the start of an entirely new generation of weapons.

Plutonium. One of the atomic isotopes from which nuclear weapons can be made. It does not occur naturally, but is a by-product of a nuclear reaction.

Positive peace. Defined in terms of harmonious relations between parties that are conducive to mutual development, growth and the attainment of goals.

Predation. The killing of animals for food.

Procurement. Acquisition of goods and services by a military establishment other than military personnel, whether by rent, lease, purchase, manufacture or requisition. Procurement spending is relevant as regards its impact in its direct effect on a nation's economy.

Productive process or labour process. Any organized system whereby the human capacity to produce results is a useful product or service. It is usually understood that such production is the specific aim of whoever establishes the system (thus 'creative play' is excluded), and that production requires collaboration. Derived from Marxian vocabulary, the concept removes some of the ambiguity of the term 'work'.

Proletarianization. The socio-historical process whereby people lose either their access to land, or their ownership of other means of production (e.g., working tools) and end up with nothing other than their labour to sell.

Race. All human beings belong to the same species, and thus the same capacities and limitations are to found in all populations. The process of evolution, however, has resulted in a wide range of minor physical differences between populations, and these inherited differences form the basis for the sub-division of our species into races. These physical differences are often adaptive, for example, the Inuit (Eskimoes) do not lose fine motor coordination in extreme cold. Some differences are hard to detect; for example, some blood groups are common among some races but unknown among others. Where race is used as a social or political concept, differentiation is usually on the basis of more obvious differences such as skin colour, which is often associated with imagined non-physical differences.

Rapier. Limited British battlefield anti-aircraft missile system intended to provide low altitude defence in both ground and seaborne roles.

Red Army Faction (RAF). Left-wing West German terrorist organization also known as the Baader-Meinhof Gang. Founded in 1967 by Andreas Baader and Ulrike Meinhof, it was responsible for a large number of attacks throughout Western Europe, often in cooperation with other left-wing groups. The founders and ringleaders were jailed in 1972 and committed suicide in 1976–77. The group is still active, especially since 1985 when the Political Military Front was founded that concentrates on bomb attacks on NATO bases and related companies.

Red Brigade. Left-wing Italian terrorist group and one of the largest European groups. It has been in existence since the 1960s and has specialized in the kidnapping and killing of Italian politicians, judges and businessmen. The leaders were jailed in 1976 but the group is still active.

Research and Development (R&D). Stands for scientific industrial, often military, research. The main source of funds is the government. Civil R&D is funded largely by private industries and trusts.

Satyagraha. A concept central to Gandhi's theories—a method of nonviolently resolving conflict. A literal translation is 'holding to the truth'. The person or persons practising *satyagraha*, the *satyagrahi(s)*, seek to demonstrate the wrongfulness of the act or decision they oppose to those who are responsible. The aim is to enable the opponent to realize that they are doing wrong without losing dignity or self-respect. The practice of *satyagraha* may involve breaking civil law, seen as inferior to moral law, in which case the *satyagrahi* willingly embraces any suffering that is a consequence; for example, imprisonment or violence.

SDI (Strategic Defense Initiative, popularly known as 'Star Wars'). A programme of research and development announced by President Reagan in 1983. An extremely complex system of weapons based in outer space which would detect and destroy any enemy missiles launched against the United States.

Settler colonies. Colonies in which people from different nations and/or continents (other than from the colonial power) came to live.

Shia (Shi'ism). One of the major branches of Islam, distinguished from the majority *Sunnah*. In early Islamic history *Shi'ism* was a political faction that supported the power of Ali, son-in-law of Muhammed; it gradually developed into a religious movement to which one-tenth of all Islam belongs. It is the majority faith in all of Iran, Iraq and partly in Yemen and it also has adherents in Syria, Lebanon, East Africa, northern India, the Indian Deccan, Bombay and Pakistan.

Social democracy. First used by various Marxist parties who believe in contesting elections and pursuing limited reforms within the existing political and economic system as a gradual means to achieving revolutionary change. Nowadays the term is applied to democratic socialist parties, such as the Labour Party, which believe that their aims can be achieved by the ballot-box but differ greatly in their definition of socialism and in their adherence to Marxist doctrines.

Socialism. There is no universally accepted definition of socialism. The two main branches of definition are: one which argues that socialism is both compatible with the continuance of private capital and that the abolition of capitalism's inhumanity and injustice is possible without abolishing capitalism itself; and the other (including Marxism) which argues that socialism is a society where productive enterprise is socially owned and managed and where the goal of production is use not profit: it requires a decisive political struggle by the working class against private capital and its bastions of power in society and state.

Spin-off. A useful product or result of a process other than the main one.

State-owned farms. Form of agricultural organization in some countries with a centrally controlled economy, in which the land is owned by the state and the farm workers are employed by the state as wage-earners. They do not have a share in the produce of the farm.

Stockpile. Refers to the practice of producing or buying and storing in the continental US in peacetime, raw materials or finished products expected to be in critical supply in the event of war.

Strategy. A plan of action which specifies the choice among available alternatives in which every situation that may arise is contingent on the history of the course of action.

Structural violence. Refers to damage that occurs to individuals or groups due to differential access to social resources and which is due to the normal operation of the social system. 'Violence is present when human beings are being influenced so that their actual somatic and mental realisations are below their potential realisations. . . . We shall refer to the type of violence where there is an actor that commits the violence as personal or direct, and to the violence where there is no such actor as structural or indirect' (Galtung).

Tax haven. A country, usually a small one, which has very low or non-existent corporate tax rates on the foreign earnings of expatriate companies. Such countries are, for example, the Bahamas, Bermuda, the Channel Islands, Lichtenstein, Hong Kong and Panama.

Terms of trade. Refers to the total of export prices and the total of import prices. An improvement in terms of trade follows if export prices rise more quickly than import prices. Developed countries have experienced a long-term improvement in its terms of trade because of a fall in relative prices of primary products.

Third World. Geographically it refers, somewhat imprecisely, to countries on the continents of Africa, Asia and Latin America. Economically it refers equally loosely to all 'poor' countries of the world. Ideologically it presents the self-awareness of emerging nations on these continents to develop different economic and social societies to that of the First and Second Worlds. Institutionally it refers to the association of those continents to the formation of a negotiating bloc (Group 77). Politically it refers to a third force in international political relations in contrast to East/West, socialism/capitalism.

Tit-for-Tat. A strategy iterated in 'Prisoner's Dilemma' which specifies the cooperative choice whenever the co-player has just played cooperatively and a defecting choice whenever the co-player has just defected.

Trident missiles. Strategic nuclear missiles launched from submarines. Two types exist: Trident II (also called Trident D5) having greater destructive power and being more expensive than the earlier Trident I (or Trident C4).

Ulster Volunteer Force (UVF). Originally a group formed in 1913 to oppose Home Rule for Ireland and subsequently to defend partition. The same name was adopted by a group started in 1964 that exists to kill nationalists.

Ulster Freedom Fighters. Particularly violent Protestant para-military group responsible for the assassination of a large number of Catholics in Northern Ireland in the 1970s and early 1980s. The group emerged in 1973 and was denounced by the UDA in 1977 for its excessive violence.

Underdevelopment. It is controversial whether this refers to a state or a process of 'backwardness' thought to be typical of the countries of Africa, Asia and Latin America. The state of underdevelopment is conventionally measured in terms of a number of economic and social criteria. The economic criteria summarize the existing and potential wealth of a nation. The social criteria assess the degree to which productive achievements are translated into improved standards of living for its people. As underdevelopment is only defined by contrast to development, critics argue that the concept has an ideological bias, being designed to sell to developing countries 'Western patent solutions to basic needs' (Illich).

Value added. Refers to the difference between total revenue of a firm and the cost of bought-in raw materials, services and components. It thus measures the value which the firm had added to these bought-in materials and components by its process of production.

Verification. The technical term arms controllers use to describe the process of assessing compliance with the provisions of particular treaties. It refers to the use of the data gathered by monitoring. The term was first used in a disarmament resolution of the UN Commission for Control of Armaments and Armed Forces.

Voltaire, Francois-Marie Arout (1694–1778). One of the greatest French authors. Characteristic of his work is his critical capacity and irony. He lived during the last years of classicism and the beginning of the French Revolution, which influenced his work in propagating an ideal of progress.

War against women. Refers to the pervasiveness of male violence against women. 'To be born female on a patriarchal planet is to be born behind enemy lines; sexism is the polite term for this war' (Sonia Johnson, 1983).

Weapon platforms. Refers to any system that delivers warheads, such as rockets, planes, etc.

Zero-zero treaty. The option of eliminating all short-range and medium-range nuclear missiles from Europe. The United States had offered this option for several years to the Soviet Union who had consistently refused it. At the Reykjavik Summit, the USSR was for the first time prepared to discuss it and come to an agreement.

Zionism. A modern ideology and movement calling for the return of the Jews to their ancient homeland, the land of Israel (also called Zion). Zionism proceeds from the assumption that the Jews form a people many of whom cannot or will not assimilate themselves to other peoples and wish to retain their identity as a national community. Theodor Herzl (1860–1904) made Zionism an international political factor by introducing the controversial programme to establish a national home for the Jewish people in Palestine.

Authors' Biographies

Rex Ambler was born in 1939 and brought up in Kent, England during the Second World War, the son of a German mother and an English father. He teaches theology at Birmingham University and is a member of the Society of Friends (Quakers) and of the newly formed Gandhi Foundation.

Peggy Antrobus was born in Granada in 1935. She is a tutor in Extra-Mural Studies and Head of the Women and Development Unit at the University of the West Indies, Barbados.

Robert Axelrod was born in the United States in 1943. He is a member of the National Academy of Sciences Committee on Contributions of Behavioral and Social Science to the Prevention of Nuclear War. Since 1987 he has been Arthur W. Bromage Professor at the Department of Political Science at the University of Michigan.

Francis Beer was born in 1939 in New York. His early work centered on NATO and international alliances. Later he turned to theory and research on more general processes involved in international violence. His major work in this area is *Peace Against War: The Ecology of International Violence* (San Francisco: W. H. Freeman, 1981).

Kenneth E. Boulding was born in Liverpool, England in 1910 and has lived in the United States since 1937. He has been at the University of Colorado since 1967 where he is now Distinguished Professor of Economics, Emeritus, as well as Research Associate and Project Director at the Program of Research and Economic Change at the University's Institute of Behavioral Science. His major interests include: economic theory, grants economics, conflict and peace studies, evolutionary theory, general systems and the study of human knowledge and learning.

Birgit Brock-Utne was born in Oslo, Norway in 1938. She holds a tenured position as an Associate Professor at the Institute for Educational Research, University of Oslo, but is currently working at the University of Dar es Salaam, Tanzania. She is on the Executive Board of the International Peace Research Association, and has been a visiting Professor in Sweden, the United States and Pakistan. She has also been a consultant to OECD, UNESCO, the European Council, the Nordic Council and the UN.

April Carter was born in 1937 in Cheltenham, England. She taught politics at the University of Lancaster from 1966–69 and at Somerville College, Oxford from 1976–84. Her peace movement experience includes being Secretary of the Direct Action Committee Against Nuclear War from 1958–61, and recently she was a member of the Alternative Defence Commission. Her latest book on arms control negotiations is being published by the Stockholm International Peace Research Institute, and she is now working on a book on peace movements.

Noam Chomsky was born in 1928 in Pennsylvania, USA. He is Institute Professor at the Massachusetts Institute of Technology. He has written and lectured widely on international affairs and foreign policy, and has been active in the peace movement for many years. Amongst his most recent books are *Towards a New Cold War, Fateful Triangle* and *Turning the Tide; On Power and Ideology.*

Richard Clutterbuck, born in 1894, was a soldier for 35 years and retired as a Major-General in 1972. From 1972–83 he was a lecturer and Reader in Political Conflict at the University of Exeter. He lectures on political violence to the police, business, and other audiences. He has written 12 books on the subject including *The Media and Political Violence* (1983), *The Future of Political Violence* (1986), and *Kidnap, Hijack and Extortion* (1987).

Sigmund Freud was born in 1856 in Moravia (now Czechoslovakia) and died in 1939 in London. He worked for many years as a psychotherapist in Vienna and became a Professor there in 1902. In 1938 he emigrated to London after the annexation of Austria by Nazi Germany. He was the founder of psychoanalysis.

Johan Galtung was born in 1930 in Oslo, Norway. His decision to register as a conscientious objector and his experience of the Nazi occupation in Norway led him to concentrate on peace studies. He has held numerous academic positions in universities throughout the world, and has been a consultant to many international bodies such as UNESCO and WHO. In 1972 he founded the *Journal of Peace Research*, and is on the editorial board of several other academic journals. In 1987 he was awarded the Right Livelihood ('Alternative Nobel') prize for his contribution to the study and understanding of peace.

Jill Gay was born in 1951 in the USA. She is currently consultant at the National Academy of Sciences where she has been organizing a conference on 'Women's Work for Health and Developing Countries'. From 1981–86 she was Associate Director of the Third World Women's Project.

Susan George was born in Akron, Ohio, USA and now lives permanently in France. She is a fellow of the Transnational Institute, Amsterdam, the international wing of the Institute for Policy Studies in Washington. Her most recent book, *A Fate Worse than Debt*, was published by Penguin in 1988.

Fred Halliday was born in Dublin, Ireland in 1946. He is Professor of International Relations at the London School of Economics. He is a member of the Council of the Royal Institute of International Affairs; a Senior Fellow of the Transnational Institute, Amsterdam and Washington; and a contributing editor to *MERIP Middle East Reports*. His most recent published work is *The Making of the Second Cold War* (2nd edn., Verso, 1986).

Brian Hamilton-Tweedale was born in Liverpool in 1953. He has been a member of the Peace and Conflict Studies Development Group since 1986. He lives in Sheffield where he is currently writing a book on the British press in Northern Ireland.

Robert Hinde was born in Norwich, England in 1923. After being Curator at the Sub-Department of Animal Behaviour at Madingley since its founding in 1950, he became a Royal Society Research Professor in 1963 and Honorary Doctor of the Medical Research Unit on the Development and Integration of Behaviour in 1972. He is a member of the International Society for Research on Aggression. His latest publications include *Social Relationships and Cognitive Development* (1985) and *Aggression and War* (in press).

Ankie Hoogvelt was born in 1941 in Jakarta, Indonesia (formerly Dutch East Indies). She is a Lecturer in the Department of Sociological Studies at Sheffield University. Her best known books are *The Sociology of Developing Societies* (Macmillan, 1976) and *The Third World in Global Development* (Macmillan, 1982). Recent research interests have taken her further afield into the areas of international capital and multinational companies (see her work with A. Puxty, *Multinational Enterprise: An Encyclopedic Dictionary of Concepts and Terms*). She has travelled widely in Africa and has taught for one year at the University of Kano in Northern Nigeria.

Girma Kebbede was born in 1948 in Soddo, Ethiopia and studied at Holyoke College in South Hadley, Massachusetts, where he has taught since 1982. He is currently engaged in research on 'drought,' famine and the political economy of environmental degradation in Ethiopia. He is a member of the Association of American Geographers, the African Studies Association, and American Association of University Professors.

Graham Kemp was born in 1954 in Chatham, Canada and emigrated to Britain in 1957. He gained his PhD at the Richardson Institute for Peace Studies through his evaluation of studies on human aggression and their relevance to peace research. He is a member of the International Society for Research on Aggression and UK Convenor for the Nonviolence Study Group of the International Peace Research Association.

Reinard Kuhn was born in 1936 in Czechoslovakia and resettled in 1946 in Hessia (now in West Germany). He studied in West Germany and Austria. Since 1971 he has been Professor for Political Science at the University of Marburg. He has also been visiting Professor at Tel Aviv University and worked at the UNESCO-funded research project on 'Social Roots of European Fascism'. During the 1970s and 1980s he has been active in the peace movement, campaigned against *Berufsverbote* in West Germany and been a leading member of the Union of Democratic Scientists.

Patricia M. Lewis was born in 1957 in Coventry, UK. She is a Nuclear Physicist and is the Senior Analyst and Information Officer at the Verification Technology Information Centre in London.

Mary Midgley was born in 1919 in London. She is a professional philosopher. Formerly Senior

Lecturer in Philosophy at the University of Newcastle-on-Tyne, her books include *Beast and Man, Wickedness, Animals and Why They Matter* and (with Judith Hughes) *Women's Choices*. She is a patron of the Freeze Campaign.

Christopher Mitchell was born in Essex, England in 1934. He is Professor of International Relations at the City University in London. He has both written about and had practical experience of unofficial mediation initiatives. He is a member of the Conflict Research Society and of the Centre for the Analysis of Conflict at the University of Kent.

Geoffrey Ostergaard was born in 1926 in Bedfordshire, England. He is Senior Lecturer in Political Science at the University of Birmingham, England. He has written numerous articles and two books about the Gandhian movement since Gandhi, the latest of which is *Nonviolent Revolution in India* (1985).

The Oxford Research Group, founded in 1982, is an independent research organization with the twin aims of researching how nuclear weapons decisions are made, and of communicating this information to the press, the public and to groups of citizens who wish to enter into dialogue with individual decision-makers. The article in this book was written by Scilla Elworthy McClean and Erica Parra. Scilla Elworthy McLean is the director of the Oxford Research Group and research fellow at the University of Bradford. Erica Parra works for the Group on a voluntary basis. She has a degree in History from Boston University and monitored the Geneva Committee on Disarmament for the Women's League for Peace and Freedom.

Anatol Rapoport was born in 1911 in Russia and emigrated later to the United States. Returning from military service in 1946, he resumed an interrupted academic career. He was associated with the Committee on Mathematical Biology at the University of Chicago, with the Mental Health Research Institute at the University of Michigan, and with the departments of Psychology and Mathematics at the University of Toronto, where he is currently Professor of Peace Studies. He writes on the philosophy of science, mathematical methods in the social sciences, the theory of games, and theories of conflict.

Betty Reardon is the Director of the Peace Education Program at Teachers College, Colombia University. She has a special interest in feminist perspectives on issues of disarmament and human rights education. She is the author of *Sexism and the War System*, and two volumes entitled *Educating for Global Responsibility* (all three books are published by Teachers College Press). She is a founding member of the Peace Education Commission of the International Peace Research Association, and of the World Council for Curriculum and Instruction.

Dorothy Rowe was born in Australia in 1930 and worked as a teacher and child psychologist before coming to England where she obtained her PhD at Sheffield University. She headed the North Lincolnshire Department of Clinical Psychology for 14 years but retired early to concentrate on her writing. Her research and therapy have always been concerned with how we create meaning and how we communicate.

Dan Smith was born in 1951 in Sri Lanka. He is a Fellow of the Transitional Institute of Amsterdam. He has written about defence and disarmament since 1974. He was a member of the Alternative Defence Commission from 1980 to 1987. In 1980 and again from 1984 to 1987 he was Vice-Chairperson of CND.

Julie Spencer-Robinson was born in 1962 in the USA. She is Associate Director of the Third World Women's Project at the Institute for Policy Studies in Washington, DC. She earned her MA in International Affairs and Certificate in Latin American and Iberian Studies from Columbia University, New York.

Hugh Tinker was born in 1921 in Westcliff, England. He gained his MA at Cambridge University. He has been Professor of Asian Government and Politics at the University of London, and Professor of Politics at the University of Lancaster, where he is now Emeritus Professor. Other responsibilities have been: Director of Institute of Race Relations; Member of Z Council, Minority Rights Group; Chairman of the Advisory Committee of SSRC Unit on Ethnic Relations; and Vice President, Ex-Services Campaign for Nuclear Disarmament.

Aguibou Yan Yansane was born in Guinea, West Africa. He received his PhD at Stanford University, where he specialized in Economic Development, Political Economy, and African Studies. He is at present Professor of International Relations and Ethnic Studies at San Francisco State University.

Index

About the Editors

Paul Smoker was born in London, England in 1938. He has worked in peace research since 1960. He is Reader in Peace and Conflict Research at Lancaster University where he is Director of the Richardson Institute for Peace Studies. He has published more than 50 academic articles and books and has taught peace studies at the undergraduate and graduate level, at various universities in Europe and North America. He is a founder member of the International Peace Research Association and the British Conflict Research Society. Currently he is researching accidental nuclear war and computer applications in peace studies.

Ruth Davies was born in 1959 in Watford, England. She was educated at the University of Lancaster where she obtained a degree in Psychology and subsequently trained as a teacher. She became involved in peace education, working first at the Centre for Peace Studies, St. Martins College and then at the Richardson Institute for Peace Studies at the University of Lancaster. She is on the steering committee of the British Peace Education Network. She is currently researching children's perceptions of nuclear war at the Richardson Institute.

Barbara Munske was born in West Berlin in 1962. She studied politics at the Freie Universitat Berlin and came to the Richardson Institute for Peace Studies, Lancaster, England in 1983 where she first worked on the issue of arms conversion. Her main interest however is on the subject of the image of the enemy about which she completed a MPhil at Lancaster. She has been involved in various areas of the peace movement both in West Berlin and Britain but her major concern is in East-West relations.